The Power of Constant Prayer and Communion With God

The Power of Constant Prayer and Communion With God

William Jeynes

INFORMATION AGE PUBLISHING, INC.
Charlotte, NC • www.infoagepub.com

Library of Congress Cataloging-In-Publication Data

The CIP data for this book can be found on the Library of Congress website (loc.gov).

Paperback: 979-8-88730-685-8
Hardcover: 979-8-88730-686-5
E-Book: 979-8-88730-687-2

Copyright © 2024 Information Age Publishing Inc.

All rights reserved. No part of this publication may be reproduced, stored in a retrieval system, or transmitted, in any form or by any means, electronic, mechanical, photocopying, microfilming, recording or otherwise, without written permission from the publisher.

Printed in the United States of America

CONTENTS

Acknowledgements vii

1. Constant-Prayer and Communion With God and Faith 1

2. Constant-Prayer and Communion With God and Joy 17

3. Constant-Prayer and Communion With God
   and Evangelism 31

4. Constant-Prayer and Communion With God and Love 45

5. Constant-Prayer and Communion With God and Humility 61

6. Constant-Prayer and Communion With God and Obedience 73

7. Constant-Prayer and Communion With God and Prayer 83

8. Wisdom and Constant-Prayer and Communion With God 95

9. God's Holiness and Constant-Prayer and Communion
   With God 105

vi • CONTENTS

10. God's Forgiveness and Constant-Prayer and Communion
With God.. 117

11. Discipline and Constant-Prayer and Communion
With God.. 129

12. Vision and Constant-Prayer and Communion With God................. 141

13. Sensitivity and Constant-Prayer
and Communion With God.. 149

14. Constant-Prayer and Communion With God
and Consistency.. 157

Biography.. 167

ACKNOWLEDGEMENTS

I am very thankful to the many individuals who played a large role in making this book possible. However, above all I want to thank my Lord and Savior Jesus Christ and taught me so much beginning at a young age, largely because I lived a challenging live in which I was forced to grow up quickly, especially beginning at the age of eight. This book was written primarily in the early 1980s and updated for publication. I want to thank my wonderful wife of 38 years, Hyelee. She is a wonderful pearl and I love her dearly. I constantly thank God for her. I also want to thank my three boys Luke, Elisha, and Isaiah for being such a treasured part of my life. I treasure my two precious daughters-in-law, Ashley and Leah. I want to thank Wayne Ruhland, who has always been a friend who sticks closer than a brother. I also want to thank his wife Janet and his son Ben. Jean Donohue was also a dear friend for decades. I also want to thank Charles & Marion Patterson, Jessica Choi, Soo Myung, and the Roger Friend family. I want to thank Dan Johnston who has played a major role in my life in so many ways. May God use this book for His glory to touch many.

CHAPTER 1

CONSTANT-PRAYER AND COMMUNION WITH GOD AND FAITH

INTRODUCTION

> Now faith is the assurance of things hope for, the conviction of things not seen.
>
> *—Hebrews 11:1*

This verse gives a precious definition of the term "faith." What a gift from God it would be if a believer had this kind of faith unceasingly! It can be done, but the requirement is that a person constantly- pray and commune with God. Constant prayer and communion with God, for the purposes of this book, means a state in which the believer is continually praying to and communicating with God and specifically aware of His presence.

An unceasing faith is never accomplished, but the more one's communication with God is without cessation, the more that individual's faith will be also. Human beings are quite an enigma when it comes to faith. One moment they can

---

The Power of Constant Prayer and Communion With God, pages 1–15.
Copyright © 2024 by Information Age Publishing
www.infoagepub.com
All rights of reproduction in any form reserved.

trust God for virtually anything, and the next moment they cannot trust Him at all (Jeynes, 2016).

Furthermore, humans find little trouble trusting God with regards to granting the eternal life which He promised in Heaven, but too often they fail to trust God to provide when it comes to daily requests and necessities. Human beings are God's greatest creation, but they are also the most inconsistent (Bonhoeffer, 1959; Chambers, 2008; Montague, 2011). Nevertheless, through constant-prayer and communion with God, there can be so much more consistency and hence, so much more faith. Sometimes believers can talk on and on with joy about their faith in Heaven, but their countenance totally changes when their electric bill is too high.

GOD VS. MAN

Confidence in God and Heaven Versus Confidence in Man and the World

It is better to take refuge in the Lord than to put confidence in man.
—Psalm 118:8

When the Christian does not possess a strong faith in God, he or she exhibits four traits:

1. Faith in man
2. Confidence in man
3. Lack of faith in God
4. Lack of confidence in God

As far as faith is concerned, the antithesis between believing in God and believing in humans always presents itself (Graham, 2015). Many of the unsaved who dwell within this earthly community will say they have faith in neither God nor people. But the very fact that they do not call to God shows that they indeed have *comparatively* a greater faith in people than in God (Graham, 2015). When Jesus said that He came for the lost, He meant that He came for individuals who entrusted themselves to men rather than to God. (Luke 19:10)

Whether an individual puts his faith in God or humankind is greatly dependent on whether he or she is aware of God or man during the day. Indeed, what a person is aware of sets the tone for the day. A person's thoughts lead that individual into action. That is, actions originate in thoughts. If then a Christian is aware of the things of man, one is trusting one's actions to originate with human thoughts. The results can only be that actions will have a human-like – rather than a God-like – quality to them. If we define *maturity as the extent to which people's actions (as well as thoughts) have a God-like quality to them, one can see that constant awareness of God is essential to maturity in Christ Jesus* (Romans 8:5-8).

How convicting! Indeed, who can say he is mature except God Himself? Praise God!

In the preceding paragraph we can see the sinful condition of humanity explained plainly. Humans are sinful because their actions originate with their human-like thoughts. Their actions, therefore, have a human -like, sinful quality (Romans 3:11-14 with Luke 6:45).

> And I, brethren, could not speak to you as spiritual people, but as to carnal, as babes in Christ... for you are still carnal.
> —I Corinthians 3:1, 3

The World and Heaven

> Thou wouldest call, and I would answer thee; thou wouldest long for the work of thy hands.
> —Job 14:15

Our world is made up of many voices. Principally though, there are four: the voice of God, the voice of Satan, the voice of the world, and the voice of self. In general, the latter two can be combined into the voice of humanity, though not always, leaving us with three voices.

Humans are nearly always aware of one or more of these voices. Constant-prayer and awareness of God is a discipline which seeks to ensure that a person will continually hear the voice of God!

If the believer is aware of God at any given point in time, that person is clearly demonstrating to God that he wants to hear the voice of the Almighty God and the voice of God only. The scene of this passage is an asylum in Hades. Think of how we would yearn for the voice of God in Hades. We would thirst for the presence of the Lord. *God and Heaven should provide such a contrast to what man offers that we thirst for God in the same way on earth!*

> O God, you are my God; earnestly I seek you: my soul thirsts for you; my flesh faints for you, as in a dry and weary land where there is no water.
> —Psalm 63:1, 2 (ESV)

Jared Brock once said that, "You have to be near Him to hear Him." It has also been stated,

Holiness is the habit of being of one mind with God." Audrey Shapoval, pastor-evangelist, shared, "The voice of God is connected with the presence of God. The stronger God's presence is in my life, the clearer God's voice is.

If only we were hungrier for Heaven! Hungry not only in the sense of desiring to dwell there permanently, but also in the sense of having a heavenly life and see-

4 • THE POWER OF CONSTANT PRAYER AND COMMUNION WITH GOD

ing our day-to-day affairs in the light of Heaven. Why, if a person is truly grateful for the fact that Jesus Christ has made an eternal life possible in Heaven, do an individual's thoughts focus on people so much? How grateful are humans really? Or is it that Heaven seems far removed from earthly living and it is difficult to take in its reality? Heaven needs to become real. If it were real, men and women would not do many of the things that they do. Yours truly often said to his children when they were growing up: "People generally don't change for the better until remaining the same becomes painful." People would change far more easily if they were more heavenly minded.

Instead, Christians should look at what first appears to be obstacles as opportunities and cry "hallelujah," that in Heaven there will never be any obstacles. Instead, there shall be basking in the Lord's presence, which brings this chapter again back to the concept of faith.

How real is God to people? How real is Heaven to people? It seems that God can only seem so real, if Heaven does not seem real. *If one has his or her ideal as basking in the presence of God in Heaven, God is real to us indeed! And if basking is one's ideal and Heaven is real, aware of God a believer will be!* The reader should note, then, that not only does constant praying and interacting with God produce faith, but it is produced by faith, i.e., the reality and ideal of experiencing the presence of God in Heaven. *Praise God*!

> For I know that my Redeemer lives, and at last He will stand upon the earth; and after my skin has thus been destroyed, then from my flesh I shall see God, whom I shall see on my side, and my eyes shall behold, and not another. My heart faints within me.
>
> *—Job 19:25-27*

Hallelujah! Here we have the verse which best sums up how Job was able to endure all of the trials that were inflicted upon him. People endure trials of God by faith, and they can have faith by constantly praying to the Lord. Trials become burdensome when instead individuals center on the events that occur in the world (Chambers, 2008). Oh, how many trials we have been in, whereupon, focusing our thoughts on the Father in Heaven and praising His most Holy Name, all thoughts of these trials vanish. *Praise God*! When trials come, we should say to ourselves, "It is time to praise the Lord." Oh, to have our minds on the illimitable nature of eternity rather than on the vagaries of life today. Oh, to think of the day that we shall see God!

I know when I may be angered or depressed or sorrowful, an important question comes to mind: "What are these circumstances in the context of eternity?" I wish to God that I could say this every time I seem to think I am on the short end of life's stick. There is such peace in knowing that in the end all of life's pain and sorrow will be taken care of. It will exist no more. *Praise the Most High! To meditate on the completeness and peace that is Heaven is to overcome life!* Because behind any thoughts of Heaven lies God's power.

Constant-Prayer and Communion With God and Faith • 5

With the Lord on my side I do not fear. What can man do to me?
—Psalm 118: 6

"Sticks and stones may break my bones...", but my soul dwells in safety (Matthew 10:28). If only the Christian could understand how secure he is in Christ, as long as he follows Him. In John 10 the Greek word for "good" as in "good shepherd" is *ka-los*, which means skillful. A Christian is secure in Christ because Christ is a skillful shepherd. He is the same God who made Heaven and earth, and protects them both, and He protects the Christian. Only upon meditating on the eternal existence of Heaven can the disciple of Christ even begin to grasp his own eternity, which he has in Jesus Christ. To be constantly aware of his own eternity, because and only because of God, is to be free from the fear of humanity. Constant awareness of Heaven helps the disciple feel secure in the midst of the onslaughts of life. How can Heaven do anything but make him stand on solid more certain ground in his relationship with the world?

In a very real sense, then, one vital component of growing is spiritual maturity is that the invisible realm becomes even more real than the visible realm. To be sure, that which is visible is real. However, even if we cannot see the extent of the power of the wind and electricity, would we be so foolish to deny their power? Similarly, would we be even more foolish than this, to deny God's power? When we become spiritually cognizant of the fact that the invisible realm is even more real than the visible realm, peace, joy, and faith come to the soul. These qualities become more inherent in our being because we develop a deeper understanding of just how omniscient and omnipotent God is.

Until we first experience the heavenly realm, in the sense of being with God in continual prayer and communion, we really cannot fully help others experience what a wonderful, miraculous, and loving God we serve. When our prayer is, "God show me your glory," and He does, it is then that we are best able be communicate to others just how glorious the Lord is.

Double Mindedness

But let him ask in faith, with no doubting, for he who doubts is like a wave of the sea that is driven and tossed by the wind. For that person must not suppose that a double-minded man, unstable in all his ways, will receive anything from the Lord.
—James 1:6-8

James 1:6 commands us to have faith. The next two verses talk about the antitheses of faith, i.e., double-mindedness. That is, if a human's mind is centered on more than just God, this is not faith, but rather double-mindedness. *The man's or woman's cure for double-mindedness is constant prayer and communication with God!* In its very essence, constant prayer requires putting our entire mind on Christ constantly. If people have their minds on God and ask the Lord to help them keep it there, these individuals will seldom experience those wandering thoughts that are characteristic of double-mindedness (Minith, 2004).

Double-mindedness is an inherent characteristic of human beings that we cannot escape. Relatively speaking, a given person may be single-minded (and it is relative to double-mindedness to which I principally speak), but on an absolute scale all humankind suffers from double-mindedness (Jeynes, 1999, 2006). *Single-mindedness is a prerequisite for faith, and constant prayer and communication God is a prerequisite for single-mindedness.* Spiritual battles within the mind are such a reality. At times people feel like they have two or three minds instead of one, each vying for control over the other. Biblically speaking, this is a battle of the flesh and the powers of darkness and light. Yet, which army wins these battles depends on where our affections are set. This does not merely mean a statement of faith, but rather an action of *true* faith, i.e., leaning on God (as defined by the Greek as trust and leaning on the Lord) To lean on God, we must have God-oriented thoughts.

The Mind We Feed is the One the Predominates

In these battles in which it seems like we have two or three minds, the mind we feed is the mind that grows and predominates over the others. In other words, if one "mind" is of God and the second "mind" is of worry, if we feed the second mind by thinking thoughts of worry, it will grow until it dominates over the "mind" of godly thoughts (author, 2015). Our thoughts, then serve as food for these minds.

To illustrate, let us say a man owns two puppies. The puppies are of the same size and strength so that when they fight, neither predominates over the other. But over time the owner takes a liking to one of the puppies and grows to despise the other. Consequently, he gives the puppy he likes much more, higher quality food. The result is that the loved puppy grows vigorous and strong while the unloved puppy becomes skinny and weak. Now when the puppies play-fight, the unloved puppy is no match for the stronger, loved puppy. It is the same with feeding our "minds." The mind we feed is the mind that becomes strong and predominates.

This lesson is especially important when it is applied to areas of our lives in which distinct drives are apparent such as in dieting and lusting. When these drives or any like them pose a threat to our spiritual status quo, it is easy to attempt to quench the drive via compromise. We reason: "If I think about the food without eating, I'll be satisfied enough and the drive will go away," or "If I think about that man/woman without having intercourse with him/her, I will be satisfied enough and the drive will go away." In each case, the reasoning is false. The longer we think about the food or the member of the opposite sex, the more the "mind" of sin will be fed and the less the "mind" of God will be fed. The "mind" of sin will predominate in such a case, which will lead us deeper into sin (Ephesians 4:27; Romans 6:12, 13; 13:14).

Constant-Prayer and Communion With God and Faith • 7

It may be quite obvious to the reader by now that constant prayer to God feeds the "mind" of God. This "mind" hence becomes larger and predominates over the "mind" of the flesh. The beautiful thing about all of this is that when the Christian is constantly aware of God, day to day, the "mind" of God builds up a large edge over the "mind" of the flesh even before the day begins. Constant awareness is not only a key towards achieving single-mindedness on any given day, but also in the long-term can serve to set a bulwark against any sinful thoughts originating in the "mind" of the flesh. What is especially encouraging is that as we practice God's presence in this way, it will eventually become harder for us to sin than it is to obey. What bliss results!

> And without faith it is impossible to please Him. For whoever would draw near to God must believe that He exists and that He rewards those who seek Him.
>
> *—Hebrews 11:6*

If single-mindedness is essential to a strong Christian's faith, we can conclude that only single-mindedness can please God. Serving God a little here and a little there will not produce a pleasing incense for our Heavenly Father, but instead only inconsistent serving. We can easily understand this in the following illustration.

If a couple goes into a restaurant, they want reliable service. They do not want a servant who will serve the appetizer and the vegetables, but then neglect to bring the meat, potatoes and dessert. The evening would become upsetting to the couple to the point that they might even have thoughts of wishing they had not gone out at all. The couple is much more satisfied, however, with a servant who is pleased to serve them their entire meal. Similarly, God is not pleased with a servant who only serves Him with half his mind, for this is in direct violation of the foremost command (Luke 10:27).

It is clear that consistent service unto the Lord is vital. Prayerless work will quickly slacken, and never bear fruit. The fire within us needs constant stirring through constant praying and communion with God, as well as feeding it to keep it burning bright.

How often does a person serve God the appetizer and the vegetables but fail to serve Him the meat, potatoes, and the dessert? In this widening world, more than ever there are many things that can occupy an individual's thoughts and serve as temptations to draw our minds from God. As the world becomes more complex, this process becomes more devastating in its potential. More than ever, we need to raise our shield of faith to the devil by being constantly aware of God. Only so long as it is raised can we hope to have an uplifting minute-to-minute fellowship with God (Ephesians 1:16). When the shield is lowered, our defenses are penetrable. We can stand firm with our shield held high for protection only through continuous communion with Him. It is not merely coincidence that the second verse following Ephesians 6:16, concerning the shield of faith, is Ephesians 6:18 which reads:

8 • THE POWER OF CONSTANT PRAYER AND COMMUNION WITH GOD

Pray at all times in the Spirit, with all prayer and supplication. To that end keep alert with all perseverance, making supplication for all the saints.

—Ephesians 6:18

Double-mindedness was a chief characteristic of many a person in the Bible, e.g., Samson (Judges 14-16); and Zedekiah (Jeremiah 37-38). One man who can hardly be accused of double-mindedness was Enoch.

By faith Enoch was taken up so that he should not see death; and he was not found, because God had taken him. Now before he was taken, he was attested as having pleased God.

—Hebrews 11:5

Enoch walked with God after the birth of Methuselah three hundred years, and had other sons and daughters… Enoch walked with God; and he was not, for God took him.

—Genesis 5:22, 24

I think it is safe to say that God was an incredibly close intimate friend of Enoch's. It is safe to say that Enoch had a life of constant companionship with God in the same way that is examined in this book. What a joy it must have been to be so close to God that in the process of reaching out to God to experience a greater relationship with Him, God reached down and took Enoch up to be with Him. If only we could seek for this kind of intimate relationship with God! I remember several times when I have felt so close to God that I felt like God was going to reach down and take me home with Him. Millions of others have experienced the same thing. What a pleasure it would be to experience this kind of relationship with God continually, just as Enoch did. Followers of Christ should treasure in the hearts of their memory those times they sense God's presence the most and are most open to what God wants them to do (the two must go together). Once Christ-followers have treasured those moments, then they know just how close they can be to God. By God's grace, they can ask God that they be that close all the time.

How often people fail to ask God to build up a consistency in them such that, by God's strength, devotees can live up to their potential and create more potential besides. People can get so comfortable in who they are that these people are slow to ask God for greater depths of relationship with the Father. Yet, this is what separates the adults from the boys and girls, so to speak. This is what distinguishes people like D. L. Moody, Martin Luther, Charles Finney, Mother Teresa, Dawson Trottman, and Brother Lawrence from the rest of the bunch. People are so imperfect that each person on earth will always need greater depth in his or her relationship with God. God always wants a deeper relationship with His children; it is up to the individual whether more enriching ties will ever form. A close walk with God, like Enoch had, is not just a matter of flicking a switch. Rather, it requires unmitigated submission to God. There is nothing like obedience today to reveal God's will tomorrow. It is the daily drill which makes mere spiritual midgets into triumphant believers.

PROTECTION AGAINST THE WILES OF SATAN

Satan Waits to Attack

My shield is God Most High, who saves the upright in heart.
—Psalm 7:10 (NIV)

The importance of a shield of faith has already been touched on. However, Psalm 7:10 indicates that a person's shield should be God. Too often a Christian's shield is something other than God. A shield spells security. As long as believers lift their shield of faith to the evil one, the Lord's followers are protected against the activities of the spiritual underworld. However, imitation shields can be raised up. Imitation shields can be most anything from financial security to "good" reasoning, to even a spouse or friends. Alcohol can be a shield, and so can other forms of escape be shields (Peterson, 2003). *But only one kind of shield can stand against Satan, and that is the shield of God!*

The kind of shield a Christian uses when faced with an onslaught from Satan tells a lot about in what that person have faith. Does an individual go for a beer? Do he or she turn on the T.V. to escape reality? Does an adult go to one's spouse for comfort? Or does that disciple go to God? Surely one will ask, "What is wrong with going to your spouse or a close brother or sister when head to head with Satan?" Nothing is wrong with it if that believer really going to God, i.e., going for counsel, intent on hearing a word from the Lord. If the counselor in any particular instance is unsure whether his or her advice is from the Lord, the value of what advice was given should decrease accordingly. If we are seeking comfort in the midst of trials, and we go to another to be comforted, it should be God's comfort which we seek, not that person's comfort alone.

For instance, if a fellow named "Bob" is having marital problems, he decides, in the course of things, to seek the advice of his best friend, "Steve." When Bob informs Steve that he is considering divorcing his wife, Steve turns to the Bible passages which state how much God hates divorce. Suddenly, Bob fumes, "Don't read to me what the Bible says. I want to hear what you say." This is an obvious case in which Bob was asking Steve's advice-not to hear from God, but rather to hear from Steve.

How frequently individuals rely on human beings and not God when circumstances get tough. This is so easy to do. When it is so natural to be aware of the physical realm that is easily apparent, men and women do not have to concentrate on the ground to know that the physical realm is there. The world is always apparent affecting one or more of one's senses at a single time. The spiritual realm is not so apparent. Although spiritual warfare is always taking place, humanity's fallen

10 • THE POWER OF CONSTANT PRAYER AND COMMUNION WITH GOD

state prevents people from being aware of it. Satan's greatest victory in the fall was seeing the mind's senses paralyzed in its perception of sin and the spiritual battles that potentially determine whether people's actions give birth to sin or not. *It is only through the restoring incarnation, death, and resurrection of our Lord that God becomes near to man and through the Holy Spirit, actually within him, and it is only through Jesus that the disciple can gain a new awareness of sin and a new awareness of the spiritual battlefield around him and within his own mind.* The path to viewing the spiritual plain of life has been opened.

Nonetheless, it takes focusing one's thoughts on God *constantly* to gain a celestial view of this plain. In short, the path to keener awareness of God has been opened by Jesus and the indwelling of the Holy Spirit. However, because this is a fallen world and spiritual sensitivity is not as automatic as physical sensitivity, a person must continually desire to set his mind and his entire being on God *so that he will be sensitive.*

> Into thy hand I commit my spirit; thou has redeemed me, O Lord, faithful God. Thou hatest those who pay regard to vain idols; but I trust in the Lord. I will rejoice and be glad for thy steadfast love, because thou hast seen my affliction, thou has taken heed of my adversaries.
>
> *—Psalm 31:5-7*

In many respects, constant awareness is the act of committing one's spirit to God, as the Psalm reads. Constant-prayer and awareness of God is an act of trust in that the individual is saying to God that he believes God can and will supply the strength needed to resist Satan and that he need look nowhere else. Most of what a person is aware of are sources! More specifically, *what a person is aware of are the sources he has faith in or trusts in!* If he is continually aware of God, he is expressing his faith in God as a trustworthy and powerful source, capable of conquering Satan. The psalmist in Psalm 31 knows that God sees what he is going through and trusts God as a believer, here. The whole section that was quoted expresses the trust that this man has in God. In fact, 31:6 states plainly "... but I trust in the Lord."

This kind of communion with God, resulting from faith, is a sure way of drastically limiting Satan's effectiveness. It follows then that Satan will attempt to break up this continual fellowship with God. Satan's goal then becomes that of convincing the disciple that God is not worthy of his faith, i.e., He is not trustworthy. *Satan will attempt to discredit God as a source so that the Christian no longer has a tremendous hunger to fellowship with God throughout the day.* Naturally, there are many ways Satan can go about this, and his multifaceted approach is one reason why constant awareness is difficult. Satan can attempt to convince a follower of Christ that God is not a just source. Satan will try to convince him that God is unfair when He permits various trials to enter his life. "Why be aware of such an unjust God?" he will say. Perhaps Satan will try to stir doubts in his mind about God's omnipotence. As a result, we think perhaps God does not have

Constant-Prayer and Communion With God and Faith • 11

everything in control. Maybe there are certain aspects of life beyond God's intervention. As a final example, Satan may try to convince him that God is not reliable enough or concerned enough about his happiness when it concerns being yielded to Him. It may be, he asserts, that God will only do what He wants to do and not what the individual wants.

On many occasions God places His children in a situation in their livres in which there is a tremendous number of trials. Satan may tempt us by saying that God is not just at such times. Unfortunately, people listen to Satan too often in this area. Satan will whisper to a person something like, "Who does God think He is? You've been trying your best to submit to Him in all areas of your life... This is the thanks you get! You call this a just God? Bring your case before Him and demand an explanation." Too many times devotees look at God's justice in terms of how comfortable they feel rather than how much they are growing in the Lord, by His grace. *If no one grew in Him, this would be an unjust God. For He cares more about our character than our comfort!*

Constant prayer is a Holy Spirit bomb which is a dangerous weapon against the evil one. The latter one will try to undermine it by trying to convince us that God is not trustworthy, but we should strike back using constant awareness itself as a means to reach God. For while Satan is on a tempting rampage by saying that God is no one special to be worthwhile being aware of, a believer can seek communion with God in such a way that God reveals to that person why He is all-deserving of an individual's thoughts. Praise the Lord! Satan has met defeat at every corner where he sought victory. For when Satan poses doubts in a certain area of a Christian's relationship with God, a disciple has only to come before the Throne, communicating with God honestly, fully, and continually, and He will tell us why He is God and that He is indeed the most faithful.

Constant Awareness – An Insurance Against Satan

By Faith a Living Sacrifice

> By faith Abel offered to God a more acceptable sacrifice than Cain, through which he received approval as righteous, God bearing witness by accepting his gifts; he died, but through faith he is still speaking.
>
> *—Hebrews 11:4*

> Behold, he whose soul is not upright in Him shall fail; but the righteous shall live by faith.
>
> *—Habakkuk 2:4*

A Call to righteousness entails offering an acceptable sacrifice to God; that is ourselves. Abel did not only offer a more acceptable sacrifice in terms of what he offered as a physical substance, but also his sacrifice was more acceptable because he gave his heart to God. The Word of God exhorts us to give our lives up as a

12 • THE POWER OF CONSTANT PRAYER AND COMMUNION WITH GOD

sacrifice to God, in the form of a full commitment to do His will (Romans 12:1, 2). In our prayer, praise, and daily life in general, we should continually ask that God work through us fully "to will and work for His good pleasure" through a totally yielded instrument (Hebrews 13:15; Philippians 2:13).

When we have an attitude that is conducive to a total emptying of ourselves that we may be of usable service to God, we are also going to be constantly aware of God. *One of the reasons why fasting is so spiritually efficacious is because what believers do when they fast is to voluntarily create a void in their lives and ask God to fill it with Himself.*

A totally submitted servant will be extremely excited about the prospect of His Master using him in very special ways, and he will not want to miss out on anything God has in store (Piper, 2011). In order to be certain that he will not miss out on anything, he will be constantly aware of any plans God should happen to reveal. *Constant prayer and awareness are necessary for a more effective and unadulterated service to God!*

Waiting on God

> But as for me, I will look to the Lord, I will wait for the God of my salvation; my God will hear me.
>
> *—Micah 7:7*

> By faith Abraham, when he was tested, offered up Isaac, and he who had received the promises was ready to offer up his only son.
>
> *—Hebrews 11:17*

Ah, yes, patience; however elusive it seems. The ability to wait on God is vital. It takes faith to honestly desire God's timing above one's own. It takes time spent with God, seeing His hand at work to desire God's timing. To be heavenly-minded as a result of time spent with God can either result from many years of experience or through constant communion with God. The former is more relaxing, but the latter more suitable for a person who really loves God.

Notice that the verse quoted from Micah reads, "I will look to the Lord" (suggesting constant prayer) followed by "I will wait..." *A believer must look to Heaven in faith and the "hope of Glory" if he is to be able to wait upon God!* Not only must he be able to wait upon God for what he wants to receive, but also upon receiving it he must realize that what he has received belongs to God, and therefore, be willing to surrender it if God calls him to do so. Abraham is a brilliant example of this. He had waited upon God for a son to carry on the seed towards the Promised Land. In Genesis 22, God asked Abraham to give up that seed. Abraham had waited decades for his son; now he would have to acknowledge God's dominion over what the Lord had given him. Abraham, by faith, passed the test. A believer has to have reached a height of communication with God to be able to pass this crucible.

Constant-Prayer and Communion With God and Faith • 13

These all died in faith, not having received what was promised, but having seen it and greeted it from afar, and having acknowledged that they were strangers and exiles on the earth. For people who speak thus make it clear that they are seeking a homeland. If they had been thinking of that land from which they had gone out, they would have had opportunity to return. But as it is, they desire a better country, that is, a heavenly one. Therefore, God is not ashamed to be called their God, for He has prepared for them a city.

—Hebrews 11:13-16

But I will hope *continually*, and will praise thee yet *more* and *more*.

—Psalm 71:4

All born-again believers have a hope which will never die; the eternal hope of Heaven. Why not be constantly aware of this constant hope?

Our Hope Is Where Our Mind Is!

1.   The believer thinks of those closest to him the most.
2.   The ones closest to him are most likely to help him in a time of need.
3.   Therefore, the ones that the believer thinks about the most are the ones that are most likely to help him.

When one talks about the believer's heavenly future, faith and hope suddenly become strongly intertwined. If a believer has faith in eternal life, he or she has a hope. The believer's God is so great, so loving, and so full of justice that having faith that God is who He says He is, that person also has a hope. There is a hope because that individual is a believer in Jesus Christ. His hope is greatly dependent on his faith. If it is true that constant prayer with God produces a greater faith in the follower, it must therefore bring forth greater hope.

Through experience and an examination of the two verses just quoted, the reader discovers two things that are requisite if one is to be a believer filled with hope:

1.   Christians must realize deep in their hearts that their hope lies not on this earth, but rather in the homeland of Yahweh (Hebrews 11:13-16).
2.   They must "hope continually" by being constantly aware of God. *A person cannot hope continually in God unless he or she is communicating with God continually.*

With reference to the first point, a majority of Christians put the greatest hope in the life which takes place on earth. If you ask these people, they will not attest to this; nor if they are in a heavenly frame of mind at church service, will they show this. However, when it comes to daily decision making, worrying about worldly concerns that are but a molecule of vapor in the context of eternity and in rejoicing over the "prosperity doctrine," their emphasis has become transfig-

14 • THE POWER OF CONSTANT PRAYER AND COMMUNION WITH GOD

ured before all who care to observe. How often does the believer meditate on this heavenly hope? Oh, but what joy awaits every believer! Hallelujah! How can he not think about it? Eternal life with God is the greatest gift humans could ever receive; *yet who bothers to shake the box and peek under the lid to try to get a glimpse of what's inside!* Many believers have such a solemn attitude about the gift of eternal life that I wonder whether God sometimes feels like taking the gift back from some people.

An important consequence of not being heavenly-minded is that humans tend to be overwhelmed by earthly problems which really are not so ponderous as they seem. It is like a teacher who is showing five-year-olds how to look through a microscope for the very first time. She tells the children that the class will be looking at small insects magnified 1,000 times under a microscope. She instructs the children to peer into the microscope with one eye but to keep the other eye set on the insects apart from the microscope. This she says, in order to give the children a proper perspective of the insects real magnified size. One of the children, however, looks at the microscope with both eyes, disobeying the teacher. To test the children's understanding of the concept of size, the teacher then asks a question. She asks, "If we were to fight these insects in a war, who would win?" Almost every child understood that humans would win because they are much larger. The child who looked through the microscope with two eyes, however, might say that the insects could win because they were so large and so many.

Many humans are much like the latter child. As long as we keep our eyes pinned to this world, the problems and elements of this planet will always appear larger than they are. As a result, they will view some of the situations encountered as overwhelming and leading to sure defeat. God wants His children to be like the majority of the students in the above illustration. He wants His children to have an eye on a situation apart from the microscope of earthly life. God wants believers to have a heavenly perspective on life. It is only then that they will see the obstacles of life on a realistic scale. Surely, the power of God exceeds all these things. Heavenly-mindedness gives devotees the faith that earthly obstacles can be conquered and the hope that because God is so great, one's heavenly hope must be far greater. For this heavenly-mindedness, constant awareness of God is the key!

Paul's epistle to the church at Thessalonica is a letter to a church without hope. The people within the church thought the rapture had already taken place. It is therefore easy to understand why their hope had deteriorated. Sad to say, we can live in a world in which the rapture has already taken place, so to speak, if we choose. We can act as if we have been left behind in this way by not consistently mediating on the hope that lies ahead, "the homeland," "the Promised Land." With the rapture having become history, a person's hope would be drowned. He or she would be in a state of bewilderment and helplessness. "Our Lord has left without us!" What one has waited for over such a long period has passed by. Only what is left on this planet remains. Oh, what an awful death sentence! Yet, this is

Constant-Prayer and Communion With God and Faith • 15

how individuals are living when they set our mind on earthly things (Colossians 2:20).

To venture to have an interminable hope, by praising God and by seeking by God's grace to meditate on eternity from sunrise until bed, is a life changer. (Philippians 4:8). Somehow as the church citizenry allows God to give them celestial meditations, earth is never the same. But the most beautiful thing is that Heaven is never the same either. Anxiety is minimized, joy is maximized, and God is better understood as the Source of all things. True, there is a heavenly-mindedness that does "no earthly good," the mind is on the unreal. But what lies within a true-heavenly minded man is a Heaven descended to earth so that the church citizenry can do "much earthly good." A person's mind is set on the real as well as the ideal. For as a Christian, one finds that the real lies within the ideal, which is Christ. Earthly living will never be the same.

REFERENCES

Bonhoeffer, D. (1959). *The cost of discipleship*. Macmillan.

Chambers, O. (2008). *My utmost for His highest*. Discovery House Publishers.

Graham, B. (2015). *Quotations book*. Retrieved March 26, 2015 from: http://quotations-book.com/quote/38480/.

Jeynes, W. (1999). The effects of religious comments on the academic achievements of black and Hispanic children. *Urban Education, 34*(4), 458–479.

Jeynes, W. (2006). *A hand not shortened*. Information Age Publishing.

Jeynes, W. (2016). *What would Christ do?* Information Age Publishing.

Jeyens, W., & Martinez, E. (Eds.). (2015). *Ministering spiritually to families.* Springer.

Minith, F. B. (2004). *In pursuit of happiness: Choices that can change your life*. Fleming H. Revell

Montague, G. T. (2011). *First Corinthians*. Baker Academic.

Peterson, J. (2003). *The insider: Bringing the Kingdom of God into your everyday world*. Navigator Press.

Piper, J. (2011). *Desiring God: Meditations of a Christian hedonist*. Multnomah.

CHAPTER 2

CONSTANT-PRAYER AND COMMUNION WITH GOD AND JOY

INTRODUCTION

From faith we move on to joy. Joy is the fuel for mature, productive Christian living (Tozer, 2013; Wiersbe, 2005). Joyful Christians are going to be Christians who seek out the love of God and are determined to find it so that God's love can poured out of them and onto others (Tozer, 2013; Wiersbe, 2005). Joy is a trait that is noticeably absent from the world, and upon seeing it in a Christian, many non-believing people will covet it and may reach a point in which they call out to God, asking for a life filled with joy. Joy, then, is an important aspect of the believer's walk with God. It is a fruit of the Lord's orchard; yet it is somehow often misunderstood by non-believers and believers alike.

JOY AS A FRUIT

The Creator and the Orchard

But the fruit of the Spirit is love, joy, peace, patience, kindness, goodness, faithfulness, gentleness, self-control, against such there is no law.

The Power of Constant Prayer and Communion With God, pages 17–30.
Copyright © 2024 by Information Age Publishing
www.infoagepub.com
All rights of reproduction in any form reserved.

18 • THE POWER OF CONSTANT PRAYER AND COMMUNION WITH GOD

—Galatians 5:22, 23

May the God of hope fill you with all joy and peace in believing, so that by the power of the Holy Spirit you may *abound* in hope.

—Romans 15:13

The first two truths that should be emphasized are that God is the source of joy and that joy is a fruit of that source with a special function performed by the Holy Spirit Himself. Joy is not an individual's own fruit, but rather it is God's. The reader should be careful to notice that the Holy Spirit is mentioned in each of these verses on joy. To be sure, one of the foremost results of quenching the Spirit is a loss of joy (I Thessalonians 5:19). The fact that God is wholly responsible for creating joy is patent intellectually, but in real life people seem to take credit for so much more than their actual contribution. It is evident that the fact that God is the only source of joy needs to be meditated on (I Corinthians 3:7-9). Yes, God is the only source of joy! People cannot produce joy by alcohol, sex, escapism, or by manufacturing an imitation of Christian joy on their own (Jeynes, 2002a, 2002b, 2003a, 2003b). Real joy comes fully from God. Hallelujah!

Regarding this searching for a fountain of joy outside of God Himself, the most prevalent form of sin is the tendency towards manufacturing an imitation of Christian joy. To experience the joy initiated by God's Spirit is to undergo a dramatic change in what is a disciple's conception of joy. It is to be so spectacular a change that a believer yearns to relive that joy again and again in his or her Christian experience. On the whole, this new ardency is precisely what God wants for His children! He rejoices over nothing more than feeding those who are spiritually hungry and giving "living water" to those who have spiritual thirst. The problem comes in when people strive to replicate that joy on their own, unable to satisfy their longing within their usual means of fellowship with God. Believers may attempt to do this one of two ways: (1) substitution, or (2) replication.

Substitution is the act of substituting another source of joy for God. Almost anything can serve as a substitute, as long as it provides a temporary lift. This can include sports, members of the opposite sex, television, food, or what have you. Many of the substitutes may not be sins in and of themselves, but once people attempt to create temporary and insufficient substitutes for God's joy, it becomes sin.

Replication is attempting to produce joy by revving up one's motor and trying to self-manufacture joy. Forced smiles or praises to God serve as examples of replication. This is not to say we should not praise God when we do not feel like it. What it does mean is that the only rejoicing that God esteems as genuine rejoicing in Him is that which comes from submitting and relying on the Spirit of God.

There is a tendency Christians can have towards being joyful all the time and using our own steam to accomplish it. Yes, it does take steam to be joyful, but it takes the steam of submission, not the steam of an engine. Much of this tendency towards *locomotive joy* accrues from a misconception of what joy in Christ really is. The Greek word for joy is "kara" which literally means "calm delight." Thomas Cock once said, "Joy is not a ceaseless rapture, but a settled quiet of the heart, the tranquility of a soul poised in harmony with divine will." One can be moving along on a real high in the Spirit for a while and then run into stiff trial(s) and the highs falls flat. In many cases such as this, the fact of the matter is that the "joy" that individual had was not a well-founded one. If the preceding pattern is characteristic of a person's walk with God, one can hardly be seen as a joyful Christian in the eyes of God. However, there are cases when a believer is close to God and is delighting oneself in Him but not experiencing a high. Once again, a stiff trial(s) may present itself, and by God's grace the devotee is not moved. When this is an individual's experience, the "joy" is substantially close to what God says is joy in Him, more than in the former example.

The difference between these two kinds of "joy" is much like the difference between a model rocket and a private airplane. As soon as the model rocket is lit, it goes soaring into the sky. It reaches great heights faster than the airplane. In fact, it may reach its zenith even before the aircraft is off the ground. The ascent of the private airplane, on the other hand, is relatively slow. However, two points are significant to note. First, the model rocket will quickly be struck down if met with adverse weather-while the plane will hold its own amidst a storm. Second, the model rocket will quickly dive down because its fuel reserve is very limited. Conversely the plane will be able to remain at great heights because it has a large fuel reserve. What kind of joy do we have as Christians? Do we have the model rocket type of joy which reaches great heights quickly but soon dives downward due to adverse conditions or a low fuel reserve? Or do we have an airplane type of joy which holds its own amidst adversity and can maintain great heights because of its large fuel reserve?

How many times Satan has fooled believers by convincing them that their "high" at a particular time and place was founded on the Rock; that it was the joy of Christ, and therefore, steadfast-when it was not indeed. And how many times Satan has attempted to make them doubt their joy because people were not leaping over bus stop benches and singing loud praises when they were indeed delighting themselves in Him and experiencing real joy. How all too human people are to swallow the lies of the evil one, when it comes to joy. Joy is a fruit. It may look perfectly juicy on the outside and not be ripe or may even be rotting on the inside. It may also appear less shiny on the outside but be very juicy indeed.

Outward Manifestations of Joy

Thou has turned for me my mourning into dancing; thou hast loosed my sackcloth and girded me with gladness.

—Psalm 30:11

20 • THE POWER OF CONSTANT PRAYER AND COMMUNION WITH GOD

> An evil man is ensnared in his transgression, but a righteous man sings and rejoices.
>
> *—Proverbs 29:6*

Though whether the fruit appears shiny or juicy may not always be an accurate indication of true joy, there is also a strong sense in which *joy cannot help but shine forth. The way that joy is best manifested is in its consistency.* Once again, the "up today-down tomorrow" Christian is not a joyful Christian, no matter how great the heights achieved may be! *As a disciple grows, the heights achieved in joy are of only slightly higher magnitude or not higher at all, but it is the consistency of joy that becomes pronounced.*

While the general term that best depicts a joyful Christian is "consistent joy," specific manifestations such as singing, dancing, bright eyes, bushy tails, and enthusiasm are no doubt evident. Singing seems to come quite naturally to most when they are joyful in the Lord. This is because God has put a "new song" in their heart. Some Christians think dancing is wrong. But I still dance, I have just changed partners! Now I dance with Jesus! Praise God! The last thing that a person should do is quench what way the Holy Spirit is attempting to express Himself (1 Thessalonians 5:19). Though outward manifestations of joy and worship are the least important aspects of each, they should nonetheless be evidenced as part of the heart's expression of its relationship with God.

CONSTANT AWARENESS AND CONSTANT JOY: A WAY OF LIFE

A Full Joy

> These things I have spoken to you, that my joy may be in you, and that your joy may be *full.*
>
> *—John 15:11*

> Hitherto you have asked nothing in my name; ask and you will receive that your joy may be *full.*
>
> *—John 16:24*

A full joy is something which God wants for all His children (Orr, 2009; Swindoll, 1998; Wiersbe, 2005). The Greek word that is used in these verses is "plaroma" and expresses "full." It is from the Greek term meaning repletion or completion. A believer can only have a complete or repletion of joy by existing within God's presence 24 hours a day. *To have a life full of joy, a Christian has to be full of God! This means allowing our heart and mind to soak in His presence.*

Why is it that Christians find it difficult to experience this complete joy when the believer knows that Jesus Christ makes it available? It seems one can only be drawn so close to God, and then the tendency is to momentarily stray from life's proper perspective, which comes from Him (Murray, 1979, 2004). *People do not experience a full joy all the time because there are times when we either think there is something else that can make us full or we doubt that God can make us as full as He claims! What utter foolishness!*

We may not think this applies to us, but if we lack joy in our life, this is by definition what is happening. Behind these deceptions that we fall victim to, lies the need for more reassurance from God. Reassurance that God is the only means to joy both on earth and eternally (John 10:10, 14:6). What is amazing is that God often wishes to reassure us, but whether it is Satan or our own spiritual acoustical ineptitude, we do not hear God's voice. Psalm 29 is entitled by many Bible scholars as "The Lord's Voice in the Storm." This Psalm describes the voice of the Lord being heard in the physical features of the storm itself. God's voice is at the forefront of trials; the latter may create doubts concerning God's ability to give us a full life and joy. If we are to hear God's voice often, reassuring us as His sheep, we must be close enough to the Lord to perceive His voice in the storm (Peterson, 2003; Piper, 2011). My own life, my dear brothers and sisters, tells me that I cannot perceive God's voice *unless I make it a point to listen for it!* Indeed, for a consistent full joy, we must *listen for God's voice from morning 'til night!*

The human tendency is to flee from "the voice of the Lord in the storm" into a house, desiring comfort rather than to stand still in silence and listen to His voice. If we would only realize in our innermost heart that when a storm comes, it is because God wants to speak to us and He wants to make His voice plain. If only we were constantly communing with God, we could understand this more than we do. Then we would apprehend that He wants to speak to us during stormy weather, when we have doubts and when we therefore look for what appears to be refuges of comfort and joy. As long as Yahweh is God of it, it will always be better to listen to Him in the storm and know His control of circumstances than to seek another refuge which looks secure, but in which we have closed the doors to the mighty and wise voice of the Lord God, Yahweh.

A Rich Experience in Joy

> Rejoice *always,* pray *constantly,* give thanks *in all circumstances,* for this is the will of God, in Christ Jesus for you.
> *—I Thessalonians 5:16-18*

The will of God is to have everlasting fellowship with His children! This is what receivers of Christ experience while living forever in the presence of God! It is God's will that this experience begin during the Christian's tenure on earth! These verses illustrate three aspects of life in Heaven: constant joy, prayer, and thanksgiving. The latter two qualities contribute to produce the first. In Revelation 4 individuals get a glimpse of what one might term "the worship leaders of the universe." In verses 4:8-11, in particular, they can see the verses I Thessalonians 5:16-18 applied in heavenly worship. How glorious it will be! Man cannot even

22 • THE POWER OF CONSTANT PRAYER AND COMMUNION WITH GOD

begin to imagine what Heaven will be like, but how blessed are God's children who get a glimpse of heaven in His Word and by His presence. That makes for "heaven on earth."

All of these three commands are founded in constant awareness of God. In these three successive verses, we find the words *"always,"* *"constantly,"* and *"all circumstances."* What could be more plain? Constant awareness of God, hence, becomes a commandment. If disciples are constantly aware of God, they are, almost by definition, praying at all times. If adherents are constantly communing with God, they cannot help but experience a vibrant overflow of joy in their lives. If people are constantly aware of God, they will see God's hand in the events of life, time and time again. Consequently, believers will be able to thank God in virtually everything that happens to them.

Christians need to talk to God more. No one can ever get enough of Him. The difference between communicating with God throughout the day and praying to Him only a few times is akin to what divergence exists between a slide projector and a movie (Bounds, 2010; Briscoe, 2013; Jeynes, 2020). In the former, a convert only gets scant glances of the hand of God performing in his life, while in the latter, it is much more continuous. Just as a person can get a much superior idea of what a story is about from a movie than a slide projector show, so he or she grows to know God more through constant awareness than "slide projector awareness." Think of a favorite motion picture of yours; let us say *"Gone with the Wind."* Would you rather see this story in the form of a motion picture or a fifty-slide presentation? In which form would we gain a better conception of what the plot was all about? Of course, we would rather see *"Gone with the Wind"* in the form of a motion picture, if we were ever to begin to appreciate its fullness.

How often people cheat themselves by glancing at the work of the Lord in their lives when He is always working. It is truly exciting to watch the ways of the Lord at work! When individuals fail to observe His hand in our affairs, they disappoint God, but they also miss out themselves. How sad it is that when a man watches a football game he makes certain that he does not miss one play. He believes that any play could change the entire nature of the game. My goodness, brethren! If one believes this is true of football, how much more is it true in God's plan. *If only human beings were as excited about seeing every phase of God's plans as they were about every play of a football game!*

> Be glad in the Lord, and rejoice, O righteous and shout for joy, all you upright in heart!
>
> *—Psalm 32:11*

> But you shall eat them before the Lord your God in the place which the Lord your God will choose, you and your son and your daughter, your manservant and your maidservant, and the Levite who is within your towns, and you shall rejoice before the Lord your God in all that you undertake.
>
> *—Deuteronomy 12: 18*

Constant-Prayer and Communion With God and Joy • **23**

If only Christians would have more of a heart for God. If only Christians would know that God is beside them and within them each moment of the day. If only Christians took complete joy in Him. If only Christians could shout for joy all day long! Though the joy of the Lord may fill the individual most of his steps, the all-too-human machinery resulting from the all-too-human fall of humanity, prevents him from experiencing a full platter of Heaven. Some people deny this and claim they praise the Lord always. I will let the Bible and their lives disprove them (I John 1:8; Job 15:14; Proverbs 20:9; James 3:2). It is my experience, as well as the experience of others, that the most joyful Christians, almost by definition, know how much they fall short of experiencing the completeness of God's joy.

Ah, yes, from the last paragraph the reader might wonder whether humility and joy tend to flock together (Clairvaux, 1940). Remember, the author does not mean joy in the often-used sense of the word, but rather with the original meaning in "kara" discussed previously. Joy in the often-used sense of the word can result from pride. This is less apt to happen when one is experiencing "kara," the true joy of the Lord. *Any gift from the Lord, in the broad sense of the term, will be accompanied by humility, and any joy beyond that is susceptible to human pride as an additive factor.* True joy from the Lord will highlight the glory of God. "God is wonderful! God is king! God has done much! Therefore, I am joyous!" In godly joy there is an acknowledgement of God as the *one* and *only* Source.

Given this background of what it is to have true and continuous joy in the Lord, it is safe to say that a substantial portion of a believer's "joy" is not from God. "Joy" is too often founded in circumstances. God allows Christians to discover just how far short they fall of the replete joy He wants for them through stiff trials. Jesus said that anyone can love the person who loves one- self and that the true test is loving one's enemies (Matthew 5:46, 47). Similarly, anyone can be "up" when circumstances are good; the real test is when his circumstances are adverse.

I recall a teenage Vietnamese boy who, though he was seventeen, because of his inexperience with the English language, had his classes predominantly with thirteen-year-olds. In all fields of athletics, he was therefore able to far exceed the abilities of his far younger classmates. Over time this teenager began to feel pretty good about his talents. He was able to wrestle his opponents to the mat without much problem at all, etc. Could one then conclude this Vietnamese boy was a superb athlete? Of course not, for he had met only with easy and not adverse situations in his athletics. He had not yet met with a situation which thoroughly tested his athletic abilities. Until such a test occurred, we could have no idea as to how good an athlete he really is.

Someone once said, "Joy is discovered in the change of conflict, disturbance, loss and confusion, which often makes other unhappy. Joy is unassailable, untouchable, undisturbable. Joy is the outward manifestation of the inner experience of grace."

24 • THE POWER OF CONSTANT PRAYER AND COMMUNION WITH GOD

The Holy Spirit and Joy

> Sing and rejoice, O daughter of Zion; for lo, I come and I will dwell *in the midst of you*, says the Lord.
>
> *—Zechariah 2:10*

This portion of scripture can be seen as a prophecy relating to Jesus Christ and His Spirit.

> Even the Spirit of truth, whom the world cannot receive, because it neither sees Him nor knows Him; you know Him, *for He dwells with you*, and *will be in you.*
>
> *—John 14:17*

God's Spirit is in the midst of His followers; what great reason for joy! Joy because it is a privilege to have God's Spirit within us, but primarily for the reason that it is God's Spirit that produces the joy (Galatians 5:22, 23; Ephesians 5:18). To experience the joy of the Holy Spirit, a Christian must open himself up to the Holy Spirit. He must seek more completely to grasp the power that is in the presence of God, that is, the Holy Spirit. For one reason or another, many believers quench the Holy Spirit so that the joy of Christ does not shine and Christ is not elevated in glory. Many congregations will allow faith, hope, and the Word of God to be manifested, but not the corporateness of joy within the Body.

I fear that within a large part of the Christian Body there is a perceptible tendency to suppress joy for fear that other believers would think certain individuals are inordinately zealous or too emotional. Be that as it may, joy does not have to be in the form of audible shouts to be joy. Yet, if an individual wishes to express the comfort and gladness which he or she experiences as an eventuation of a heart which is surrendered to the Lord, why should that person be discouraged from expressing himself? How sad that these inhibitions are within the Church itself to limit the extent to which God can guide His people in the direction and at the magnitude that He so desires to work. How much more then will there be inhibitions within believers themselves among nonbelievers? God means that the Church be a vessel through which He can strengthen His people in their continuous struggle with the outside world. When a church does not encourage the liberty of joyfully worshipping the Lord in an individual way, we need to wonder how much strength the Body, in fact, acquires. The Scripture is clear that a follower derives his greatest source of strength from the "joy of the Lord" (Nehemiah 8:10). To the extent which this is true, what does this say for the people who are involved in spiritual warfare who are moribund when it comes to evidencing the joy of the Lord?

I have found it very important to sing a hymn or really become involved in praising the Lord in my morning devotional time. I find that if I do not go out the door spiritually exalted in my Lord, I am "dead," so to speak, as soon as I shut the front door. If the approaching day is like so many others, the events of the day will

Constant-Prayer and Communion With God and Joy • 25

eventually catch up with me. This is why I make certain I am spiritually lifted in Jesus, when I start the day. In this sense, joy is a preventive medicine. Joy serves to protect the Christian from the unexpected turn of events that can so easily send him down an emotional ski slope. The 10, 000 decibel joy from God will safeguard His people against any shock waves Satan can whip up, in a given day. The joy that is purely from the Lord is TNT to Satan. This is why Satan rarely attempts to fight this joy directly, but rather uses indiscriminate means. Satan's usual plan of attack will be to dilute the joy and attempt to make it less founded on God. He will endeavor to bring to affect a joy founded on pride, or circumstances, or emotions. The devil will attempt to make a person think he is really applauding God, when he is actually concentrating more on the blessings themselves rather than their source. Satan will attempt to dilute or pollute the joy that a person has from the Lord, and then he will manage to find an opening through which he can attack and sabotage the joy absolutely.

How often it seems that a person's joy is initially of God, but then it is taken by the wind so that one's joy soon becomes based on little foundation at all. A believer begins by giving praises to God, which are pure white in nature. "Praise God! He is the only true glorious King." Satan meanwhile defiles this praise, i.e., dilutes it by planting thoughts in his head along the lines of: "He has done so much for *me.*" As time rolls along, his emphasis becomes more and more on the "me," rather than the "*He*"! The ploy is obvious; and the results are even more obvious. "Joy," then, can be deceptive. *Satan can use even weapons of God against God's children!* If a child of God does not hold steadfastly to God's Word, i.e., the Sword, Satan will use the Sword as a weapon. If he does not check whether his joy is from God, Satan can potentially use the joy against him to set the stage for a surprise attack (I Peter 5:8).

> And they kept the feast of unleavened bread seven days with joy, for the Lord had made them joyful, and had turned the heart of the king of Assyria to them, so that He aided them in the work of the house of God, the God of Israel.
>
> *—Ezra 6:22*

> And they offered great sacrifices that day and rejoiced, for God had made them rejoice with great joy; the women and children also rejoiced. And the joy of Jerusalem was heard afar off.
>
> *—Nehemiah 12: 43*

What a tremendous joy God offers His friends (John 15:14, 15). It is evident that joy in these verses results from feasting with the Lord in the first case and sacrificing to Him in the second. Though communion is generally thought of as the time when God's body feasts with the Lord (Matthew 26:26-29; I Corinthians 11:23-26), believers should continually be feasting with the Lord.

26 • THE POWER OF CONSTANT PRAYER AND COMMUNION WITH GOD

….. a cheerful heart has a *continual feast.*

—Proverbs 15:15

The man or woman who feasts with the Lord senses the presence of God wherever one goes. This does not mean this devotee has some extra-sensory perception, but rather that the person is constantly aware that God is near and acts upon that knowledge by communicating with God. When an individual is studying the Word of God fervently and is communing with God unceasingly, that person will be feasting on God's meat and this is a feast indeed. *A Christian does not get just milk, when he is continually feasting with God!* And how Jesus loves to feast with His children. This is likely a major reason why the glorious celebrations in the Old Testament were in the form of feasts (Deuteronomy 16:13; Exodus 12:12, 23:16; 34:22; John 7:2, 10:22, 13:1). Even when Christ offers to come into a person's heart, it is for the purpose of having supper with His children (Revelation 3:20). What a personal God! God does not want just worship and praise, He wants to *feast with His children!*

The verse in Nehemiah refers to sacrifice. The church's responsibility as a body of believers today is not to sacrifice animals, but instead for each member to sacrifice his or her own life. A person sacrifices oneself so that the Lord may be able to feast on that person so that that disciple might bring glory to His Name! In sacrificing, Nehemiah 12:43 is quite clear about the joy resulting. How appropriate it was in the years before Christ that feasting was accompanied by sacrifice. *The festivals were meant to promote a spiritual feasting on God by man and a spiritual feasting on man by God. In this mutual feast, one finds the rudiments of a continual abiding joy in the Lord!*

What a feast God offers us as followers of Jesus! Jesus desires to have a feast unto eternity with His children; yet His followers seem to hesitate not at declining His invitation! They often say, "But I have to work to do Lord, even work for you. I have not got time to feast. I'd hate to eat and run!" How foolish the church citizenry is indeed! *For we cannot do the work of God unless we feast with Jesus both before and during work for him.* I fear that even if His servants accept Christ's invitation to feast *before* the day and His task set before us, most decline Christ's invitation *during* the day and *during* our tasks. The latter is the continual feast God desires to fill His children's hearts with and is entirely reposed upon constant awareness of God in the fullness of joy.

It is like a wife who is starving to have some time with her husband. The husband, not desiring his wife to get in the way of his daily tasks, decides he will set aside an hour each morning to spend with his wife. However, situations arise during the course of the day in which the wife needs to talk to her husband. But her husband says, "No, I haven't got time to talk with you now. I already gave you an hour; let it go until tomorrow." This example may seem quite ridiculous to reader, but this is exactly the way humans often treat God. Believers may have an hour's

Constant-Prayer and Communion With God and Joy • 27

quiet time with the Lord in the morning, but because they are not constantly communing with Him, they do not hear His voice during the day.

JOY DESPITE CIRCUMSTANCES

The Fountain and the Heart

Rejoice in the Lord always; again I will say, Rejoice; let all men know your forbearance. The Lord is at hand.

—Philippians 4:4, 5

Rejoice and be glad, for your reward is great in heaven, for so men persecuted the prophets who were before you.

—Matthew 5:12

If Christians are to rejoice in all circumstances, they must be able to rejoice in adversity (Agich, 2003; Bergman, 2004; Jeynes, 2009). The reason why believers are not more consistent in their walk with God is largely because they are not constantly communing with God enough. If these Christ-followers experienced communion with God on a more consistent basis, they would be more prepared for a Satanic onslaught of tribulation. As long as believers fellowship with God, there is hardly a chink in their armor.

When individuals are constantly praying to God, they are receiving a fountain of God's joy that our cup may overflow with joy, in the midst of turmoil (Daley, 2009; Graham, 2015; Minith, 2004). *We cannot have a flow of joy in turbulence unless we have our heart filled with God's fountains of joy on a consistent basis!* There is no other true fountain. There is no other true source of joy.

Born-again Christians must open up their vial to the everlasting fountain of God to receive more of the Living Water which they already have in their heart. If they do not open up, lifting up his vial to the Living Water of the Lord, God's fountain of joy cannot enter one's heart. We lift up our vial insofar as we are aware of God and pray to Him. We are not blocking the thoughts of God as long as we are talking and listening to God. Our own thoughts just will not do; for God's thoughts are vastly superior to man's (Isaiah 55:8, 9).

Matthew 5:12 emphasizes that God's joy is a heavenly joy. A heavenly joy is nothing other than heavenly directed. An individual cannot be high in "spirit" on the things of the world and have heavenly joy. Joy points man's eyes upward. There is nothing on earth which can justify such extensive joy as that joy which is from God's heavenly fountain. Ah, that we might partake and know that Heaven is ever so close. Close, not as a result of what we reckon with the seven senses, but by uncorking the lid of our vial which is the heart.

Our Perspective and God's; The Path Resulting

> Then he said to them, 'Go your way, eat the fat and drink sweet wine and send portions to him for whom nothing is prepared; for this day is holy to our Lord; and do not be grieved, for the joy of the Lord *is your strength.*
> —*Nehemiah 8:10*

> Thou doest show me the path of life; in thy presence there is *fullness of joy, in thy right hand are pleasures forevermore.*
> —*Psalm 16:11*

Where else is joy but in the presence of the Lord? Where else is there strength but in the presence of God? Psalm 16:11 makes it plain that a *complete* joy is found when we have complete fellowship with God. As a human being, a person has an unfortunate tendency to look for a strength that one can see. Even when individuals seek out God's foundation, they still want to be able to see it. Christians want an indication from God that He is with us. Thank God that He has given us His Word!

It is not surprising that a devotee goes wayward with respect to God's plan when his strength is not the joy that results from a mature and hence, a continual fellowship with God. One of the main areas in which a Christian needs strength is in terms of his mind. Satan attacks the mind of the Christian in order to confuse him as to what the will of the Lord is. Satan baffles his mind by changing the street signs, so to speak. Satan moves the Main Street to Broadway and vice versa. One of two things can take place here:

1. God's direction may have been to take Broadway on the Main Street—Broadway intersection. As a result, the person takes the wrong street and strides along the wrong road.
2. God's directions may have been to go east on Broadway on the Main Street—Broadway intersection. Upon reaching this intersection, the Christian becomes disturbed because Broadway runs North-South due to the shenanigan of Satan. The result of this experience is doubt.

"God, you gave me the wrong directions! What is with you?! Why did You do this to me?!"

Yes, this is the way Satan deceives God's people. Minds are susceptible to such chicanery. Only the counsel of God can save people from this fate. Counsel from the Lord comes only through communion with God, in whatever form. Strength comes from this, and where there is strength and communion with God, there is joy. Joy and spiritual direction have a high positive correlation with each other.

Surely, there is joy if a Christian is going in the direction and at the speed which the Lord wants him to go (Offner, Larsen. & Larsen, 2013). The devotee can best understand that joy is from the Lord when his perspective is from the

Lord's eyes. Joy is so certainly a part of God's will for His people that true joy and walking in the will of the Lord almost invariably go together. This is not to say that God *expects* a Christian to have joy at all times. After all a Christian is only human. Nonetheless, in trusting that God is going to provide for his future, the disciple necessarily has some element of joy. The reasoning along these lines is simple. A child of God is heaven bound with regards to his direction when he is constantly practicing the presence of God. Psalm 16:11 gives a true declaration that there is joy in the presence of the Lord; there is joy in walking in the will of God. No true full joy lies outside God's will. Happy is the man or woman who seeks God's will, for the resultant joy shall be eternal.

What joy people miss when they are out of God's will, especially when they know they are out of God's will. Why do humans rebel against the will of God at times when they cannot see beyond to the joy that waits? With respect to the Chapter on Faith, *we must trust in God for the joy that we cannot see.* That is, the joy that waits as one follows God's path. And too bad it is the case that men and women are not always joyful on God's path; and as a result, they drift away from the path! Too often, Christians do not trust God, for either the joy to come nor receive the joy that is at hand! Thus, what develops is a two-fold problem of joy here:

1. People should trust in God that following God's path will lead to a joy in the Lord.
2. Individuals should receive the joy that God can give us while we are walking in the way of the Lord.

In the latter case, God does not promise Eden, but He does promise a joy (remember the aforementioned definition of joy), from God in the midst of all weather, thunderstorms, etc. It has never been attained, but by Christ, and it never will. But the joy is there for the taking (Augustine, 2010, 2015a, 2015b). The plain truth is that believers can partake of this endless joy only insofar as we have continued communion with God.

A full joy, a rich joy, an actual joy, the joy—it comes from an unyielding desire to consistently talk with and listen to God!

REFERENCES

Agich, G. J. (2003). *Dependence and autonomy in old age: An ethical framework for long-term care.* Cambridge University Press.

Augustine of Hippo. (2015a). *Brainy quote.* Retrieved on April 2, 2015 from: http://www.brainyquote.com/quotes/quotes/s/saintaugus 124552.html

Augustine of Hippo. (2015b). *Brainy quote.* Retrieved on April 2, 2015 from: http://thinkexist.com/quotation/do_you_wish_to_rise- begin_by_descending-you_plan/263998.html. , p. 1.

Augustine of Hippo. (2010). *City of God* (Dods, M. Peabody, Trans.) Henrickson Publishers.

Bergman, G. (2004). *The little book of bathroom philosophy: Daily wisdom from the greatest thinkers*. Fairwinds Press.

Bounds, E. M. (2010). *Purpose in prayer*. Blackstone.

Briscoe, S. (2013). *Time bandits: Putting first things first*. Multnomah Press.

Clairvaux, B. (1940). *The steps of humility*. Harvard University Press.

Daley, R. J. (2009). *Sacrifice unveiled: The true meaning of Christian sacrifice*. T & T Clark.

Graham, B. (2015). *Quotations book*. Retrieved March 26, 2015 from: http://quotations-book.com/quote/38480/

Jeynes, W. (2002a). A meta-analysis of the effects of attending religious schools and religiosity on Black and Hispanic academic achievement. *Education and Urban Society, 35*(1), 27–49.

Jeynes, W. (2002b). Educational policy and the effects of attending a religious school on the academic achievement of children. *Educational Policy, 16*(3), 406–424.

Jeynes, W. (2003a). The effects of Black and Hispanic 12th graders living in intact families and being religious on their academic achievement. *Urban Education, 38*(1), 35–57.

Jeynes, W. (2003b). The effects of religious commitment on the academic achievement of urban and other children. *Education and Urban Society 36*(1), 44–62.

Jeynes, W. (2009). *A call to character education and prayer in the school*. Praeger.

Jeynes, W. (2020). A meta-analysis of the relationship between prayer and student outcomes. *Education and Urban Society 52*(8), 1223–1237.

Minith, F. B. (2004). *In pursuit of happiness: Choices that can change your life*. Fleming H. Revell.

Murray, A. (1979). *Abide in Christ: The joy of being in God's presence*. Whitaker House.

Murray, A. (2004). *A life of obedience*. Bethany House.

Offner, H., Larsen, D., & Larsen, S. (2013). *A deeper look at the fruit of the Spirit: Growing in the likeness of Christ*. InterVarsity Press.

Orr, C. E. (2009). *How to live a holy life*. Floating Press.

Peterson, J. (2003). *The insider: Bringing the Kingdom of God into your everyday world*. Navigator Press.

Piper, J. (2011). *Desiring God: Meditations of a Christian hedonist*. Multnomah.

Swindoll, C. R. (1998). *Joseph: A man of integrity and forgiveness: Profiles in Character*. Word Publishers.

Tozer, A. W. (2013). *The pursuit of God*. Gospel Light.

Wiersbe, W. W. (2005). *Devotions for renewal and joy: Romans and Philippians*. Honor Publishing.

CHAPTER 3

CONSTANT-PRAYER AND COMMUNION WITH GOD AND EVANGELISM

ZEALOUS TO SHARE OUR FAITH

Love for the Lord

> But may all who seek thee rejoice and be glad in thee; may those who love thy salvation say *continually*, 'Great is the Lord'!
>
> *—Psalm 40:16*

> Epaphras who is one of yours, a servant of Christ Jesus, greets you, *always remembering you earnestly in his prayers*, that you may stand mature and fully assured in all the will of God. For I bear him witness that he has worked hard for you for those in Laodicea and Hierapolis.
>
> *—Colossians 4:12, 13*

Constant awareness of God is imperative for the most effective form of evangelism. It is those who treasure their salvation that share it. It is those who treasure

---

The Power of Constant Prayer and Communion With God, pages 31–44.
Copyright © 2024 by Information Age Publishing
www.infoagepub.com
All rights of reproduction in any form reserved.

32 • THE POWER OF CONSTANT PRAYER AND COMMUNION WITH GOD

their God who are praying continually to Him. A Christian who loves God loves salvation, and the reverse should also exist, though it often does not. How little we love God; how little we love our salvation! (Augustine, 2010, 2015a, b). The relationship nonetheless exists ideally. Inevitably, constant prayer leads to the sharing of our faith, as it so often leads to other fruits. Evangelism, on the other hand, does not always lead to constant prayer. *Christians today do not share enough because their love for God is not deep enough.* The Christian will share out of his love for salvation, but this is only one aspect of a complete love for God. *Love of salvation is not synonymous with a complete love for God!* In fact, a love of salvation can sometimes be a self-centered type of love. A more mature love of salvation is God-centered.

Psalm 40:16 calls upon him who loves his salvation and truly loves God to share his faith and continually utter words of love and praise to God. The person who shares his faith should then have a continual communion with God of praise and conversation. When he does this, the love of God more totally fills him, and he is able to be used more effectively for God. The most beautiful effect of this continual communion upon those who evangelize is that it gives them a greater desire to share the gospel. There is no more natural and glorious process than to have the love of God spur an individual on to witness to the hundreds of people around him. Because the result of sharing out of a pure love for God is that God's love flows out of his heart upon the one he is sharing with. *It is God's love flowing out of oneself from a nearness of relationship with God which is one of the most important factors in bringing people to the Lord!* A person must be certain to notice that the source of this love is God, and a strong fellowship with God only serves to release the love of God's Spirit. *A believer's main goal in sharing the Gospel should not be to win an argument, but instead to affect a release of God's spirit of love upon that individual!*

A follower of Christ who is serious about sharing the gospel knows that although the gift of evangelism is indeed a gift and therefore separate from any real sense of maturity, still his relationship with God will play an essential role in drawing people to the Lord in addition to this gift. Love has just been mentioned as significant in this regard (Brady, 2003). The joy, peace, and faith which a devotee transmits by the power of God will also affect the person he is witnessing to, to an extent greater than he probably imagined (Froehlich, 2014; Hayford & Bauer, 2011)

Upon seeing a Christian's joy, peace, faith, etc., in sharing, many a non-believer will say to himself, "I want that for my life!" Constant prayer to God then becomes important with regards to a life that can be used to a high potential by God. A receiver may have been blessed by God with the gift of evangelism and is being used effectively by God, but how much more effectively will he be used as he draws closer and closer to God in his own personal life. The question, then does not so much become "Is God using me to effectively witness now?" but whether God is using him in evangelism to his highest potential. *A person's potential in any area of his life cannot be met unless one is constantly communing with God!* A righteous instrument can always be more effective, given the same degree of the gift that a person has received as a result of God's grace, than a not-so righteous person.

Constant-Prayer and Communion With God and Evangelism • **33**

In Colossians 4:12, 13, we have the example of Epaphras as a man zealous to share the word and one who "worked hard" to see to it that the spiritual welfare of people had been achieved. *Let it be known that a man who works hard for the welfare of others, has worked hard to achieve a closeness of relationship with God!* The very fact is implied in illuminating the strength of his prayer life. If he is "always" remembering the members of the Body in prayer, he must have a pretty solid relationship with God. Notice here that the person committed to evangelism not only has a fire for seeing people saved but constantly is praying for their growth. The man or woman of God will not only do the work on the front lines, but also will do the work of God behind the lines by praying that the power of God come upon the new converts. The apostle Paul himself realized the importance of follow-up and prayer for new converts (Daley, 2009), knowing full well that the decision to follow Christ is but 5% of the actual act of following Christ (I Thessalonians 3:5).

> But for me, it is good to be *near God*; I have made the Lord my refuge, that I may tell of *all* thy works.
>
> *—Psalm 73:28*

> After this the Lord appointed seventy others, and sent them on ahead of Him, two by two, into every town and place where He Himself was about to come. And He said to them, 'The harvest is plentiful, but the laborers are few; pray therefore the Lord of the harvest to send out laborers into His harvest.'
>
> *—Luke 10:1, 2*

If one cares to stop to think about it, the Christian will ascertain that *the more we are called to go out from the Lord, the more we are called to draw near to Him!* If we draw an analogy between the warmth of the Son of God and the warmth of the sun, we can see this more clearly. As a person goes out from the sun, the warmth that he receives directly from the sun decreases. For warmth then that individual must turn to the sun often and seek to receive all of the warmth one possibly can. Now, this is true in relation to the Son as well. For as a man leaves his comforts at home and plunges into the jungle of life, his relationship with Christ is a good deal different than it was in the security of his own niche. No longer is he basking in the teachings of Christ in his rocking chair, but he has been sent out as Christ's ambassador. He can look back to what Christ taught in his home to retrieve some of the lost warmth, but somehow this is not enough. Surely, the individual is where one most needs the Lord; yet in spirit, he is miles away. This is why people are called to draw near to God when they are called out. Fortunately, the analogy between the sun and the Son ends at this point because unlike the sun, although Jesus has sent us out, He is nonetheless always near (Peterson, 2003). But the point remains when we are sent out by Christ we need Him more. For this quandary, constant awareness is the answer.

The zealousness that Epaphras has in the passage from Colossians previously quoted is not something only he possessed but which radiated out of the lives

34 • THE POWER OF CONSTANT PRAYER AND COMMUNION WITH GOD

of other saints as well, such as Titus (II Corinthians 8:16, 17) and Epaphroditus (Philippians 2:25-30). Zealousness, in fact, is something that Christ demands of all His children (Titus 2:14). Surely, many believers pray that God will send forth more servants to preach the gospel, but far too few think of themselves as the object of Christ's prayer request (Orr, 2009). The Psalm 73 passage points to a man who desires to be close to God and under His wing that he might be in the harvest fields telling non-believers about the accomplishments of God. How wonderful to be closer to God that more might be brought into the Kingdom! The Body of Christ must allow itself to be called out by God and respond to the people whose souls are starving for the true bread of Heaven (Mark 6:7; Acts 13:2, 3; 15:27; II Corinthians 8:18, 23). May God stir up the Christian people of the world, nation, state, town, street and most importantly, in the depths of one's very own hearts, to move in a continual communication with God (Psalm 70:4). A communication which does not exist only for its own sake, but also because of what results from it, so that God can be glorified. Truly, our response to the Great Commission (Matthew 28:16-20) and Christ's challenge in Luke 10:1, 2 ought to be as thus:

> And I heard the voice of the Lord saying, Whom shall I send and who will go for us?' Then said I, 'Here am I! Send me'.
> *—Isaiah 6:8*

Boldness

> …. That I may declare it *(the gospel)* boldly, as I ought to speak.
> *—Ephesians 6:20b*

> If I say, 'I will not mention Him or speak anymore in His name, there is in my heart as it were a *burning fire* shut up in my bones, and I am wearing with holding it in and *I cannot.*
> *—Jeremiah 20:9*

Boldness in sharing the gospel, as well as other instances of living in God's will, is an entity that results from a strong fellowship with Jesus Christ (Wiersbe, 2005). Boldness should be a goal of every Christian's life. Ephesians 6:20 tells us this and Jeremiah 20:9 illustrates why indeed it does result from a strong vertical fellowship. Paul, in a final few words of Ephesians 6, states, "as I ought to speak." How can anyone know how he ought to speak apart from communing with God? How will a person fulfill the words he ought to speak, by actually saying them, except by an extraordinary relationship with God? A Christian does not become a person with a tongue that proclaims God's message by angelic cue cards. The message that he shares is one which God produces within that person. If the gospel messenger allows God to work as He desires in this area of his life, the result will be boldness. Make no mistake about it—boldness is a commandment (II Timothy 1:6-8; 4:2). This simply follows from the fact that love is bold in nature, not timid. Neither is God's love timid; it must be expressed.

Constant-Prayer and Communion With God and Evangelism • **35**

As Christians, it is so easy to say that one is eager to serve. Yet, undoubtedly, since actions speaks louder than words, most who so vivaciously say they are eager to serve are even more eager to be selfish (Ezekiel 34:7-10). So many times in speaking firm words, people forget the power of the enemy to remove the fuel behind those words, until there is no action (Jeremiah 37:9, 10). Individuals can raise our hands in church to praise to God and submit to Him thereby, but how much submission is this really if those same people not raise our hands to fight the enemy? We can speak boldly about evangelism within Christian circles, but if we do not follow up by speaking with the same boldness in the world's domain, our words are in vain. Teddy Roosevelt's motto: "Speak softly and carry a big stick" is applicable to Christians as well. In this case, it is much better to share the gospel much and boast little than to share the gospel little and boast much!

If disciples are to be serious with Jesus, they must choose to be bold in sharing the gospel more than being bold in talking about sharing the gospel!

The Christian must be constantly open to God's prompting concerning the spreading of the Good News! If the Lord says speak, then the believer should speak. If the Lord says wait, then the disciple should wait. The gospel must not "be hidden, for a love such as God's was not meant to be hidden" (Mark 4:21, 22; Jeremiah 26:1-15). *To hide that of God which is not meant to be hidden is an insult to God!* If one sees Jesus as the actual Lord of his life, he will not be soft in sharing this. The consequences of not being willing to share are quite strong, i.e., Jesus will be ashamed of that believer before the Father (Mark 8:38). Yet, even if we are not ashamed, we miss so many opportunities, don't we? The woman sitting next to us on the bus, the businessman who just passed us on the street, etc. Granted, we would be going out of our way if we were to share about Jesus with those with whom we do not normally converse. This would be especially so if there was but one person on the bus, and we sat next to that person for the sole purpose of showing God's love and His gospel both in life and in word. *But Jesus went out of His way for us, didn't He?*

As much as in any dimension, constant prayer and communion with God has helped me become far more effective in sharing my faith than I was when I first started witnessing in college, for example. When I was in college, I would go door to door witnessing with between one to two other dear friends of mine. By the grace of God, a considerable number of the hearers came to Christ. However, there were two other outstanding results of sharing the gospel in this way that really stood out to me.

First, many of those who came to the Lord came via constantly praying to God through the process. As we witnessed to a variety of people, I would pray that God would lay the words on my hearts and lips that were the right ones that would bring these listeners to Christ. One after another God proved Himself faithful and would give this servant the precise actions and sentences that would be key in seeing these hearers come to Christ.

One example is I recall that my witnessing partner and I encountered a brilliant man, who had memorized many of Plato's writings. He could even give the page number and location on the page of many of Plato's famous quotes. He was far more knowledgeable than I was, especially of Plato. "How could I possibly be used to reach him for Christ?" I asked of the Lord. After a very short period of time, the Lord gave me the answer I needed. The Lord quickened to me that the answer was not having an intellectual battle with him about Plato or anyone else. The key was to unmask him and share that he was putting up a front with regards to Plato, because he was empty inside. I shared these words with the man and suddenly he burst into tears and admitted to me that it was a front. He then gave his heart to Christ. It was all accomplished by constant prayer and communion with God.

On another occasion, there was a fellow that shared with me and my witnessing partner that "Christianity is for wimps." I asked God how to go about addressing that attitude. The witnessing we did was done at a major university that was known for producing national champion wrestlers. I approached the heavy weight champion of the team, who almost never lost and was known as the university's finest wrestler. I knew that he was a devout Christian and asked him if he would be willing to hide behind the corner, as I witnessed to the same fellow the following week. The wrestling champion replied, "That is right up my alley." I contacted the fellow we had witnessed to and asked if he would be willing to again state "Christianity is for wimps" to a friend of mine at the same time next week.

The next week, at the scheduled time, the wrestler hid behind the corner from the door of the fellow who had stated, "Christianity is for wimps." I asked him if he had remembered what he had claimed the week before, i.e., that "Christianity is for wimps." He said that he remembered. I also asked him if he recalled promising that if I brought my friend to meet him a week later that he would be willing to make the statement to my friend., Yes, he remembered making that promise. I then introduced him to my heavyweight university wrestling friend, stating that his lifetime wrestling record was nearly undefeated. When I asked the fellow to repeat the statement he had made he replied, "Well, don't the statement out of context, I mean…." Within a minute he prayed the sinner's prayer and gave his heart to Christ. Praise God!

WHAT IS REQUIRED OF AN EVANGELIST

Laborers Fishing for Men

My mouth will tell of thy righteous acts, of thy deeds of salvation *all the day*, for their number is past my knowledge.

—Psalm 71:15

So David left Asaph and his brethren there before the ark of the covenant of the Lord to minister continually before the Ark as each day required.

Constant-Prayer and Communion With God and Evangelism • **37**

—I Chronicles 16:37

The most successful fisherman, whether a fisher of fish or a fisher of men, is a person who fishes constantly. Fishermen, who go out for fish but once a month, do not see as many fish caught due both to the lack of time they put into their trade and a lack of practice. The former who reaps the greatest harvest spends much of his time in the fields rather than at home. God must say, "How sad it is that fellowship dinners and Christian sports leagues attract more interest than evangelism." How the Holy Spirit Himself must be grieved by our hardness, for the Body, at present, does not have the compassion of Christ for those that are perishing. *Many will fish for a living, but so few will fish for the dead!*

The reader is probably acquainted with some of the verses in the Bible in which Jesus sends out His disciples. Several of these verses, including the often quoted Matthew 9:38, contain the Greek word "ekbala" which means to cast forth or drive out (Matthew 9:38; 12:20; Luke 20:21). How much this Greek word reveals to us about how anxious Jesus is to send His followers out so that souls would be saved. Servants of the Lord are sometimes not willing to be thrust out by the Lord. How great a problem this is within the Christian body today. The resistance those of faith surmount to being cast forth by our Lord is rooted in their lack of submissiveness to Him and an emptiness of understanding concerning their actual relationship to God (Clairvaux, 1940). For we are but a bond slave to our Lord and have value only because of His blood. Who are we to resist one who paid so high a price for our soul? And yet we still resist Him who loves us so much. We seem to understand not the depth of God's knowledge of us. He knows our stubbornness and is well acquainted with our desire for comfort. Who cares, at first, to be thrust out on the oceans with only the gospel. That is, who desires to be thrust out on an unfamiliar boat as well as called to walk out on the sea. God knows His children's hearts; He knows they are but landlubbers who desire safety from the storm rather than to venture out in it (Jeynes, 2007; Murray, 1979, 2004; Piper, 2011; Tozer, 2013). Yet in the spirit there is an eye of that storm where all is peaceful while the storm rages around. In our hand is the gospel of peace, and it is this peace that will pierce our heart again and again, as we share the gospel. Ah, if only we could appreciate the peace that God is ministering to our hearts each time we share the gospel. The non-believer is not the only one the Spirit is touching.

Upon the oceans of the dark spiritual jungles of the world, people must be aware of God as Christ was aware of His Father. Christians are "ambassadors" for Christ in these spiritual jungles and called to walk as He walked (II Corinthians 5:20; I John 2:6). Out in the very depths of the oceans, we must rely on God to be our substance (Ephesians 3:7; II Corinthians 3:6), allowing God to direct us to as many people as possible (Colossians 1:23). Evangelism is important to the up-building and maintaining of the Church (Ephesians 4:11; II Timothy 4:5). If only believers would realize how important evangelism is and allow God to cast them forth! Sea fishing men do not have delicate scientific instruments to help them

38 • THE POWER OF CONSTANT PRAYER AND COMMUNION WITH GOD

locate fish, nor is it a wise use of time to relax and wait until the bait is snatched. Instead, a religious adherent must rely on the hand of God and one's own experience. As an individual grows, we will even ask God which ones can be caught by the Lord and those God desires most to be caught. And, lo, the joy when the "fisherman" latches on to the first whopper, at first straining to haul him or her in, and then turning the situation completely over to God so that God Himself can bring in the catch.

Aspects of An Evangelist's Personality

Willing to Preach the Word

On the oceans of a paganistic world the Christian is subject to grave attacks by the world and the Evil One (Ephesians 6:12; I Peter 2:11). Satan will work to discourage the believer from sharing Jesus. Ah, the various ways he will seek to do this! If Satan knows God's "evangelist" plans to go out sharing Wednesday afternoon, he will make Wednesday morning a series of small disasters, irritations, and frustrations. If not, Satan may tack on a sickness or a body ache. Perhaps Satan will bring to mind all the times an "evangelist" failed to present the gospel clearly and the fact that few have come to decisions for Christ. Have no fear, my friend. Let it be known that if Satan should attempt such ploys, a soul-saving adventure is right around the corner. "Mon ami," if I sense that a sickness or pain intensifies as I enter the final hour before that in which I am to share, unless otherwise directed by the Lord, I make a special point to venture out into the fields. And if I were to share that some of the most powerful, remarkable, and plentiful conversions took place on such days as these, the reader need not be surprised.

Oh, how necessary it is to share about the life humans can have in Jesus so that others may have power in their lives rather than perish (Romans 1:14, 15). Few receive Christ without hearing the words of others uttering the gospel message. Thus, the responsibility is laid on Christians to answer the challenge, rather than sit back and relax while others do the work of allowing God's hand to save people from fire (Romans 10:14). Certainly, if Jesus Christ and Paul recognized the imperativeness of this, it is of prodigious importance (Matthew 10:7; Ephesians 3:8-12).

> But we will give ourselves continually to prayer, and to the ministry of the word.
>
> *—Acts 6:4*

Being willing to preach the word to God's standards demands devoting ourselves to consistently to doing the will of God. This requires constantly praying to God. Sharing God's word is not merely a series of actions but a thorough "giving" of ourselves to the will of God. This is so much of the essence of constantly communing with God. Only as we give ourselves to God will God be able to use us as microphones pronouncing the Good News. We may also notice that prayer is closely connected to spreading the Word. Prayer lays the groundwork for evangelism. If we are genuinely devoted toward the sharing of God's Word, we will commit ourselves strongly in prayer toward the prospering of God's word. The fruit that results from the sharing of God's word ensues from prayer. Without the foundation of prayer, the sharing of the word of God may indeed be in vain. The continual prayer that is mentioned in Acts 6:4 refers to praying in the actual process of sharing as well as praying beforehand. Ah, what power there is in activating the Holy Spirit through prayer and sharing the Word at the same time! Praise God! Our words become inundated with vigor of the utmost magnitude ministering to the people's hearts. We can talk all we want, but in the end it is prayer that supplies both the words and their meaning.

Willingness to Admonish, Warn, and Reprove

Cry aloud, spare not, lift up your voice like a *trumpet*; declare to my people their transgression, to the house of Jacob their sins.

—*Isaiah 58:1*

Upon your walls, O Jerusalem, I have set watchmen *all the day* they shall never be silent. You who put the Lord in remembrance, take no rest, and give him no rest until He establishes Jerusalem and makes it a praise in the earth.

—*Isaiah 62:6, 7*

Few are the "trumpets" of Isaiah 58:1; few are the "watchmen." Fewer are those who "take no rest" and give the Lord no reason to rest. Admonition in love stirs up the waves of revival. Reproof must be done in love (I Corinthians 13:3). Trumpets send waves which vibrate beyond human recognition. Blessed are the trumpets, for revival will begin from them. Blessed are the watchpeople, for they shall watch the Lord roar forth in Spirit. Blessed are we? That is, are we that trumpet and are we that watchperson? I would love to hear someone respond to the question, "When is there going to be a revival?" in a more laudable way than is common. An answer like "I've been having a revival for five years, and I have a revival meeting every morning when I wake up, I believe it's going to spread." Glory to God; that is the answer! If only a person could have that attitude each day, i.e., to think of each and every Quiet Time as a *revival meeting*! Also, to think of each prayer one prays to God as an opportunity for revival in our life is truly beautiful! Glory to God!

When Jesus comes for His people, when the trumpet sounds, I believe there will have been many trumpets that have been sounded beforehand. That is, God's instruments sounding His message of warning before His people in the church as well as the unrepentant (Ezekiel 33:1-9)! Before every spectacular act of God, there is a trumpet! Noah was the trumpet before the flood. The angels were the trumpets before the destruction of Sodom and Gomorrah. Moses was the trum-

40 • THE POWER OF CONSTANT PRAYER AND COMMUNION WITH GOD

pet before the Exodus. The prophets were the trumpets before the destruction of Jerusalem. Before God works, there must be trumpets! How often we are too cowardly to blow the horn of God. i.e., not too meek or humble, but too cowardly. For meekness and humility are conducive to warning and reproof not at odds with these. Here lies the truth that we are but dust before God and what is it but pride which prevents us from uttering the truth which God wants us to speak. *Is not cowardice pride in disguise?* Is not what the world deems as meek and humble really a misrepresentation and often prideful at the root? How can we not warn, if we love? For on whom we have compassion, we immediately take on a responsibility. Especially for those whom we love, we have a responsibility to blow the trumpet (Ezekiel 33:6). If we have the love of God implanted in our heart, and if truly His love springs upon those who are lost, we must declare the word of the Lord no matter what it may be; no veritable humility will prevent God's reproof from leaving our tongue (Ezekiel 33:7). If agape love is the tear of our heart, then reproof cannot be a commandment to be refused but one to be done (Ezekiel 6:11, 34:2-31). Shall we then continue to suppose that we should perform what we most desire or shall we fulfill the desire of the Most High (Jonah 3:2)?

Whom do we reprove? Do we reprove those who seem to most need it? Those who are most likely to respond? Those to whom we are close enough to do so? Those we will not offend? Those whom we like? Those whom we offend? Those who, we dare say, may even attempt to offend us? Those who offend us because we so choose? Those who offend no one? Yes? Indeed, yes, for we should at least be willing to reprove all. Terribly put, as it may seem to be, we should address the question, "Whom do we reprove?" to none other but God Almighty, not to those of our own preference. Of course, it is so important that if and when we give reproof that it be done in a spirit of love or else it will yield little fruit and could be inappropriately hurtful.

> Do not reprove a scoffer, or he will hate you; reprove a wise man, and he will love you. Give instruction to a wise man, and he will be still wiser, teach a righteous man and he will increase learning. The fear of the Lord is the beginning of wisdom and the knowledge of the Holy One is insight.
> *—Proverbs 9:8-10*

The righteous need to be recipients of reproof also. If they indeed are righteous, they will respect loving and honest rebuke. The good King Hezekiah was reproved by the prophet Isaiah for a small misjudgment when contrasted to many of his predecessors. Yet, Hezekiah was rebuked nonetheless (Isaiah 39:3-7).

Willingness to be Used of God to Win Souls

> Ask, and it will be given you; seek and you will find; knock and it will be opened to you. For everyone who asks receives, and he who seeks finds, and to him who knocks it will be opened.

Constant-Prayer and Communion With God and Evangelism • **41**

> —*Matthew 7:7, 8*

…he who wins souls is wise.

> —*Proverbs 11:30 (NIV)*

So we are ambassadors for Christ, God making His appeal through us.
> —*II Corinthians 5:20a*

A willingness to see souls saved is one of the areas of greatest deception within a believer's own mind. Any Christian gets excited when a soul is saved. He or she claps one's hands and praises God though he sometimes forgets what he's getting so excited about. There is in the average Christian believer a marked similarity to Pavlov's dog. But instead of salivating whenever someone comes to the Lord, the Christian gets excited instead. Excitement is not wrong; it is good. But so often an individual's commitment to souls ends with excitement (salivation). Not to say this happens all of the time, but it occurs often enough so it is disturbing. Too easily believers fail to have the deep compassion that Christ had for the masses and a strong realization, at that time, of what the person who has received Christ has been saved from. How often people respond like Pavlov's dog than like this. There is a second level at which individuals can be deceived concerning seeing the Lord save souls. A person can applaud the saving of souls, but that hardly weighs equally with actually going out into the fields himself. A fire to see souls saved does not consist in merely applauding the feats of those who reach down to lead someone out of the tunnel to the light which exists at its climax. The definition of "fire" in respect to evangelism requires action, not merely applause. At the first level of deception, *if a follower is really moved with the compassion of Christ when a soul is saved, it will be impossible for him not to be stirred to action to go out and see God fetch those straying sheep that trudge toward a destination intended only for the most evil of evil ones.* At the second level of deception, if the follower's applause is truly based in his heart, he will be incited towards the same type of action. Hallelujah!

The third type of deception is a person imagining that just because he or she is sharing the gospel, that person is doing enough. This is what sin is all about, for we can do nothing enough as long as we have a Savior and example who has done everything well (Mark 7:37). It may be that we share the Good News more than most but hardly share it enough (Piper, 2011; Swindoll, 1998). There are times when we use our time selfishly in ways which go beyond the realm of Christ-like leisure, i.e., leisure that is either not edifying or beyond the time that God desires us to spend in leisure. Devotees must not fool themselves concerning this area of weakness in their lives. For while people leisurely go about our business, souls are sinking into the miry, forbidding clay. Rise up, dear soul, and see reality and avoiding the presence of God. It is here where we fall. There are too many Christians who are but freeloaders on the train to heaven. Freeloaders, because they want the joy of God's benefits but not the responsibility of His tasks. Herein lies the irony; for God bestows His greatest benefits to those who undergo a transformation in being an enlightenment by their very concentration upon His presence and in their communion with God. Communion with God is the instrument through which we can be lifted up to God's most heart-felt desires. This comes to those who are closest and must united to Him.

IT IS GOD WHO SAVES

God is the Source

> Seek the Lord and His strength, seek His presence *continually!* Remember the wonderful works He has done, His miracles and the judgments He uttered.
>
> *—Psalm 105:4, 5*

> No one can come to me unless the Father who sent me draws him; and I will raise him up on the last day.
>
> *—John 6:44*

It is far more than coincidence that whenever believers are living in the presence of God, they become far more aware of the fact that God is the source of all things. This relationship is suggested in the Psalm 105 verses above. When we see the source of anything good as coming from ourselves or anything outside of God, one's service for God is practically in vain. For a disciple's primary thrust as an instrument of the workings of God is to glorify God in all things. When we fail to point to God without exception, and evangelism is a part of it of this tendency, we pretend that it is not God who works the miracle of bringing a soul to Christ. This is unadulterated 100% pure pride. Pride can be so subtle in evangelism, and this fact may be why pride is especially poisonous in evangelistic endeavors. Yes, subtle is a key word in respect to pride concerning evangelism. Note:

> Now the serpent was more *subtle* than any other creature than the Lord God had made.
>
> *—Genesis 3:1*

Pride is quite a battle for evangelists, both great and small. The same temptation of pride that strikes leading evangelists can strike the layman in his daily encounter with non-Christians and his attempts to lucidly share the gospel.

One of the most common manifestations of subtle evangelistic pride occurs in the phrase, "I brought someone to the Lord." This is one of the most common cries of Christians who have shared the gospel. Yet, it is such a false claim. More appropriately, the claim of any evangelist on any level should be, "The Lord brought someone to Himself." The phrase "using me" may be added without taking the glory away from God. The point remains that God is the source, while his disciples are the vessels. By the very words people use to express various events, another person can tell a lot about who is receiving the glory. John 6:44

is clear about who the source of salvation is. Are we clear? Are we aware of who the power behind the gospel is when we share? Too often we are not aware. We know we are not aware because we are not praying continually. Ah, we see now the importance of continual prayer. In continual prayer we are acknowledging God as the source. The power of constant communion with God in evangelism is that in it believers can recognize the power of the gospel lies not in themselves, but in God Himself.

Tapping the Source: Prayer

The Prayers of other Christians

> Pray at *all times* in the Spirit, with all prayer and supplication. To that end keep alert with all perseverance, making supplication for all saints.
> —*Ephesians 6:18, 19*

Prayers of other saints have a tremendously beneficial effect on any evangelistic outreach. The same humility in an individual which causes him or her to continually pray to God and seek His presence while witnessing, will also urge that individual to seek the continual prayers of others (James 5:16). Now is the time we must grow into an everlasting realization of the life-giving nature of prayer (Genesis 10:7; Jeremiah 29:7). Notice how Samuel (in I Samuel 12:23) knew the importance of intercession so that he would not cease to intercede for the Israelites. Oh, that believers would not be so foolish as to venture out in ministry without strong foundational and continual prayer support (Bounds, 2010). No one is such a lone ranger as to be able to go out into the fields without the support in prayer of members of the body of Christ. Do believers dare to even venture to believe they live up to their potential without the power of prayer behind them? Disciples can do nothing without the Lord, so it is in Him that they should take refuge and cling to His presence, believing that His power will be unleashed through the prayers of the saints. Without God's response to the prayers of His saints, I wonder what fruit there would be. I need not wonder, for I know.

The Prayers of Ourselves

> But we will give ourselves *continually* to prayer, and to the ministry of the Word.
> —*Acts 6:4*

> Seek the Lord while He may be found, call upon Him *while He is near*.
> —*Isaiah 55:6*

The apostles serve as a good example of falling down before the Lord and earnestly desiring His hand to guide all forms of spiritual outreach. Praise God! Believers must in heart continually follow the examples of the apostles. The Lord's hand is not shortened to save the straying sheep (Isaiah 59:1), but human hands are, and if a follower reneges on God's urgings that His hand may be extended, the hand that goes out to the lost is now shortened because it is no longer God's hand that goes out, but one's own.

It is prayer that allows God to extend His hand entirely. It is pride that limits the mobility of His hand. It is not that God cannot overrule this pattern but rather He chooses to act within it, for this is His supreme desire. It is God who draws in lost souls, and it is prayer that affects His action, not apologetics. The Christian is to call upon the Lord to bring a *soul* home, not a theologian home. Much less should the Christian call on himself to save a soul. Instead, God's desire is that we call on God to use us to bring a lost sheep into the heavenly kingdom. A prayerful outreach is the only outreach and one based on constant prayer is the best outreach. For it is God's hand that is not shortened, but our own.

REFERENCES

Augustine of Hippo. (2010). *City of God* (Dods, M. Peabody, Trans.). Henrickson Publishers.

Augustine of Hippo. (2015a). *Brainy quotes.* Retrieved on April 2, 2015 from: http://www.brainyquote.com/quotes/quotes/s/saintaugus124552.html

Augustine of Hippo. (2015b). *Brainy quotes.* Retrieved on April 2, 2015 from http://thinkexist.com/quotation/do_you_wish_to_rise-begin_by_descending-you_plan/263998.html

Bounds, E. M. (2010). *Purpose in prayer*. Blackstone.

Brady, B. V. (2003). *Christian love*. Georgetown University Press.

Clairvaux, B. (1940). *The steps of humility*. Harvard University Press.

Daley, R. J. (2009). *Sacrifice unveiled: The true meaning of Christian sacrifice*. T & T Clark.

Froehlich, M. A. (2014). *Courageous gentleness: Following Christ's example of Restrained strength*. Discovery House Publishers.

Hayford, J. W., & Bauer, R. H. (2011). *Penetrating the darkness: Keys to ignite faith, boldness, and breakthrough*. Chosen Books.

Jeynes, W. (2007). *American educational history. School, society, and the common good.* SAGE.

Murray, A. (1979). *Abide in Christ: The joy of being in God's presence.*Whitaker House.

Murray, A. (2004). *A life of obedience.* Bethany House.

Orr, C. E. (2009). *How to live a holy life*. Auckland: Floating Press.

Peterson, J. (2003). *The insider: Bringing the Kingdom of God into your everyday world*. Navigator Press.

Piper, J. (2011). *Desiring God: Meditations of a Christian hedonist*. Multnomah.

Swindoll, C. R. (1998). *Joseph: A man of integrity and forgiveness: Profiles in Character*. Word Publishers.

Tozer, A. W. (2013). *The pursuit of God.* Gospel Light.

Wiersbe, W. W. (2005). *Devotions for renewal and joy: Romans and Philippians.* Honor Publishing.

CHAPTER 4

CONSTANT-PRAYER AND COMMUNION WITH GOD AND LOVE

THE CALL TO LOVE: A CHALLENGE
THAT ONLY GOD CAN MEET

What Love God Demands That His Children Have Towards
Himself

> Then the King commanded, then Daniel was brought and cast into the den
> of lions. The King said to Daniel, 'May your God, whom you serve con-
> tinually, deliver you… O, Daniel, servant of the living God, has your God,
> whom you serve *continually* been able to deliver you from the lions?' Then
> Daniel said to the King, O King, live forever. My God sent His angel and
> shut the lions' mouths, and they have not hurt me because I was found
> blameless before Him…
>
> *—Daniel 6:16, 20b-22*

To love the Lord and to serve Him continually; what a joy it would be to accomplish this! To do this would be to glorify God continually. To do this then

---

The Power of Constant Prayer and Communion With God, pages 45–60.
Copyright © 2024 by Information Age Publishing
www.infoagepub.com
All rights of reproduction in any form reserved.

46 • THE POWER OF CONSTANT PRAYER AND COMMUNION WITH GOD

would be the greatest series of actions that we could do. Again and again through His Holy Scripture God makes the request, though it is also a commandment, to love Him with everything we have to offer (Deuteronomy 6:5, 11:1, 22). This is quite a commitment God calls for. This is a commitment few believers have ever made. On top of this, God makes it sound simple and easy (Jeynes, 2012b).

> And now, Israel, what does the Lord your God require of you, but to fear the Lord your God, to walk in *all* His ways, to **love** Him, to serve the Lord your God with *all* your heart and with *all* your soul.
>
> *—Deuteronomy 10:12*

Born-again believers can make a basic but destructive mistake. It lies in the misunderstanding of one central fact: a mutual God-human love relationship is quite different from a mutual human love relationship. There are two ingredients of differences. First, the love a believer has towards God has a different texture and quality than the love that exists among human beings. Second, the love relationship a believer has with God is the only relationship he has in which *the object of his love is also the source of his love.* Naturally, now that these two points have been stated, they seem to be quite obvious. However, the believer's failure to acknowledge these differences, meditate on them, and interact with the divergencies has produced a void within the Body of Christ and within the individual believer.

The believer's love towards God and God's love towards the believer are anthropomorphized by humans much of the time in a miscomprehension of the "fullness of deity" that is the Godhead. This fact was anticipated by God and, to an extent, solved in Jesus Christ, God incarnate. But although a child of God may believe and receive Christ in all His deity, because he or she has only learned to love humanity all of one's life, that person loves God as only he or she knows how. Though the devotee hardly likes to be reminded of it, the Christian's love towards God is only in certain respects easily distinguished as existing in a higher quality and nature than one's love towards humanity. What is required to love God is made more difficult by most than it actually is, because after people have received Christ, they believe that once they have made the decision to love God and receive God's Spirit in their lives, all they have to do is increase that love for God and they are on their way to experiencing the abundant life God promised (Kruschwitz, 2001). What a mistake this is (Kruschwitz, 2001)! Starting from this assumption, devotees now must seek to enter into heavenly love with human's love machinery (Kruschwitz, 2001). This plan is bound to fail (Kruschwitz, 2001). Even though believers who are looked upon as loving God the most, would probably admit that there is a major barrier to be broken through in their love relationship with God; additional time in the Word will not totally crack the barrier. Neither will "The fullness of the Spirit" and "positive confessions." The answer lies in the *heart*!

My son, give me your heart and let your eyes observe my ways.

—Proverbs 23:26

God desires that His children each to give their entire heart to Him, but not in the usual sense of the term. As it is now, a Christian gives one's heart to Christ upon receiving Him as Lord and Savior and asks God to increase one's love for Him. What I am referring to is giving our heart to Christ in this manner, as well as asking God to totally change the nature of the love that proceeds from our heart. That is, to ask God to help us *unlearn* many ways humanity is prone to loving God and ask Him to help us *learn* of the heart of love that Christ has towards His Father. I trust that the Lord, through this book, will proceed to explain more specifically what He requires of His people and the ways the love relationship of humanity loving God is different from people loving people.

The love we have towards God has a different texture and quality than the love that exists among human beings. Mothers and/or fathers often tell their children that the love between a husband and wife is "different" from that between a parent and child. The child may not understand what is being said, but indeed what the parents say is true. God, through His Word, has told His children that the love between God and His children is different from that between earthlings. I do not think anyone would disagree with the fact that God desires a higher quantity of love than people show towards their fellow man (Matthew 10:37; Luke 10:27, 9:59, 60). While nearly everyone realizes that God wants a higher quantity of love, few realize in their hearts that God also demands a higher quality. Matthew 10:38 and Luke 14:33 are good examples of this *command*.

He who loves father or mother more than me is not worthy of me; and he who loves son or daughter more than me is not worthy of me; and he who does not take his cross and follow me is not worthy of me.
—Matthew 10:37; 38

so therefore, whoever, of you does not renounce *all* that he has cannot be my disciple.
—Luke 14:33

Matthew 10:37, 38 is one of the clearest verses in asserting the love that Christ demands of His disciples. In verse 37 Christ commands that His followers have a larger quantity of love for Him than anyone else. Christ says in essence, that unless we love Him in greater quantity than anyone else, he is "not worthy of Me." In verse 38 Jesus enters another dimension by demanding that His followers love Him with a higher quality of love than anyone else in their life. No human would ever make the request of verse 38 to another human being. Verse 38, then rises above the love God requires among human beings but represents a higher form of love all together. Again, in Luke 14:33, Christ makes a request which exceeds the bounds of human relationship. No one but God would require this of another human being. In John 21:15-19, Jesus requires that Peter's love have a quality of

48 • THE POWER OF CONSTANT PRAYER AND COMMUNION WITH GOD

other-orientation which, again, no other human being requires of another. *In no human relationship are we called to love everyone and everything out of love for that individual.* What God desires in a disciple's fellowship with Him is in its very foundation texturally different from any human interaction no matter how close.

At this stage in the book, the ways that a person's love association with God are qualitatively and texturally different are probably pretty obvious to the reader. What occurs psychologically within the born-again believer's heart and mind is something quite disparate to what he understands intellectually. For if one loved in God in a sense well beyond the human realm of association, devotees would not complain in the midst of trials, would use all their time to further the exaltation of God; would not hesitate to love the most belligerent individual; would not stop to think of their own comfort, but would instead trust God to meet all their needs; would be in a constant state of humility, giving the glory where it belongs, etc. (Clairvaux, 1940).

The born-again believer fails at executing the above because the very make-up of his or her love for God is at an elementary stage of spiritual development. Those in the general populous grumble in trials because they treat the one who is using these trials (i.e., God) in their lives as a human being rather than the Almighty God. People have difficulty seeing or even trusting in God's purpose because they are accustomed to purposeless and unpredictable homo sapiens and view God accordingly (Bounds, 2010). A human does not use all of his or her time to the glory of God because that person treats God like his spouse and/or friends. If one needs to have his periods of relaxation apart from the daily demands of other people, similarly he believes he needs periods of relaxation apart from what God daily asks of his life. This is not to say that God does not want His children to relax, rather quite to the contrary. However, on the one hand there is a relaxation apart from God, i.e., a relaxation with oneself in mind; and on the other hand, there is a relaxation in the presence of God in which one communes with God nonetheless and has a strong conscious knowledge that we are glorifying God even at that very moment.

People generally do not love the most bellicose of individuals whom God wants them to, because they respond to God as they would an earthly parent (Tozer, 2013). As a child, a person often asks questions either of the parents or himself. A child's obedience to his parents is usually far from unconditional. If a parent requests that his or her child do something, which is demanding, the child is often very reluctant to fulfill that request. Jesus Christ proclaims a radical obedience of His disciples, and few Christians live by a radical obedience because they obey Christ as they would an earthly parent. In the midst of parents, when a child is called upon to obey in a very demanding way, the child rebels, and I fear in the believer's humanness he reacts the same way with God. It takes a higher quality love to respond constantly to the leading of God in loving our enemies. Yet, often believers react to the commands of God as if God were merely a human being. Think of the child who is asked of his mother or father to clean up his room so it is spic and span and then help clean the yard. The child sighs and says, "But I want to go out with my friends. And besides there is not enough time." In fact, any parent knows that children become experts at making excuses. Often Christians respond in similar ways to God. "But God…" is so often our cry, as we begin our excuses (Chambers, 2015).

Individuals have difficulty living in a state of continual humility before God because they treat God like a human being. It is far more difficult to humble ourselves before a human being than before the Lord because in the presence of God, there is more to be humble about. Church adherents need to meditate deeply on the greatness and omnipotence that is God so that they may honestly acquire a greater understanding of our relationship to the Lord. Humans cannot humble themselves before God as the Lord requires of us because we think of Him as "too equal" to ourselves. Many anthropomorphize God to the point of reducing His significance, His wholeness, and His majesty (Bonhoeffer, 1959). In our failure to be humble before the Lord God, we fail to glorify Him. To the extent that we fail to humble ourselves before Him acknowledging Him as the great "I AM," we do not glorify Him. Glorifying God requires firstly a deep actuality of humility. Sadly, people have grown accustomed to living in a world in which credit for notable deeds goes to human beings. Yet we struggle enough in being able to give credit to others. In our humanness how much more we fail to give glory to God. I do not think we realize how short we fall here. Usually the words "I, me, my" float out of the man's mouth as in Job 29. The challenge, beloved is to ask ourselves how often he says "me," "my," and "I" and how frequently he refers to "God" in respect to the events of everyday life. The frequency of our usage of each will reveal more than we would most likely be pleased to admit. I fear that our love for God is far too human-like than we would prefer to admit. But truth is truth, and it is known in Heaven.

Total Love of God with Respect to Mankind

> If anyone says, 'I love God,' and hates his brother, he is a liar; for he who does not love his brother whom he has seen, cannot love God whom he has not seen. And this commandment we have from Him, that he who loves God should love his brother also.
>
> *—I John 4:20, 21*

> I thank my God always when I remember you in my prayers, because I hear of your love and of the faith which you have toward the Lord Jesus and all the saints.
>
> *—Philemon 4, 5*

If the love for God is difficult for those that are human, the love of our fellow man appears almost to be an impossibility. For with God, the love to which we are

50 • THE POWER OF CONSTANT PRAYER AND COMMUNION WITH GOD

receiving will always be far greater than what we can give in return. Such is not the case with human beings. Hence, the challenge is great. It is wise to remember that the one who has given this commandment is not an ordinary father but a Heavenly Father.

Love is one of those things that a person cannot forge. Love for the brethren and all of humankind, in the highest "agape" sense, can only grow out of a close walk with the Lord. Other facets of holiness can be imitated up to a point, but not love. Some people can go through the outward signs of holiness, sharing the gospel because the pastor told him to, singing in the choir so other Christians will think he or she "involved," but love is much more difficult and virtually impossible to imitate.

An individual is blessed to have the fortune of being able to allow the love of Jesus to flow through him (Brady, 2003). How often the receiver neglects and forgets this privilege (Rosberg & Rosberg, 2013). What greater honor are believers given than to allow the love of Christ to flow through them (Brady, 2003; Elliot, 1992). Yet, somehow, we do not always treat it as a privilege. Even the church faithful sometimes complain when they are called on by the Lord to love someone who is difficult to love. If one could only make it the greatest of joys to love their enemies, an opportunity to follow in the steps of Christ and to allow His love to flow.

To love as Christ loved is the beginning and the end of obedience. That is, the very foundation of obedience is love (John 14; 15, 21, 23). To love, as Christ loved, necessarily requires a heavenly attitude and perspective (II Corinthians 5:6, 8). How can we love with a continuous flow of love from the Spirit apart from a continuous communion with God? We cannot even begin to grasp the privilege we have, by God's power, of loving those for whom Christ died unless we permit God to continually remind us of this fact. Who and what we meditate upon and interact with determines what or who will control us.

> For the love of Christ controls us, because we are convinced that one has died for all; therefore all have died.
>
> —*II Corinthians 5:14*

While to a degree the love of Christ controls all believers, it has the greatest influence on those who submit to His love the most. This submission comes as a result of continual interaction with the Lord, giving one's heart over to Jesus in an even fuller way, in the process of communion.

In the Philemon passage quoted, the reader should observe that he who loves in the Lord in the truest sense appreciates others within the Body of believers who do the same. If we are, on the other hand, jealous or critical of others who love with the bold love of Jesus, our love, so far as it stems from God, lacks depth and therefore lacks significance. This section of the letter to Philemon without question tells us about the love of Philemon but in a greater degree is revelatory of the sincerity of Paul's love.

The love of both the saved and the lost, the proud and the humble, the beautiful and the ugly, the loving and the unloving, and everything in between is the greatest challenge that confronts the Christian (Jeynes, 2012a, 2018). It is nothing less than a test of the reality of his faith. For whether a Christian is able to love those around him is the test of the quality and depth of his Christian character and his love for God (I John 2:15). The task set before each Christian is far greater than any individual can take. A person can only hope to come anywhere near the love of Christ by a daily and minute-to-minute, second-to-second reliance on God. God helps us all in the Body who desire to love as He loves.

CHARACTER TRAITS OF A LOVING CHRISTIAN

Patience

> Be still before the Lord and wait patiently for Him…
> —*Psalm 37:7a*

> And so for that in the good soil, they are those who, hearing the Word, hold it fast in an honest and good heart, and bring forth fruit with patience.
> —*Luke 8:15*

Few understand the importance of patience in the Christian vocation of service to the Most Holy God. I often wonder how much sin has its root in impatience, although it is not realized by the individual believer. Impatience often causes anger, remarks of pride, a failure to reach out to other people, rushing into things rather than waiting on God, etc. Only God knows the extent to which people stunt potential communion with the Lord Jesus by their incessant impatience. To whatever extent, impatience burdens the heart-to-heart relationship that we have with God, I believe God wants to share with His children some important insights about patience which will help all believers.

Patience is one of the central most themes in love (I Corinthians 13:4). The reader should notice that patience includes nearly all the traits mentioned in I Corinthians 13:4, 5. If we are patient, we will not be jealous, boastful, arrogant, or rude. This fact is one of the primary reasons why I Corinthians 13 is such a challenging and elusive chapter in terms of every day spiritual application.

Impatience results from a misunderstanding of the human condition. It is a misunderstanding of humanity's relationship to God and humanity's relationship to humanity. Whether our impatience occurs with people or with God, it results essentially from this. A man or woman is a fallen creature who bathes in sin and is too often in alliance with his or her flesh and too often compromises with God. Most people are convinced that if they follow the desires of their flesh, they will achieve the highest level of satisfaction. From the world's perspective, the flesh is *supposedly* man's number one ally. Satan and the world can either attach them-

52 • THE POWER OF CONSTANT PRAYER AND COMMUNION WITH GOD

selves to flesh or remain separate from it, depending on how deep the sin may be. If Satan and/or the world remain detached from the flesh, the Christian does not fall as heavily into blatant sin. But because he still lives by the flesh, he is consistently being forced into situations in which he must compromise with both Satan and the world. These people do not inherently love evil or love the world, but because they do not rely on God they are often nonetheless swept up by Satan and the world. To whatever extent Satan and/or the world attach themselves to the flesh, that person is actively used of Satan and the world on a regular basis. This is the human condition. Man is a slave first to his own self and secondly to Satan and the world. In all cases, he is a slave to sin (John 8:34; Romans 6:17-20). A person is helplessly lost without God among these circumstances. It is no wonder that existentialism thrives today. Only pride prevents an individual from acknowledging one's lost state. *Pride is a protective mechanism man himself creates to protect himself from his own awareness of his fallen state!*

This is the creature we are so often impatient with. This is also the creature that we are ourselves. God is far above all of this. Now when the believer is impatient, he is doing one or more of the following things (see Figure 4.1):

1. They are misunderstanding or forgetting the fact that humans are in a fallen state and that all sorts of sin and faults are to be expected from them. They therefore do not understand humanity's- nor their own- relationship to God.

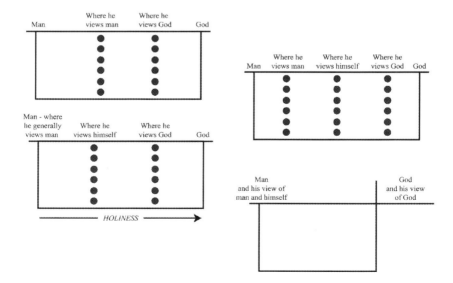

FIGURE 4.1- When a Believer is Impatient, One of the Following is Happening.

Constant-Prayer and Communion With God and Love • 53

2. They comprehend the fallen state of humanity, as a whole, but they nevertheless have not come to grips with the fact that they too are fallen. They therefore neither understand their relationship to God nor their relationship to other people.
3. They neither comprehend their relationship to humanity, nor humanity's relationship to God, nor their relationship to God.
4. They may understand humanity's relationships and their relationship to people, but nevertheless become very frustrated in the very knowledge of humanity's sinfulness.

Wherever we most often fall with respect to these categories, we must decide between us and God. In acknowledging our lack of patience, a devotee should seek God to first understand and accept his relationship to God and humanity and secondly, to help us to be in continual prayer before God that we would be ever-mindful of that relationship and its beauty. If we can do this, we will be more patient both with God and the overall populace. We would do well to read and meditate on Isaiah 55:8, 9.

Beloved, I fear that born-again Christians fail to understand the commandments to love the Lord and love their neighbor. God is clear again and again that they go together. *If it is true that a man cannot claim to love God if he does not love his neighbor, we can hardly claim to be waiting on God and patient with His purposes if we are not patient with our neighbor.* It is wise to meditate on Psalm 37:7a quoted at the start of this section and take note that this is still a truth if we replace "Him" (referring to God) with "him" (referring to our neighbor).

Kindness

> Thus says the Lord of hosts, render true judgments, show kindness and mercy each to his brother, do not oppress the widow, the fatherless, the sojourner, or the poor, and let none of you devise evil against his brother in your heart.
>
> *—Zechariah 7:9, 10*

> As the Father has loved me, so have I loved you; abide in my love.
>
> *—John 15:9*

Kindness is such a general term. I fear that as a result the overall population can use the word so haphazardly that men and women neglect to see this quality bloom to full extent in their own lives (Brady, 2003; Swindoll, 1998). Very related to the trait of kindness is thoughtfulness. To be kind is to be full of thoughts geared towards other people (Murray, 1979, 2004). *Our love is manifested only to the point in which our thought life is geared towards the maximization of the well-being of those around us!* "Kind" is an interesting word because to be kind

54 • THE POWER OF CONSTANT PRAYER AND COMMUNION WITH GOD

results from viewing others as the same "kind," as ourselves. If a person is genuinely interested in the maximization of other peoples' benefit, he will not only have certain hopes along this line, *but also he will do everything possible to make the hope into a reality* (Jeynes, 2009, 2019). He will pray, encourage, sacrifice, and rebuke when necessary, so that that person's ultimate benefit may be achieved (Orr, 2009). A constant desire to see another's bests interests fulfilled will beget a constant dialogue with God to the end that all that we can do towards this end may be accomplished within the bounds of God's wisdom and love. For we know if we depend on our own abilities, we will fail (Jeynes, 2016, 2018, 2020a). Hence, for the sake of the other person, we should rely on God. This constant dialogue with God will beget an overflowing of love that cannot be gainsaid (Jeynes, 2012).

The challenge for the Christian is then to be in full and constant communion with God so that the other person is the subject on his dialogue with God as often as God would have, which is quite constant. To commune with God with other people always in mind is to truly abide in love of Christ. This call is no doubt challenging, for it includes giving many aspects of one's life over to the Lord (I Peter 3:8, 9). It includes being merciful in even the smallest matters and to those whom society views as small (Ruth 2:8-16; Proverbs 14:21). In a most challenging sense, it means being kind to one's enemies (Exodus 23:4, 5). To be continually aware of God to the end of working so that our enemy may receive what is best for him is a tall order (Murray, 1979, 2004). I dare say that no one lives up to this call. I praise God that Jesus has paid the price for our many failures in this whole area of kindness (Jeynes, 2003, 2006). Hallelujah!

Before ending this section, I want to point out that to desire the best for all human beings is not necessarily synonymous with desiring what they themselves desire. A rebuke may sometimes be the most Christ-like act that a person can do for another (though it is important that it be done in love). A believer may have the kindness of Christ in pleading with God to take away the riches or glory that an unsaved individual has, that his heart may be softened enough to receive Christ into his life. Nevertheless, if such kindness is to be constant, he must be constantly pray to God.

Compassion

> What do you think? If a man has a hundred sheep and one of them has gone astray, does he not leave the 99 on the mountains and go in search of the one that went astray? And if he finds it, truly, I say to you, he rejoices over it more than the 99 that never went astray. So, it is not the will of my Father who is in heaven that one of these little ones should perish.
>
> *—Matthew 18:12-14*

I do not think there is any verse which more greatly exemplifies compassion than this. Certainly, there is no greater example of compassion than the Lord Je-

Constant-Prayer and Communion With God and Love • 55

sus. Through Matthew 18:12-14, the follower can come to an understanding of the steps involved in the biblical concept of compassion.

First, the Christian must be sensitive to certain sheep going astray and therefore, demanding his attention.

Secondly, the Christian must have a love for that sheep so that he will go to the extremes to see that the sheep resumes its proper position in the flock.

Thirdly, the Christian must have a heart of rejoicing when a member of the flock is restored. Though Jesus is the Chief Shepherd and the person who functions as pastor has a special shepherding function, all believers are called to have a shepherd's compassionate heart and therefore often function as a shepherd (Jeynes, 2016, 2018). For a greater insight into what it is to be compassionate, the believer should, at each of these steps individually, be:

1. **Sensitive to sheep going astray**—If the disciple is truly compassionate, he will sensitize himself to whether Christians allow obstacles to sidetrack them or even willfully stray from the flock (Jeynes, 1999, 2003a). He will also sensitize himself to non-Christians who, by definition, are lost sheep. This is quite a large task and to pretend otherwise would not fall into the scope of reality.

   There are a lot of people hurting in the world. At the same time, very few of their hurts are revealed by the people themselves. People fear being transparent. To be able to hide one's feelings and hurts is considered a sign of steadfastness. The disciple cannot assume, therefore, just because hurts are not revealed that they do not exist. The Lord's child can only gain the type of sensitivity required by being constantly sensitive to God's own voice and direction. The faithful follower needs to become in tune with God's heartbeat, for His heart pumps when His children have themselves a heart that pains. As believers fellowships with God, God will point out to them those who have wounds and those who are undergoing difficulties beyond what they can bear alone. The adherent should remember that God is often willing to reveal about the inner life of the brethren what they themselves are not willing to reveal nor may even be aware of.

2. **An extreme love that will work to see that the sheep return to the flock**—The Lord knows that it is not enough merely to know when a member of the flock is in trouble. The devotee must do something about this fact. Anyone who has ever seen what happens when one member of a flock roams away from the majority of the sheep (whether it be as an eyewitness or in a movie, etc.) knows that it is often very difficult to retrieve the lost sheep. Even if the sheep is retrieved, too often it will no sooner return than go off course again.

   The Christian must then be committed to offering his entire self to work towards the re-establishing of the sheep in the flock (Swindoll,

THE POWER OF CONSTANT PRAYER AND COMMUNION WITH GOD

1998). No halfway efforts will do. The Lord's child must have committed oneself to being used of God in any way the Lord chooses to bring that person back into proper fellowship, both horizontally and vertically. No such commitment can be expected of any men or women unless they have a Christ-like compassion for that individual. If such a compassion rules people's hearts, they would not merely spend their spare time guiding sheep by God's grace back into the flock. Rather, they will take time to be certain that sheep do not go astray. They will stand by a soul until that time when they are quite certain that person is steadied enough to function in the proper role within the flock. Compassion cannot help but manifest itself in dedication.

3.   **Rejoicing when a member of the flock is restored**—Hopefully, when God has used His adherent to return a lost sheep into the flock, the adherent will be overjoyed. Because of human frailties, however, people often have a little more trouble rejoicing when someone else is used to accomplish the same end. There may be several reasons for this. Certainly, because he has not been a witness of this beautiful work of God, he may not be as excited.

It is more unfortunate when the reason is comparison or competitiveness with the person who has been used by God to secure the sheep into the fold. If the believer has such feelings towards another instrument of God, he need wonder whether one is desirous of being used by God for the glory of God or one's own glory.

If a Christian is deficient in any of these three areas, the believer needs to lay prostrate before the throne of God and ask for more of the compassion of Christ.

A MEDITATION ON LOVE

A Real Love is Everything

I will establish his kingdom forever if he continues resolute in keeping my commandments and my ordinances, as he is today.

—I Chronicles 28:7

A friend loves at *all* times.

—Proverbs 17:17a

How fitting it is that Christ, who loved at all times, whose love is everlasting, should have a kingdom that is everlasting. The love of God is incomprehensibly important. *The eternal life of the believer lasts only as long as God's love lasts!* It is a cause for rejoicing that God's love is eternal. *If God's love would cease even for one moment, all creation would perish, for God's creation was created in love and is sustained through love.* People are totally dependent on God's love for their sustenance and in fact, his total existence. Love is this important!

Love is a life support system for humanity that it has rejected to a very large degree. It is so that if humankind is totally denied of God's love, it will cease to exist. However, it is also true that to the extent individuals are denied can result from a person's rejection of what love is offered. Moreover, it can also result from an unwillingness of those around that person to love with the love of Christ. *Each time we fail to show love, we deny another person of that love in Christ.* Now it may be that God may intervene another way to manifest His love to this person and increase their potential in Him, but the above fact stands ceteris paribus (i.e., other things equal). There is a tremendous responsibility attached to love (Bergman, 2004). If we truly have the love of Christ in our heart, we will seek to make other people the best they can be. It will be our constant desire to see people reach their very highest potential. It will be a desire which overflows from the Christian's life continuously, as a fruit of the Spirit of God and unable to be snuffed by any human or Satanic opposing force (Froehlich, 2014). As the believer witnesses and becomes a part of those around him, meeting up to their fullest potential, he will know and rejoice in the fact that love has been victorious.

Meditations on Loving God

> Then Paul answered, 'What are you doing, weeping and breaking my heart? For I am ready not only to be imprisoned, but even to die at Jerusalem for the name of the Lord Jesus.'
>
> *—Acts 21:13*

> But *whatever* gain I had, I counted as *loss* for the sake of Christ. Indeed, I count everything as loss because of the surpassing worth of knowing Christ Jesus my Lord. For His sake I have suffered the loss of *all* things and count them as refuse, in order that I may gain Christ.
>
> *—Philippians 3:7, 8*

To love God is to desire to glorify Him in all ways possible and at whatever costs conceivable, as well as desire to see Him glorified in all events and in all people around us. *The love of God does not rest in the praise, obedience, or love of others in and of itself unless it is preceded by, occurs with, or is followed by the unrelenting desire to see God glorified!* So many people who live lives of what the populace terms "obedience," "love," and "worshipful" believe that they are living strongly upright lives before God. However, sometimes they are not as spiritual as they presume because each is not motivated purely by a desire to glorify God. Even the most beautiful of Christians fall victim often at this intersection.

Among those believers who are faithfully following God, knowing that their whole life depends on following Him, there is still a sluggishness in allowing God

58 • THE POWER OF CONSTANT PRAYER AND COMMUNION WITH GOD

to spawn a life not only a radical obedience but also of radical glorification. Many Christians over the century have asked the question, "What did the church have in the first century that the church doesn't have today?" I will state frankly that I think this question is very much related to what is being discussed in this section. For the lack has now existed for many centuries.

Some pose that the lack is due to the fact that Christians are not allowing the Holy Spirit to move in the way He did in the first century. Others say it is because of the absence of first century church structure. Others believe the reason is boldness. The list continues. I do believe there is truth in each of these claims. I think there is truth especially in the first claim but in a different way than is commonly thought.

The major problem in the Christian body today insofar as loving God is concerned is that most seek to please God as a/the major priority and count pleasing God as synonymous with glorifying God, when in fact it is not!

Let me expand on this idea a little since at first it is probably confusing. First, let me present an analogy of a "D" student in a classroom who is trying to please his teacher. He knows that if he gets a "B" he will please his teacher and an "A" will please his teacher very much. But if this student's success in getting higher grades pleases his teacher, the teacher does not get much glory for it. People will see that and give most of the credit for the grade to the student. It is this way in the world today. Too often, if only a few lives are changed drastically by becoming born-again, the glory is given to the individual and not to God. Now, returning to the analogy, what would the student do if he was trying to glorify the teacher rather than just please her? He would do everything to help and encourage the other students to get "A's." If all the students learned a great deal and got "A's," people would give the credit to the teacher as having phenomenal teaching abilities rather than to each individual student. The student would do everything in his power to make sure that the teacher received all the credit for his improvement, as well as the improvement of his classmates.

We can see by this analogy that there is a vast difference between merely pleasing God and glorifying Him (Jeyes, 2015; 2016). Glorifying encompasses pleasing, but pleasing does not encompass glorifying Him. Yet this has been throughout the years a major problem among believers. Even believers are often consistently pleasing Him but not consistently glorifying Him. Two large words make for the difference between "pleasing" and "glorifying": love and humility. Many believers may have enough love and humility to often please God but not to continuously glorify Him in the way mentioned in the analogy. Do we have this kind of love and humility? No. But God can help us.

Comparison and a desire to do the best we can in relation to others result from a desire only to please God and not a sincere heart drive to glorify Him. If we are truly loving and humble, i.e., truly desire more than anything to see God glorified, we will give 100% of the credit for various accomplishments to God, not 95%, but 100%. If we truly have our heart totally out for God's glory, we will do all we

Constant-Prayer and Communion With God and Love • 59

can to see that everyone we can reach in the Body of Christ is built up, moving rapidly toward reaching their full phenomenal potential that God may be glorified. Having all Christians as tremendous lights is the ideal rather than have individuals glorified, because only a few people are lights. We will see our life on earth as wholly geared towards other people that this goal of full glorification of God may be realized (Philippians 1:20-23). We will love all that we see that is good within the Body of Christ. We will not merely criticize the evil, but also do everything in our power to see the evil removed, because God is not glorified in the growth of evil (Psalm 97:10).

In the following section by God's grace, God will elaborate on this principle through this writer's pen and show how directly the love of the brethren relates to the importance of glorifying God and not just pleasing Him.

Meditations on Loving One Another

> For God is my witness, whom I serve with my Spirit in the gospel of His Son that without ceasing I mention you *always* in my prayers.
>
> —*Romans 1:9*

> Do not rejoice when your enemy fails, and let not your heart be glad when he stumbles.
>
> —*Proverbs 24:17*

Glorifying God, more so than just pleasing God, involves committing our entire being to God's children as a living sacrifice of God's. We realize in so doing that God is best glorified when all of God's children are at their highest potential in Him through a love that reaches out and desires the best for other individuals. The verse in Proverbs, just quoted, strongly relates to this. God will be glorified if we have the same attitude toward our enemies (Matthew 5:32-48) and strangers (Leviticus 19:34; Deuteronomy 10:19), as well as fellow believers. If our attitude in general is to desire the best possible thing for other people, then we will find ourselves "turning the other cheek" and showing the love of Christ to all people. For in such a case, we act according to what is best for the whole person.

As children of God continue to seek to building up of others into the people that God meant them to be, they will notice a lot of changes taking place in the lives of others (Jeynes, 2007). Ninety percent of the time, one's contribution of loving, wholly geared toward the glorification of God, will not be appreciated for what it is by all except God. This fact separates the men from the boys. A believer who is totally committed to the glory of God will not mind this fact. Others will mind it.

To live such a life wholly dedicated to glorifying God, far above pleasing Him, is a tremendous task. Among humans, no one can truly achieve this. People fall way short; a person's flesh too often grays pure intentions and desires (Offner et al., 2013). To the extent to which this way of life can be accomplished, it requires a constant dependence on God to do it. God's faithful must continually commune with God and be forever asking God to glorify and enhance Him.

REFERENCES

Agich, G. J. (2003). *Dependence and autonomy in old age: An ethical framework for long-term care*. Cambridge University Press.

Bergman, G. (2004). *The little book of bathroom philosophy: Daily wisdom from the greatest thinkers*. Fairwinds Press.

Bonhoeffer, D. (1959). *The cost of discipleship.* McMillan.

Bounds, E. M. (2010). *Purpose in prayer*. Blackstone.

Brady, B. V. (2003). *Christian love*. Georgetown University Press.

Chambers, O. (2008). *My utmost for His highest.* Discovery House Publishers.

Clairvaux, B. (1940). *The steps of humility.* Harvard University Press.

Daley, R. J. (2009). *Sacrifice unveiled: The true meaning of Christian sacrifice*. T & T Clark.

Elliot, E. (1992). *The shaping of a Christian family.* Revell.

Froehlich, M. A. (2014). *Courageous gentleness: Following Christ's example of restrained strength*. Discovery House Publishers.

Graham, B. (2015). *Quotations book*. Retrieved March 26, 2015 from: http://quotationsbook.com/quote/38480/.

Kruschwitz, R. B. (2001). *Forgiveness*. Baylor University.

Murray, A. (1979). *Abide in Christ: The joy of being in God's presence*. Whitaker House.

Murray, A. (2004). *A life of obedience.* Bethany House.

Offner, H., Larsen, D., & Larsen, S. (2013). *A deeper look at the fruit of the Spirit: Growing in the likeness of Christ*. InterVarsity Press.

Orr, C. E. (2009). *How to live a holy life*. Floating Press.

Peterson, J. (2003). *The insider: Bringing the Kingdom of God into your everyday world*. Navigator Press.

Swindoll, C. R. (1998). *Joseph: A man of integrity and forgiveness: Profiles in Character*. Word Publishers.

Tozer, A. W. (2013). *The pursuit of God.* Gospel Light.

CHAPTER 5

CONSTANT-PRAYER AND COMMUNION WITH GOD AND HUMILITY

This chapter continues where the last chapter left off. Sensibly speaking, it takes both humility and love to live a life which is glorifying to God (Clairvaux, 1940). The two work together to create a life of holiness pleasing to God (Daley, 2009).

They work close enough so that it is not necessary to repeat some of the key ideas of the former chapter. Hence, we continue with new ideas.

GOD'S RELATIONSHIP TO THE HUMBLE

God's View of Man

What is man that thou art mindful of him, and the son of man that thou dost care for him?

—Psalm 8:4

We have all become like one who is unclean, and all our righteous deeds are like a polluted garment, we all fade like a leaf; and our iniquities, like the wind, take us away."

The Power of Constant Prayer and Communion With God, pages 61–72.
Copyright © 2024 by Information Age Publishing
www.infoagepub.com
All rights of reproduction in any form reserved.

—Isaiah 64:6

but you are a chosen race, a royal priesthood, a holy nation, God's own people, that you may declare the wonderful needs of Him who called you out of darkness into His marvelous light.

—I Peter 2:9, 10

If we understand God's view of humanity, we will have taken the first step towards godly humility. True humility, in essence, is seeing ourselves as God sees us (Romans 12:3, 16). God views man as he is. Man is fallen and in and of himself is totally separated from the perfection which is God. There is a second part as well, however.

In Christ people are born anew and become a part of a wonderful process of transformation into greater Christlikeness. Despite the all-too-obvious fact of who humans are, God has chosen to overstep this fact by participating with people in their earthly experience and surrendering to the life of Christ on the cross. In His blood each individual may have life in spite of his sin. In fact, in Christ the believer is exalted to a position of authority and responsibility.

While there are two aspects of God's view of humanity, Christians tend to emphasize one or the other. Some insist that people are but dust and stress man's unworthiness in comparison to God's worthiness. Others like to treat the exalted position of humanity as far more important and say that a Christian can hardly have a victorious Christian life if he or she has a "worm theology." The problem that few people confront, however, is that the two are inseparable concepts.

Humans are indeed but dust, but they are also exalted in Christ. The important truth to remember, in regards to this, is that hu*mans can only understand their exalted position in Christ insofar as they understand their depravity without Him!* As the devotee grows in insight concerning his or her wretchedness without God, one is more able to receive the position of exaltation in Christ as the act of grace that it is! *Understanding our depravity is essential to understanding God's grace.* The disciples who best comprehend their sinful state before God understand just how saved they are. Disciples of Christ grow into a deeper realization of the meaning of salvation as they come to grips with their utter inability to please God. An interesting conclusion comes from these facts:

The person who knows in one's heart his or her depravity is much closer to understanding and enjoying one's exalted state in Christ than if the individual lays emphasis only on exaltation.

It is like a boy who is being taken on a tour of the Western states. He has also had a vague knowledge of how fortunate he was to be walking on level ground far above the canyons, the bottom of the sea of the molten center of the earth. But the child never realized just how exalted he was above these things until he looked into the depths of the Grand Canyon. When the child walked out of the Grand Canyon and upon level ground, it was then he realized how exalted he was on level ground to begin with. Before then, his understanding was only an intellectual one. So it is, with understanding our exalted state in Christ. We cannot truly understand how exalted we are unless we also experience the depths of depravity.

The challenge to Christians who desire constant communion with God is then to be cognizant in heart of both their wretchedness and priesthood continuously during the day. In so doing, they will acknowledge God's transcendent love for them and act upon the power invested in God's love as it works through them.

God's Nearness to the Humble

> But He gives more grace; therefore it says, 'God opposes the proud, but gives grace to the humble'... Draw near to God and He will draw near to you.
>
> *—James 4:6, 8*

> For though the Lord is high, He regards the lowly, but the haughty He knows from afar.
>
> *—Psalm 138:6*

> Blessed are the people who know the festal shout, who walk, O Lord, in the light of thy countenance, who exult in thy name all the day, and extol thy righteousness.
>
> *—Psalm 89:15, 15*

The last verse probably best sums up the relationship between nearness to God and humility. The people who walk closest to God, in His light, are those who are most likely to lift up the name of the Lord. The humble will raise up God's name not only once, but throughout the day. The meek man or woman of God will lift up God's righteousness, light years greater than one's own. It is no coincidence that the individual who glorified God in his daily living will not only be attracted to God more in the process, but God will also be more attracted to that person. It is also true that the believer who is walking rightly before God will have an overwhelming desire to see God glorified and God alone!

The humble may almost entirely be defined as they who lay aside all aspects of themselves to take on the person of Christ, they do everything out of whole dedication to God and a heart of total self-denial that brings God and the humble into a nearness of fellowship. God can only fall behind the work of a Christian who is allowing God's Spirit to manifest Himself to declare the glory of God. There was never a person, with the exception of Jesus, whose work God totally fell behind. God can only be entirely for a person's work if God's glory is the main object and also the main result. Such work lives in the heart of a humble man or woman of God.

64 • THE POWER OF CONSTANT PRAYER AND COMMUNION WITH GOD

People of humility are the first to recognize their absolute dependence on God (Augustine, 2010, 2015a, 2015b). They know that they can do nothing of eternal value for the kingdom out of their own adamic nature (Agich, 2003; Murray, 1979, 2004). It is the humble servant of God, then, who is the first to turn his or her attention to having a continuous communion with God. Without a constant fellowship with God, a devotee realizes one can hardly begin to please God in any type of consistent fashion. Recognizing his inability to meet up to the tasks and paths that God had laid before him, the lowly individual prostrates himself before God. He prays to the Lord to give him a tremendous love for Him such that he has never known so that he may have a continual awareness and communion with the Most High. Such a person says, "For how can I even begin to glorify your name as you both desire and deserve if my mind is not totally engrossed in your love and awed by your majesty throughout the day."

Such should be our prayer, my beloved (Bounds, 2010). I do not know why we are forgiven and raised up to a kingship because of our belief in Jesus (Hayford & Bauer, 2011). Yet we receive, and instead of trying to understand it in our most finite mind, we choose instead to act upon this fact. In acting upon it, God will be glorified and others will experience a life with many parallels to ours and those of other believers. It is only God who can fill us with this love that we so desperately need to love God as He ought to be loved. And indeed, we can never love God as He ought to be loved nor even come close. Such a love is only found in perfection; and we will always fall vastly short of this (Brady, 2003).

There are several important results of God's nearness to the humble that should be noted:

1. **With humility comes wisdom**—The Bible associates humility with wisdom quite frequently (Proverbs 11:2, 12:5). Wisdom results from spending a large part of our time conversing with the Lord Jesus, as our very best friend. The more we converse with the very source of wisdom, which is God, the wiser we will become. Humility is conducive to wisdom because it leads us to throw ourselves into a rich communion with God.

   First, we realize our complete need to rely on God, and secondly, we desire to glorify God more than anything else and realize that we must seek a strong bond of friendship with God if this is to be accomplished. As we give ourselves over to the beginnings of the everlasting communion that God eventually desires, wisdom will surely result.

2. **The humble are used of God mightily**—As the Christian comes to fathom the magnitude of his undeservedness, God will look for him more and more as a useable instrument to set into operation His glorious purpose.

   It is mind boggling that God, in fact, chose each Christian to share in His glory (John 15:16). If a Christian has any modesty whatsoever, that

Constant-Prayer and Communion With God and Humility • **65**

child of God will no doubt ask, "But why of all people would God chose me?" The fact that a devotee opens himself up with this question shows that it is already chipping away his pride. Though this is a key question that every believer should ask himself, it cannot be over-emphasized that posing this question is but a shallow beginning to living a life of humility before the Almighty God. As a Christian grows, this question should take on a great immensity of depth so that this frame of mind and heart over-flows to revolutionize every aspect of one's Christian life (I Chronicles 17:16-18; 29:14).

All these things my hand has made, and so all these things are mine, says the Lord. But this is the man to whom I will look, he that is *humble* and *contrite in Spirit* and trembles at my Word.

—Isaiah 66:2

It is the servant of God of lowliness and meekness whom God uses in the mightiest ways (Offner et al., 2013). This does not necessarily mean that he's a great soul winner or is used to perform spectacular miracles or has a large ministry involvement with the media. This may be man's concept of what it is to be used mightily of God, but it is often not God's. (Man emphasizes results that can be seen with the human eye, but this is but a small percentage of the total picture which God sees). It is the humble instrument of God who will inevitably stand as first in the Kingdom of God (Matthew 18:4).

Even among those whom Christ followers have labeled "people used of God," there are some who down the years have stood out as tremen-dous lights amidst the rest. I remember, in my day, I viewed Billy Gra-ham as being in tune with God, way above his contemporaries. There have been others before this time: Andrew Murray, Tozer, Brother Law-rence, Martin Luther, Augustine, Thomas Merton, etc. (Augustine, 2010, 2015a; Graham, 2015). It has always intrigued me that while many com-mentaries have had important spiritual insights and other contributions throughout the years, it is still Matthew Henry's writing hundreds of years ago that is considered especially spiritually enlightening. Why do these instruments of the Lord stand out as light among their contem-poraries? I would not hesitate to say that a major part of the answer is humility. I would encourage the reader to peruse the works of these men and see what one thinks. It is true that the people gifted rightly in evan-gelism, teaching, prophecy, etc., will be used by God greatly. But show me one who is humble and is as gifted as these, and God will show the believer much more.

3.   **God has favor towards the humble**—This is a great catch-all phrase, but it is nonetheless true. God loves nothing more than to be recognized for who He really is in love, power, and grace, etc. It is the humble Chris-

tian who comes the closest to seeing God as He truly is. God will show favor toward those who see themselves in their rightful place before God (Isaiah 51:15).

CREDITING GOD AS THE SOURCE

Seeking God's Glory Affects the Memory

In God we have boasted continually, and we will give thanks to thy name forever.

—Psalm 44:8

Let him who boasts, boast of the Lord.

—II Corinthians 10:17

It depicts well the human condition, the fact that boasting is most often associated with pride rather than humility. This fact also depicts the truism that God receives very little of the glory that He deserves. The cry of Psalm 44:8 can only be said by a very humble man. In fact, this can only be cried by the person who in constant prayer with God, such that constant humility results. Constant humility results from a constant fellowship with God in which an individual is continually seeking His glory. If a Christian is habitually seeking God's glory alone, one will see God's hand in most every circumstance and event that comes his way. An imprint of what God has done in each situation will be left on this person's mind. If, however, the receiver is caught up in his own gifts and achievements, an imprint of what he himself has done will be etched well into his mind. When the time comes to give credit where it is due, either within a man's own mind, in prayer, or in sharing these events with others, whatever has been imprinted on his mind will be what is emphasized in his recall.

If what God has done is imprinted, God will receive the glory. If what the believer himself has done is imprinted, he himself will receive the credit. *To the extent that a Christian gives the credit to God for all good in his life and in the lives of others, this person actively seeks God's glory. In the end, a person can only be called a servant of God insofar as he actively seeks and succeeds at glorifying God in his life!*

Daniel sought the glory of God and therefore had no curse concerning a short memory of what God had done (Daniel 2:3). Proverbs also warns the Christian against seeking to uplift himself rather than God (Proverbs 27:2; 30:32). It would be wise to meditate on these verses. I fear that no person really knows how to glorify the Lord, as one should (Offner, Larsen & Larsen, 2013). Few even know where to start, though they think they do. If our hearts are honest in glorifying the Lord, we will be glorifying God unceasingly, never attracting attention to ourselves but always pointing to God as the source (Peterson, 2003; Piper, 2011).

Constant-Prayer and Communion With God and Humility • **67**

If we utter a few "praise the Lord" declarations or glorify God only intermittently; we can hardly say that we are living a life glorifying to God. *Glorifying God is a lifestyle; it is putting aside ourselves totally for the sake of Christ* (Briscoe, 2013; Daley, 2009)!

Thanksgiving and Humility

And do you seek great things for yourself? Seek them not…
—Jeremiah 45:5a

But far be it from me to glory except in the cross of our Lord Jesus Christ, by which the world has been crucified to me, and I to the world.
—Galatians 6:14

The consequences of a life void of an overflowing of thanksgiving are one of the most underestimated footholds of Satan in modern society. As nations become more advanced, there is along with this "progress" a tendency towards the fatal disease of "unthankfulness." Being spoiled and complaining are results of this disease. People complain if the thermostat is a few degrees off or if the refrigerator door is difficult to close. *Unthankfulness is grounded in pride!*

If a person is NOT thankful, he or she is therefore asserting the fact that one is deserving. Whatever we have failed to thank God for, we have indirectly said to God that we deserve what He has given us! If I do not remember even thanking God for the fact that I have a shower, for instance. Up until now, I have not been entirely grateful for its existence in my home. This is another way of saying, "God, I don't need to be thankful for it. I deserve it." Now certainly a person can take this principle to the point of neurosis in which he thanks God for every kind of bird, insect, and piece of dust. I do not advise this. There is much, however, that the believer is blessed with time and time again whose existence he assumes.

Thanksgiving results from humility (Clairvaux, 1940). We have a long way to go in both these areas. We thank God for so very little of His acts of grace during the day. God answers all sorts of little prayers every day. God gives us food, wakes us up, gives us air to breathe, shelter, talks to us, sings with us, comforts us, gives us a good night sleep, keeps our friends and family safe, keeps our hearts pumping, gives us green trees to look at, etc. Yet, how many times do we thank Him for these things each day? Very few. We can hardly claim to be humble. We assume certain blessings because underneath we think we deserve them. We are presumptuous fellows at best. *Constant thanksgiving is acknowledging and appreciating the moving of God's hand of grace in everything, in every day, and at every turn.* Just picture going along in life and every few moments seeing a hand reach down from heaven and give graciously, providing constantly all the day long. There would be very little room for pride. In a life of constant thanksgiving, the case is much the same, for the Christian is indeed seeing God's hand move again and again and again.

Constant thanksgiving is especially important in those areas of life in which the follower tends to, or has the potential to, take glory and honor away from God. If the believer is a good businessperson, that individual should constantly thank God for that talent. If the person is intelligent, loving, wise or helpful, the individual should be thanking God very often for these gifts. When a compliment comes a person's way, one's attitude should be one of humility and thankfulness to God. If we have not been thankful, we will naturally assume the credit (Deuteronomy 15:15). There is nothing wrong with expressing appreciation for a compliment, but the glory must surely be God's. *It is good to accept encouragement from others, but when we take some of God's glory and claim it as ours, we have gone beyond the bounds of allowing others to encourage us and are now encouraging ourselves.* The bottom line is this—*if we spent more time receiving God's encouragement, we would have little need to encourage ourselves. It is a fact that too many people seek the encouragement of people because they do not know what it is to allow God to encourage them.*

ADDITIONAL TRAITS OF THE HUMBLE

Servanthood

Seek the Lord and His strength, seek His presence *continually*.
—*I Chronicles 16:11*

So you, by the help of your God, return, hold fast to love and justice, and wait *continually* for your God.
—*Hosea 12:6*

Oh, that we might be a servant of the Lord continually! To be a true servant of the Most High is to seek His presence without interruption, for only in His presence can we know His desire moment-to-moment. And only when we know His desires each moment can we hope to serve Him as He should be served. By the grace of the Lord *only* can we develop a love for Him in which there is not a minute we do not want to be by God and not a minute we do not want to converse with Him, either to talk or to listen. As His servants, we cannot serve Him if we are afar off. Lead us into your presence, Lord.

Any servant must have two qualities to please his master (Froehlich, 2014; Orr, 2009, Wiersbe, 2005). First, he must know his Master (to have any chance to please his Master wholly, he must know his Master's every desire). Second, he must be diligent in acting upon what he knows of his Master. One of these qualities by itself can be fruitless. For the servant who knows his Master but does not act upon that knowledge grows only in hypocrisy.

Constant-Prayer and Communion With God and Humility • 69

The disciple must have a respect for the knowledge of the Holy One. For though humans are designed to build, in its lack of application, humans can only be hurting themselves. Second, the servant who does not know his or her Master but seeks to diligently please Him, may succeed in his quest at times but despite his well-intended heart will often appear as a fool.

Even those relatively quite mature in the Christian body believe they can grow to know God a good deal by spending an hour with Him in the morning, praising Him, or praying to Him a few times during the day, and fellowshipping with Christians. But it has come to my attention that nothing could be further from the truth! To think that we can truly grow to know an infinite God by spending 1 to 3 hours communing with Him during the day is, for the lack of a better word, amusing. There is not a person on earth who has ever come close to totally knowing his spouse despite the many hours of contact. How much less could he ever come to know God! Twenty-four hours of communion every day is not sufficient to come to know God. Even those days when we have not failed to be aware of God but for one minute, we know our knowledge of God is but a speck.

If even the "mature" Christian spends but a mere 1–3 hours in communion with God each day, it is no wonder why the world has not been turned around for Christ, as it was in the first century. In his letter to churches, Paul spoke many times of constantly praying (Colossians 1:9, II Thessalonians 1:11; Romans 1:9, Philemon 4:1; Thessalonians 3:10, etc.). How often can we make such a claim, if we so desired, in our letters?

The world would be turned upside down for Christ if all the members of the Body of Christ were continual lights of the world (Augustine, 2010; Tozer, 2013). Alas, we forget this fact. A light bulb needs a continuous link with the source of electricity to shine, or else a split second later, it will go out. What remains is a light bulb that when approaching it you can detect its warmth. And yes, to some extent, this stands out before the world as a testimony for Christ. This is the extent of the testimony. But the Lord Jesus did not call us to be a warm light but a shining one. And we can be a latter only if we are constantly praying to the Lord. I detect there is too much warm in us, and not enough light.

The second facet of an effective servant for Christ is diligence in putting into practice what he does know. If the Christian is truly as diligent as he supposes he is, his diligence will always lead him back to God until he has attained a continual communion with Him. The Christian's diligent heart will lead him into a desire to know God more by communicating with Him more that he might more effectively work toward the furthering of the kingdom and the glory of God. In servant-hood, does the follower gain right to the authority of royal priest? Until he serves, though he be a royal priest in Christ, he has not experienced the priest's authority (Luke 17:10, Matthew 3:15). Woodrow Wilson once said, "The princes among us are those who forget themselves and serve mankind." In the Christian context, we might say that, "the true royal priests among us are those who forget themselves and serve the Lord and mankind."

70 • THE POWER OF CONSTANT PRAYER AND COMMUNION WITH GOD

The true servant of God acts when his Master tells him to and waits at the command of his Master as well. The servant must be willing to act or wait as long as the Lord requires him to (Hosea 12:6). It takes humility to be able to wait upon the Lord. For in the process of waiting, God may ask him to do some very menial work that one would otherwise prefer not to do. The ceremony of the washing of feet seemed at the onset quite insignificant, but in the eyes of the Lord was unquestionably significant (John 13:14-16). In humility, the servant must trust the Lord Jesus that in waiting there is a salience which transcends human understanding, much as children should trust their parents that various guidelines they set for his behavior have an importance which the children do not yet appreciate (Matthew 18:2-4). Someone once said, "We need not nervously pace the deck if the Great Pilot is at the wheel." Also, "Little faith will bring your soul to heaven; great faith will bring heaven to your soul."

Brokenness

> Be thou to me a rock of habitation, to which I may *continually* come; thou has given commandment to save me, for thou art my rock and my fortress.
> —*Psalm 71:3(NASB)*

> I, I am He that comforts you; who are you that you are afraid of man who dies, of the son of man who is made like grass, and have forgotten the Lord, your Maker, who stretched out the heavens and laid the foundations of the earth, and fear continually all the day, because of the fury of the oppressor, when he sets himself to destroy? And where is the fury of the oppressor?
> —*Isaiah 51:12, 13*

To be a broken vessel before God is to be in a position of purposeful, self-negligence of self. Brokenness is a release of the sin that lies waiting to subvert our Christ consciousness into the hands of God that it may be both cleansed and uprooted. The broken spirit is the ultimate sacrifice that God desires (Psalm 51:17, 69:32). Nevertheless, brokenness is an uncommon state among contemporary believers.

The two verses quoted at the beginning of this section are used to form a contrast of a continual refuge in God verses a continual fear of humanity. May I say that in my early years as a believer, I was in the habit of fearing humans more than fearing God. I wrestled with the cares of daily life more than I enjoyed the peace that God offers. *Brokenness is laying aside the fears we have toward the world, and even Satan, that we may fear God alone!*

Lord, help us to be broken before You, for indeed it is but our nature to desire to have all things "together," not only within ourselves but apart from ourselves. We desire so much to see with whole eyes and hear with whole ears and to love people with a whole heart. But here is where our foolishness rests, for our whole-

Constant-Prayer and Communion With God and Humility • 71

ness is but emptiness which tries to disguise itself to us and others. *We must first become broken before we can truly be made whole.* Let those who have been hurt in life rejoice for hurt can lead to brokenness and only brokenness can lead to wholeness!

A wagon cannot run right with square wheels though we pretend otherwise at times. We must be willing to remove the square wheels, thereby rendering the wagon incapable and motionless, before the round wheels can be added to make the wagon whole.

Brokenness is essential to humility. Upon examining Romans 12, a believer will see that brokenness/humility is essential to each command in the chapter. Brokenness is the key to a glorifying and harmonious Christian life.

Few understand the believer who is living a life of growing brokenness. Such a person knows his or her purpose in life. He knows that if the Christian is to glorify God and wants nothing more than to see this goal accomplished, who cares about recognition for what an individual does? He would rather have only enough recognition as to sustain him in the form of encouragement that His Lord may receive all the glory. He knows he receives much more recognition than he deserves and even attributes this fact to God's grace (Ezra 9:13). The broken vessel always points his finger upward when receiving favor. This person does not desire fingers to be pointed at him or her. The broken vessel is much more prone to love than to talk, knowing his or her relationship to God (Ecclesiastes 5:2). Even in one's talk, the specially broken vessel tends to be more concerned with the other discussant rather than oneself. The broken vessel's conversation has more questions of love than answers of knowledge. This is not true because this Christian lacks wisdom; but because in this close relationship with God, this person possesses much wisdom (Proverbs 12:23). In his humility, the broken vessel is constantly confessing his pride and humbling oneself before God that he might always become more broken (II Kings 22:18, 19).

In the Bible, Joseph was such a man (Genesis 4:16; Swindoll, 1998). If only we had more of the broken spirit of Joseph (Swindoll, 1998). Oh, Lord, that you might break us more completely, for we are proud vessels who still too often wish to think we are whole by our own design and strength when we are nothing!

REFERENCES

Agich, G. J. (2003). *Dependence and autonomy in old age: An ethical framework for long-term care.* Cambridge University Press.

Augustine of Hippo. (2010). *City of God* (Dods, M. Peabody, Trans.). Henrickson Publishers.

Augustine of Hippo. (2015a). *Brainy quotes.* Retrieved on April 2, 2015 from: http://www.brainyquote.com/quotes/quotes/s/saintaugus124552.html

Augustine of Hippo. (2015b). *Brainy quotes.* Retrieved on April 2, 2015 from: http://thinkexist.com/quotation/do_you_wish_to_rise-begin_by_descending-you_plan/263998.html. , p. 1.

Bounds, E. M. (2010). *Purpose in prayer.* Blackstone.

Brady, B. V. (2003). *Christian love.* Georgetown University Press.

Briscoe, S. (2013). *Time bandits: Putting first things first.* Multnomah Press.

Clairvaux, B. (1940). *The steps of humility.* Harvard University Press.

Daley, R. J. (2009). *Sacrifice unveiled: The true meaning of Christian sacrifice.* T & T Clark.

Froehlich, M. A. (2014). *Courageous gentleness: Following Christ's example of restrained strength.* Discovery House Publishers.

Graham, B. (2015). *Quotations book.* Retrieved March 26, 2015 from: http://quotations-book.com/quote/38480/

Hayford, J. W., & Bauer, R. H. (2011). *Penetrating the darkness: Keys to ignite faith, boldness, and breakthrough.* Chosen Books.

Murray, A. (1979). *Abide in Christ: The joy of being in God's presence.* Whitaker House.

Murray, A. (2004). *A life of obedience.* Bethany House.

Offner, H., Larsen, D., & Larsen, S. (2013). *A deeper look at the fruit of the Spirit: Growing in the likeness of Christ.* InterVarsity Press.

Orr, C. E. (2009). *How to live a holy life.* Floating Press.

Peterson, J. (2003). *The insider: Bringing the Kingdom of God into your everyday world.* Navigator Press.

Piper, J. (2011). *Desiring God: Meditations of a Christian hedonist.* Multnomah.

Swindoll, C. R. (1998). *Joseph: A man of integrity and forgiveness: Profiles in Character.* Word Publishers.

Tozer, A. W. (2013). *The pursuit of God.* Gospel Light.

Wiersbe, W. W. (2005). *Devotions for renewal and joy: Romans and Philippians.* Honor Publishing.

CHAPTER 6

CONSTANT-PRAYER AND COMMUNION WITH GOD AND OBEDIENCE

WHAT IS OBEDIENCE?

Our Limited Understanding of What is Meant by Obedience
Limits the Depth and Scope of Our Obedience

> I do not reprove you for your sacrifices; your burnt offerings are *continually* before me.
>
> *—Psalm 50:8*

> And Samuel said, 'Has the Lord as great delight in burnt offerings and sacrifices as in obeying the voice of the Lord? Behold to ***obey*** is better than sacrifice, and to hearken than the fat of rams.
>
> *—I Samuel 15:22*

"To obey is better than sacrifice" is an often-used term to illustrate that God desires us to live a life of obedience over living a life merely of sin and claiming

---

The Power of Constant Prayer and Communion With God, pages 73–81.
Copyright © 2024 by Information Age Publishing
www.infoagepub.com
All rights of reproduction in any form reserved.

salvation, by the blood of the Lamb (Piper, 2011). This is an accurate correspondence. However, while this fact is true, it is also true that most people fail to go a step or two further in applying this verse to different levels of obedience. In the most general sense of the term, obedience is not an all or none exercise. Rather, it is one of degrees.

In any given command that God may give to one of His children, that person must decide to what extent he is going to obey or is not going to obey and therefore, in the latter case, merely claim the blood of Christ. We should note that every Christian should claim the blood of Jesus as his only means of justification. However, there is a difference between depending on the blood of Jesus for justification and merely claiming the blood of Jesus and not obeying the Lord, i.e., not acting upon his relationship with God. Many times it is not a willful decision to fail to obey God fully, but one which results from a certain deficiency in the knowledge of God. Nevertheless, to whatever extent a Christian does not obey God, he is disobeying Him, and this is sin (Murray, 2004; Offner et al., 2013).

Here is an illustration of the idea of degrees of obedience. Say there is a woman who lives down the block from a believer, who asks the believer to come over to her apartment to listen to a problem that she desires to share. The believer knows it is God's will for him to listen to her, so he goes to visit her. The believer listens to her problem, although not as closely as he should have. During the course of the conversation, he also has a rather self-centered urge to counsel her quite strongly concerning her difficulties when all she really needed and asked for was to be listened to. The believer never quite catches on that she really does not care for his advice. However, upon leaving he does make it clear that he is available whenever she may need him and urges her not to hesitate to call him. Before going to bed that night, the believer prays for the woman.

Now there are a few important points that should be noted about this illustration. First, on a general level, the believer obeyed the Lord. He went to see the woman to counsel her when the Lord had desired. On a more specific level, the time that he spent with the woman was marked both by obedience and disobedience. The battle had not been won merely as a result of answering the call for help. God desired that the believer show the love of Christ to her in a very definite way. Central to this theme of love, the believer should have listened intently to her to show her that he really cared about her dilemma. Unfortunately, at this specific level of obedience, the believer failed and rather than listen was more concerned with being used mightily by the Lord than showing Christ's love. Many people may have been obedient to God's general call to counsel, but far fewer will respond to the more specific call, in this case, listening in love. One may go a step further specifically and ask the question—"Did the believer tune himself into what Christ would have said in every sentence he spoke?" Naturally, the latter would be very difficult to live up to. The more specific one gets in talking about obedience, the less that person is able to claim that he has been obedient.

Obedience today is gravely misunderstood, and too much of an emphasis on it can lead to legalism. "Most Christians," says Kenyon, "have lost their fellowship and are putting duty in place of it." Obedience, for the most part, is looked upon as following the commandments of God as they are written in the Bible. But this definition is highly misleading (Murray, 1979, 2004; Tozer, 2013). The definition is rather *the result of obedience rather than the act of obedience. The actual act of obedience is the vision of our heart with God so that the will of God becomes our own will!* The only way that a union of hearts with God is possible on a continual basis is through constant prayer and communion with God. Too often humans attempt to see others convicted by the idea living up to the commandments of the Lord. However, if preachers would stress the true act of obedience is in the uniting of man's heart with God, there would be less legalism, more conviction, and an actual increase in obeying the commandments of God. For it is true that most people think that they keep the commandments better than they actually do.

If the average Christian were to rate himself on how loving he was versus how God would rate him, nine times out of ten the former rating would be higher. When emphasizing the union of man's heart with God the question now becomes how often does man have his heart united with God and thereby act in love. Kenyon once said, "Walking in the light of the Word means walking in love. Every step out of love is a step into the dark." If a devotee attempts to have a life submitted to God in union with God's will, he will soon discover just how far short he actually falls of complete obedience.

It is the union of hearts that is the New Testament concept of obedience. In its essence, it is obedience in the sense of union of hearts that Christ says those who love Him will manifest (John 14:15, 21). The fact that a believer's heart is united with God that leads him to keep the commandments of God. The heart that is one with God is a heart offered to God in all yieldingness, as a gift and pleasing fragrance to Him who has died for all men (Psalm 76:11). The heart that is usually in a state of softness and openness to God will lead a Christian to a habitual recognition of his sin and hence, a repentance of heart-felt reality and a more complete heart of submission to the specifics of God's will (Jeremiah 26:13; Ezekiel 7:23). Love, courage, and an awe of God's greatness will pervade the life of a Christian who through a continual communion with God comes to have a union of his heart with God's (Hosea 6:6; I Chronicles 17:13-16; Leviticus 19:36, 37).

It is much like the contrast between our conception of our two-year-old's obedience and his conception of his obedience. When a neighbor asks our two-year-old whether he is obedient and respectful of his parents, the child will most likely say, "Yes." But we know better. While the child might be obedient more often than other kids his age, and we would like to think of him as "a good boy;" memories of various incidents lead us to a somewhat different conclusion. A more likely conclusion is more along the lines of "some days he is, some days he isn't." so it is in our own conception of obedience versus God's. We view obedience in terms of generalities. God views obedience in terms of specifics. We view obedi-

76 • THE POWER OF CONSTANT PRAYER AND COMMUNION WITH GOD

ence in terms of achieving a self-satisfying level, God views obedience in terms of wholeheartedness. Oh, that we might surrender our superficial way of viewing obedience and move on to greater heights.

Obedience as Relationship

> Bind them upon your heart *always*, tie them about your neck.
>
> —*Proverbs 6:21*

Obedience is not success in following a bunch of laws and rules; it springs out of the joy of a close friendship with God. We may have trouble obeying when commandments are placed in front of us to "obey or not." On the other hand, we will have a good deal less trouble obeying someone who talks to us and to whom we talk most of the day. Obedience is to be a joy, and joy only comes from closeness of relationship, not falling in line with various regulations. It is clear in Christ's prayer in Gethemane that Jesus Christ's sacrificial death was an act of obedience which radiated out of relationship rather than abiding by God's rules (Matthew 26:39-42).

We become especially aware of the difference between obedience as a result of following regulations versus as a result of relationship, when we are in the midst of trials (Jeynes, 2022, 2023; Murray, 2004). In such cases, the motivation for abiding in God's commands is at a low ebb. Apart from a heart-to-heart relationship with God, a believer cannot hope to advance above trials and rejoice in the Lord amidst them. Every believer has probably heard many a Christian share with him how it is nearly impossible to truly rejoice amidst our trials. Yet it is clear that this is exactly what the Word of God says the Christian is to do (James 1:2-4; Romans 5:3-5; Philippians 4:4-7).

The reason why rejoicing amidst trials seems so impossible for Christians is because believers seek to rejoice either out of the fact that it is a commandment or the other extreme—out of feeling. Yet when it comes right down to it whenever we try to rejoice because it is a commandment, if we know ourselves at all, we will often reach the point of recognizing that we have been fooling ourselves. While the person who seeks a joy based on feelings will find the joy very short-lived. An authentic rejoicing amidst diverse trials must be based on trust in the Lord Jesus. This trust does not result from a determination on the Christian's part to have faith amidst all circumstances but out of relationship. *The more quality time we have spent with God in prayer and communion with Him, the more we will be able to trust and hence rejoice in Him on the day of adversity!*

The Greek word for believe is "pistaooo" which actually means to trust or lean on. The concept of trusting and leaning on are strongly related, if we picture the following illustration.

If a man stands erect with a person standing behind him, if he trusts the person behind him, he will not fear to lean/fall backward and allow the person behind him to catch him. The same fact is true in our relationship with God. If we truly trust the Lord we will not fear leaning back and allowing the Lord to catch us. As time has passed, my brethren, it has become all-too-clear to me that to trust God so as to fall back into His loving arms is not possible through anything but relationship. In getting to know the person behind me, if I find that person to be loving and trustworthy, I will have less fear to lean back. The more that I come to know this person, the more willing I will be to fall back. The conclusion then is all too plain.

Rejoicing (and obedience as a whole) comes from faith, and faith comes from relationship. The result is that rejoicing (and obedience as a whole) must ultimately come out of relationship.

Rejoicing amidst our trials is being emphasized, because it is in the midst of trials that it is most difficult to obey.

If we can be steadfast in obedience amidst trials, we will be obedient in most situations. Sometimes God seems to be distant from the depth of our own trials. To some degree, this is to be expected, but I fear that we too frequently accept this as part of the normality of the Christian life. The normal Christian life is indeed far from this.

If a disciple's obedience to God is based on a direct reliance on following His commandments, the periods when God seems far away will be frequent. On the other hand, if his obedience is based on communing with God, those periods will be far fewer. To better explain this point, I'd like to share another analogy.

Picture two servants who are each left with the huge task of caring for both farm and home. The first servant has very little communication with the master but has only a list of jobs which need completing. The second servant has a very strong bond of friendship with his master. In fact, he and his master talk most of the day while he is working. Come the day of trial when the servant are confused as to what his task is and lacks confidence with regards to accomplishing even what he does understand, the second servant will not sense that his master is as far away as the first even if both masters are away. We need to meditate on this fact often.

Constant prayer and communion with God builds a relationship so that a Christian can live a life of steadfast obedience even in the midst of trial.

OBEDIENCE AS FOUNDATIONAL TO GLORIFYING GOD

Blessed are they who observe justice, who do righteousness at *all* times.
—*Psalm 106:3*

I will keep thy law *continually*, for ever and ever.
—*Psalm 119:44*

How can God possibly be glorified if His people are not lights unto the nations? Of course, He really cannot be. Non-believers will come to see God as

78 • THE POWER OF CONSTANT PRAYER AND COMMUNION WITH GOD

somehow above the world only if they see that His people are above the world. At the beginning of Christ's ministry, the foundation of His ministry was laid with the calling of the disciples (Mark 1:16-18). Human beings are essential for the completion of the work of Christ. Those especially chosen to be leaders by the Lord Jesus must be strong in Him, being important to the foundation of the Body and therefore to the growth of the entire Body of Christ (Luke 6:46-48).

The Glory of God is accomplished when the reality of God is manifested! That is, when God's true character is made known in the realest sense that it can be, this is glorifying God! Naturally Jesus, being God incarnate, glorified God more than all other human beings combined. Nevertheless, to the extent that the true character of God is made known by believers having the character of God, God is glorified. The way this applies is simply that the more of the reality of God a person is exposed to and receives, the more he will take on the character of God, and therefore the more he will glorify God. This does not merely mean in a supernatural sense, but also in the sense of spending every moment of the day communing with God. I confess I do not approach 100% continual prayer. I do not believe this is humanly possible. However, the more a disciple allows himself to be exposed to the glory, the more he will take on God's character and glory. This truth is most aptly demonstrated when Moses was descending off the mount after being immersed in the glory of God, shining like a light (Exodus 34:29-35; II Corinthians 3:7-9). If a seeker immerses himself in the presence of God by praying and communing with Him, he too will shine as a light. The incident of Moses is not too extraneous from the scope of the Christian's daily experience as one might imagine. Undergoing constant prayer and communion with God is the most direct means by which a Christian can shine as a light.

Jesus says that the only solid foundation is one that is built on Him (Luke 6:46-48). Furthermore, any foundation must be built on obedience. If we seek to glorify God without placing an emphasis on quality and constant prayer, our building will not fare well. Many enjoy communion with God in their praises, but if this communion is not continued and developed into a union of hearts, it is in vain. If worship does not lead us into a more substantial submissive relationship with God, it can hardly be called worship (I Timothy 2:8; Hebrews 13:15). It is not a prayer with God which "feels nice" which glorifies God but a prayer life that leads to obedience. A prayer which "feels nice" can be turned into an experiential emphasis which is nothing short of selfishness. Continual communication with God is not a relationship with God in which we seek for a sensational experience. Rather it is a relationship which is based on faith and one which seeks in everything to please God with feeling as very secondary.

CONSTANT AWARENESS AS NECESSARY TO HAVE OBEDIENCE COME OUT OF A RELATIONSHIP RATHER THAN COMMANDS

Joy of Obedience

Hold me up that I may be safe and have regard for thy statues *continually*.
—*Psalm 119:117*

There is a joy in obedience which God wants us to discover in a deeper way. God wants to talk with us that we may understand how we tend to make obedience less enjoyable than God intended. God's joy and definition of discipleship is quite different from the human definition. Only God chooses disciples. It is not people who do the choosing, for only God knows what is required for discipleship.

I *delight* to do thy will, O my God; for thy law is *within my heart*.
—*Psalm 40:8*

Delight is opposed to imposition. Delight does not deal in a "have to do" but rather a "want to do." The Christian full of delight is a Christian who lives immersed in the enjoyment of the glory of God and His kingdom's furtherance (Orr, 2009; Wiersbe, 2005). He loves to see His Lord exalted. There is no greater delight than this. His delight is so strong that he will even be willing to suffer personal setback that God may work through others and therefore be glorified.

Hail the Name of the Lord! Rejoice in His Name! Help us, Lord, amidst our trials and lift up by thy grace that we may rejoice in your kingship and thereby comprehend how we are to rejoice in the kingship you have given us (Hayford & Bauer, 2011). For we are your children. If our head is in Heaven, we will abound in a joy which is apart from our earthly experience (Daley, 2009). If our head is in the world, we will be joyful only when our life's earthly condition gives us reason to be. The way we live can only be conducive to obedience in the former case. *Obedience results from a joyful heart in the Lord!*

God's commandments are to have a warm spot in the heart of the believer. This is difficult to do unless we live in the Lord in joy. It cannot be denied that a marriage which does not produce joy is a difficult marriage for loving, honoring, and obeying to bear much fruit. A marriage which abounds in greater and greater joy will grow continually in love and obedience. The Bible, too, emphasizes that service and obedience grow out of joy (Ephesians 6:6-8). The relationship between joy and obedience is a universal truth whether in our work, our friendships, or our intimate relationships. That is, man serves best those who give him joy. Someone once fittingly said, "Joy is the keynote of all discipline." And since obedience is a discipline, joy must also be the keynote of all obedience.

The fact that the extent of a Christian's obedience is pointedly correlative to the amplitude of his joy is a disconcerting fact for such as we (Offner et al., 2013). For is it that automatic that our potential for obedience is immediately hindered

80 • THE POWER OF CONSTANT PRAYER AND COMMUNION WITH GOD

if we do not have a keen sense of real joy? Yes. It is therefore tragic that our supposed joy can be built upon feeling with very little solid rock faith (Froelich, 2014). The fact that so-called joy based on feeling is so commonplace within the Christian body is one of the many reasons for lack of obedience among Christians. As a believer develops a joy based on faith, his joy will not fluctuate as much. Instead, he will be steadfast and therefore eager to obey.

Celebrating God's Presence by Obedience

Obedience is best manifested in a believer's life when he is joyously celebrating the glory and exaltation of God. Such celebration is hardly ever interrupted. The servant of God wants to do what the Lord would have him do in every circumstance. Two questions the celebrating servant will ask are: "What would Jesus do in this situation?" and "What can I do that would best glorify God?" The person who practices Constant-Prayer and awareness of God will not just ask these questions once in a while but again and again during the day. God knows that we do not ask these questions as often as we should. If we were really celebrating the glory of God, we would find it difficult to cease from such activities. Nevertheless, it is assuring to know that in the process of growing in Him, this celebration will arise more continually (Graham, 2015; Murray, 1979; Tozer, 2013).

Ah, the joy of celebrating with God and as a friend asking Jesus what He would do if He were in the situation we are in! Praise be to His Name, for He answers so willingly. Even if Jesus answered, "You know what I'd do. You're on your own," He does answer. Jesus is a true friend. He will always answer even if the answers rest in His silence. What an honor it is to be able to celebrate side by side with a friend such as this.

REFERENCES

Brady, B. V. (2003). *Christian love*. Georgetown University Press.

Daley, R. J. (2009). *Sacrifice unveiled: The true meaning of Christian sacrifice*. T & T Clark.

Froehlich, M. A. (2014). *Courageous gentleness: Following Christ's example of restrained strength*. Discovery House Publishers.

Graham, B. (2015). *Quotations book*. Retrieved March 26, 2015 from: http://quotations-book.com/quote/38480/

Hayford, J. W., & Bauer, R. H. (2011). *Penetrating the darkness: Keys to ignite faith, boldness, and breakthrough*. Chosen Books.

Jeynes, W. (2002). A meta-analysis of the relationship between cannabis, opiates, cocaine, heroin or other illegal drug use and academic and behavioral outcomes. *Education and Urban Society, 54*(6), 631–655.

Jeynes, W. (2023). A meta-analysis: The association between parental involvement and students and parental variables. *Education and Urban Society,* in press.

Murray, A. (1979). *Abide in Christ: The joy of being in God's presence*. Whitaker House.

Murray, A. (2004). *A life of obedience*. Bethany House.

Offner, H., Larsen, D., & Larsen, S. (2013). *A deeper look at the fruit of the Spirit: Growing in the likeness of Christ*. InterVarsity Press.

Orr, C. E. (2009). *How to live a holy life*. Floating Press.

Peterson, J. (2003). *The insider: Bringing the Kingdom of God into your everyday world*. Navigator Press.

Tozer, A. W. (2013). *The pursuit of God*. Gospel Light.

Wiersbe, W. W. (2005). *Devotions for renewal and joy: Romans and Philippians*. Honor Publishing.

CHAPTER 7

CONSTANT-PRAYER AND COMMUNION WITH GOD AND PRAYER

GOD, THE BEST FRIEND HUMANS HAVE AND ALWAYS DREAMED ABOUT

The Nearness of God

> And He told them a parable to the effect that they ought *always* to pray and not to lose heart.
>
> —*Luke 18:1*

> Draw near to God and He will draw near to you.
>
> —*James 4:8a*

To practice the presence of God is to practice God's nearness. The person who successfully fellowships with God on an uninterrupted basis will know in his heart that God is ever near. God is always near us and yet how often we fail to acknowledge this fact. God is near to us for a reason (Chambers, 2008; Piper, 2011; Tozer, 2013). He knows that we need Him to be near us (Murray, 1979, 2004; Peterson, 2003). We should act upon His providential nearness to us (Chambers, 2008). In His nearness to us, God is telling us that we need him. God knows this

---

The Power of Constant Prayer and Communion With God, pages 83–93.
Copyright © 2024 by Information Age Publishing
www.infoagepub.com
All rights of reproduction in any form reserved.

84 • THE POWER OF CONSTANT PRAYER AND COMMUNION WITH GOD

and therefore supplies His presence (Murray, 1979). To what extent do we act upon our knowledge of our need to fellowship with God in this way? God's presence reminds us of our need. We know that He is there. He does not hide Himself evasively behind the bushes or the furniture. It is we who hide from God. If it appears that God is concealing Himself from us, it is only because our sight is one dimensional; we see only on an earthly dimension. We can only see white light in our natural man. Just as in our physical being, we can neither perceive infrared or ultraviolet light, the same can be said for our spiritual man.

Physically speaking, when we cannot see certain wave lengths of light, it is not because the light so desires to hide itself from us but because we are limited in the span of light which we are capable of seeing. To practice the presence of God is to grow in the degree which can comprehend all manner of spiritual light.

First off, the Christian grows in his assimilation and comprehension of white light. Most believers are limited to this range. For those who are disciplined in practicing, new horizons appear. "There you are God. I can see You now. You were not hiding after all. You were only beyond the scope of white light, challenging me to exercise my spiritual eyes that I might attempt to see beyond the range of white light that you might show me more of yourself." In constantly communing with God, a devotee's spiritual eyesight undergoes a tremendous widening in scope. God almost never seems to be hiding anymore. Even when times occur in which God seems far from his heart that man of God knows surely God is not hiding but is in a realm which in beyond what his spiritual eyes can perceive.

It must be pointed out, however, that there are spiritual light horizons not open to humanity, and others while they are open to humanity, have not yet been achieved; and still others while open to humanity theoretically, because of humans' fallen nature, cannot practically be achieved.

While on earth there will always be much that is hidden from humanity.

Continual prayer is an important key for breaking down the barriers for the degree of spiritual light which people can see. Most of this prayer involves listening to God. In a person's relationship with God, as well as one's relationship with people, he or she should seek to listen more and speak less (James 1:19). In Luke 18:1, the verse quoted at the beginning of this chapter, Jesus says a follower must be in a continual prayer in search of God's presence despite discouraging circumstances by which a devotee could conclude that God is not near but at a substantial distance. As a Christian seeks God in prayer, his spiritual light spectrum will widen and hence God will seem nearer. Therefore, there is more depth to the second verse cited in James 4:8 than is apparent on the surface. God is always near, but He will seem nearer as an individual's spiritual light spectrum expands.

The Spiritual Light Spectrum

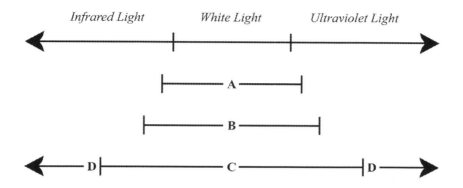

A – The range open to man that has been achieved.
B – The range open to man that can practically be achieved.
C – The range throrhetically open to man but cannot practically be achieved due to man's fallen state.
D – Range not open to man, but only to God.

The arrows signify extension into infinity.

FIGURE 7.1- The Spiritual Light Spectrum

Having the Prayer Life of Both a Friend and a Slave

No longer do I call you servants, for the servant does not know what his master is doing; but I have called you friends, for all that I have heard from my Father I have made known to you.

—*John 15:15*

Paul, a slave of Christ Jesus, called to be an apostle, set apart for the good news from God.

—*Romans 1:1*

Long may he live, may gold of Sheba be given to him. May prayer be made for him *continually*, and blessings invoked for him all the day.

—*Psalm 72:15*

86 • THE POWER OF CONSTANT PRAYER AND COMMUNION WITH GOD

It is a paradox, but the servant of Christ is both a friend and a slave of Jesus Christ. The born-again believer is not just a slave nor just a friend; the born-again believer is both. This paradox is one of the most crucial aspects of having a close walk with God. There are a good sum of people who can resolve this paradox intellectually, but it is another thing to apply this principle so that it has a thorough effect on this life. The difficult object for the Christian is this: *to desire that his best friend also be his master*. The general tendency is just the opposite. Human nature views "slavery" and friendship as almost entirely an exclusive relationship. Our human nature views the matter as one in which a person is either a slave or a friend, in bondage or free. On the surface it would appear from the carnal perspective, that one cannot be both a friend and a slave of God.

It is a sword in our pride to have our best friend be our only Master. Yet this is what we have in our lives, and this is what we should desire more. The road to achieving a friend/slave relationship is found in prayer. In fact, the more a believer prays, the more of a friend he will find God to be, and the more he will enjoy his function as a bondslave of the Lord Jesus Christ. One essential element of developing an attitude of rejoicing amidst this unique relationship is sincerity in his prayer (Psalm 130:1) *A disciple can only develop a real friendship when there is sincerity in the relationship.* Sincerity in a believer's fellowship with God means he can share his heart to God when he feels like sharing and come boldly before God with various requests and any confessions and questions that he may have (Hebrews 4:16; Psalm 146:1, 2). Both David and Abraham experienced the intimate fellowship with God that they had largely because they had a sincere prayer/conversational life with God (Psalm 55:17; Genesis 18:23-32). A follower will find himself praising, complaining, sharing, pouring out his anguish and sending up thanksgiving from his heart if he is sincere. "Sincerity," says Thomas Merton, "is perhaps the most vitally important quality of true prayer."

With regards to sincerity, the Christian *either desires God's nearness more or desires to impress God more*. If we desire God's nearness more than impressing God, we will be sincere. If we do not desire God's nearness that much with respect to impressing God, we will not be that sincere with God. *The extent to which we emphasize sincerity with God demonstrates how important God's nearness is to us.*

There can be a tendency among Christians to desire to think positively and so not openly share either with God or with others what trials they are facing. But this is quite contrary to God's word and *hardly conducive to experiencing continual communion with God.* If the committed individual is not sincere with God about what one is really feeling and thinking, it is no wonder why God seems to be far away.

It is much like a situation involving two astronauts who are half-way to the moon. Then all of a sudden their rocket ship malfunctions. Consequently, there is panic among the astronauts in the ship. Do they tell mission control about their problem, or do they pretend to be able to work it our themselves? They eventually decide not to tell mission control about the rocket's malfunction, and now, as a result, they feel very alone in space.

In a Christian's openness before God, the Christ follower has an acute awareness that God will hear a heart-based prayer (Psalm 17:6). To such people, it is important that God's presence surround them that they might dwell together with God in prayer (Psalm 35:22). It is the presence of God the Christian must seek in order that all anxieties be relieved from his bosom so that one neither experience sleepless nights, or what is often worse, wakeless days (Psalm 22:2).

It is beyond doubt that humility is the key ingredient needed in having our best friend be our master (Clairvaux, 1940). Specifically, to experience a beautiful co-relationship, the disciple should be in a position so that he comes to the spiritually dynamic realization that God is not only behind all events and subsistence but is required for His interaction with all creation (Psalm 57:12). The paramount conscious apprehensions and not this only, but also the appreciation of God's reign in respect to creation, will drive the follower to the cross, pleading before the Almighty with most fervent desire that he may have a constant active relationship with Him. For in gratitude of God's active persistence to accomplish His perfect will through His creative influence covering all the universe, the believer, too, will want to activate this inertia towards the full accomplishment of God's will in his own life. The disciple has then recognized that all his mindless attempts are feeble apart from God.

Most of people's actions are so ingrained that they are in fact mindless. Yet God calls them to a life continually mindful of Him that His power may be released in their lives as it has been and will continue to be in all of creation. For this is the ultimate design of God for His people, that the same glorious hand of God that created the heavens, raised Christ from the dead, and poured forth His Holy Spirit on Pentecost, might be made a reality in every moment of the seeker's existence on earth.

ONE ASPECT OF PRAYER:
LISTEN TO GOD SPEAK THROUGH US

In all these days He went out to the Mountain to pray, and all night he continued in prayer to God.

—Luke 6:12

It is in many respects true that there are two central aspects to prayer: talking to God and listening to Him. But this is too simplified a model of what actually takes place. For while such a bifurcation exists, listening in prayer is not always what it is assumed to be. Listening in prayer does not always necessitate a closed mouth and open ears. My beloved, I see that there are times when we hear God speak to us while we are in fact speaking to Him because His Holy Spirit rests within us. There are times when in the midst of our words to God, come golden truths which we know do not proceed from our own mind but are from God's Spirit. We must be careful to listen to our own words, otherwise we might conclude that God has withdrawn in silence when indeed He has not.

The longer children of God remain in a time of quality prayer, the more they will discover that God chooses to even speak through their lips of ash. It is not to be disputed that God has bestowed upon God's own a great honor in this. For Christians hardly deserve to speak forth words originating from the thoughts of the Almighty. It is a wonder that God does not strip His followers of this privilege since people tend to take the credit for words that find their only source in God. God's adherents might even convince themselves that breakthrough was achieved as a result of talking things through with God and not because God chose to direct them via speaking a truth by which they could act. Such is humankind.

There are numerous examples in the Word of God of the Lord intervening in the prayers of the saints to speak a word of truth. A saint may stand in a congregation of believers of his own church, filled with anxiety and hardness of heart. Suddenly, however, the Holy Spirit prompts him to look up a verse of Scripture. The example just given is most likely the intervention of God. God wanted to be worshipped, so the Holy Spirit moved to release the message in spite of this man's hardness of heart. The reason why God's intervention is possible in this type of situation as well as in Christian's prayer is because though prayer is in essence man speaking to God, it is also usually Spirit led. This means that the words a child of God utters within his prayers *are often the very words that God has led him to speak.* Christians are frequently the recipients of "anointed" prayers not because of the person speaking but *because of the Spirit's leading.* If it be that people can be ministered to by the Lord as they listen to truths being spoken in the prayers of others, there is no reason why they cannot listen to their own prayers that they, too, can be ministered to by the Lord through them.

It should be an integral part of the Christian's life to key in on his prayers to God in his minute-to-minute interactions with God. As a disciple draws nearer to God, he will discover that more and more his prayers will consist of the freshness of the reality of truth which God so often has spoken directly to his ears. As this individual conforms to the image of the Father, the truth of God will emanate from his lips as an increasingly high percentage of the words which he speaks. The very truth of God will emanate from his life. As the Christian submits to God in prayer, he will take on the character of God (Daniel 9:13, 19; II Chronicles 33:18, 19). In fact, a Christian need not be surprised as his life in Christ becomes a living prayer.

FAILURE TO PRAY CONSTANTLY

The Christian's Failure

Watch and pray that you may not enter into temptation, the Spirit indeed is willing, but the flesh is weak.

—Matthew 26:41

Constant-Prayer and Communion With God and Prayer • **89**

Praying earnestly *day and night* that we may see you face to face and supply what is lacking in your faith.

—I Thessalonians 3:10

Constant prayer is one of the most important pillars to constantly communing with God. In fact, constant prayer and constant communion are almost inseparable. The reasons members of the body fail to constantly act and pray within God's presence are firstly, because their flesh is weak, and secondly, in respect to intercession, few have the compassion that they should have for those weak in faith (which in essence includes everyone). The ways constant prayer should manifest itself are manifold and all together clear when a believer meditates on them openly before God's presence but whose existence that individual often likes to deny in his flesh. *We must face the fact once and for all that our lives cannot be a prayer in its appearance unless our lives are a prayer in its innermost activity.*

Leonard Ravenhill said, "The prayer chamber is a mirror reflecting our spiritual condition." There is no reason why, if we are truly immersed in prayer, that dozens and sometimes hundreds of people cannot be prayed for in the midst of our daily activities. Prayer is the most powerful weapon that the Christian has against the powers of spiritual darkness, and it is a disgrace that no one uses it as he should.

I find the unleashing power of prayer amazing, and yet I know that I have only skimmed the surface. "It has been often said," says F. J. Huegel, "that prayer is the greatest force in the universe. This is no exaggeration, it will bear constant repetition. In this atomic age when forces are being released that stagger the thought and imagination of man, it is well to remember that prayer transcends all other forces."

There are so many people and situations to pray for; it boggles the mind. No one can possibly begin to cover the vast array of prayer needs in pithy little prayer times and prayer meetings. If God is to win mighty spiritual victories, constant prayer is required. Ah, yes, but one is reminded once again that the Spirit is willing, but...

If people would spend as much time praying as watching television or reading the newspaper, God would work miracles that would bring atheists to their knees. Reading the newspaper is hardly valuable unless we are praying for the situation a person is reading about. The same is true of television and the internet. The same is even less valuable than the newspaper. Very little of the viewing of television on most stations edifies.

If a fellow human being shares a problem, the first action we should take is prayer. If we see an ambulance go by, why should not we try to pray for the individual inside? If we do not, who will? We must not stop to pray only for those things for which we will see answers. We should have a prayerful spirit so that as soon as we think of a person, our foremost desire is to pray for him; whenever we give a prayer request or are the recipient of a prayer request, we should have a longing to pray.

90 • THE POWER OF CONSTANT PRAYER AND COMMUNION WITH GOD

Jesus said in the verse in Matthew quoted at the start of this section that His disciples must watch in an attitude of prayer. *This is the only way we watch—if we pray. Praying constantly gives us heavenly eyesight!*

Constant prayer is a source of immunization against the dangers of temptation. Through immersing ourselves in the word and constantly praying, we can avoid a lot of needless temptation.

Many believers wonder why they are plagued so often by large doses of temptation. The fact of the matter is that there is really little reason to wonder at all. Believers experience temptation so frequently because they are not watchful. *Watchfulness is required to guard ourselves against temptation, and continual prayer is required for watchfulness.* When we are in a position of continual fellowship in the Lord's sphere, we will pick up movements of Satan like radar. As we grow in the depth in which we fellowship with God, we will be amazed at the extent to which the devil's moves can be picked up by our prayer radar. This fact alerts us to prepare to do battle against Satan and start swinging our Sword—the Word of God.

In every aspect of a Christian's life, the disciple is called to a life of prayerfulness (Romans 12:12; Colossians 4:2; I Thessalonians 5:17). *If the Christian desires that one's life be a prayer, prayer must be his life (Psalm 42:8).* God often chooses those who are constantly in prayer because they are almost by definition, in their very act of prayer, the most open to Him (Acts 10:2; Luke 2:37). It is interesting to note that there are many disciples of Christ today who complain of a lack of direction in their life and want the knowledge of God's will for their life. I have compassion on these people, for when I am distressed in such a predicament, I know how great a compassion my Lord has for me. We seldom discover just how strongly and frequently we are called and how regularly God divulges His will until we are in a state of perpetual communication with our Creator. God makes calls upon our lives each day, sometimes in extremely minute matters. Nevertheless, they are still calls, and out of love for God we cannot help but be obliged to respond to them. Now there may be those who quip, "I'm not interested in God's calling concerning small things but rather important matters." How often I know of this attitude within myself. By God's grace it disappears slowly. For in the first place, to God there are no small matters. If God calls a servant to do something, it can no longer be considered a small matter. If God has taken time to call a person to action or to speak forth (or listen), it must be something important. The small things *are the big things.*

Secondly, it is in obedience in the small matters that the servant will discover what God's call is in the large matters. The Christian cannot determine the latter unless he has uncovered the former.

This process is very similar to the growth process of a child. A mother would be totally foolish to ask her six-month-old child to cook Lobster Thermidor for dinner. At six months of age, the infant can barely eat. Instead, the mother teaches the child to eat, and as the child grows, slowly introduces additional experiences as the child's develops. Over a period of time, the mother teaches the child to feed him- or her-self and then to sit down among the adults, and eventually, to cook. If the infant had been only interested in learning to cook and nothing less significant, he would have learned neither of these. It is similar with the Christian. If the Christian refuses to learn submission to God in small things, that believer will never learn obedience in the larger ones (Orr, 2009; Wiersbe, 2005).

It is typical of a large array of Christians that they desire to do great feats for the Lord and get discouraged when they discover that God neither seems to be opening the doors nor providing the grace and power for these great feats to be accomplished. The reason is simply that they are too proud to seek to do the little seemingly insignificant "feats" for the Lord. In fact, if I or anyone else were that intent on doing the small for the Lord, I could not help but be aware of God almost every single minute of the day. We are not as intent as we like nor intent as we should be in accomplishing God's will in small ways. This reveals pride in our heart. If we were truly humble, we would realize our inability to fulfill God's will in any degree outside of establishing an uninterrupted communion with Him.

I remember a plethora of instances in my life when, in the midst of talking unceasingly with my Lord Jesus in prayer, He quickened to me to do some small act(s). One instance was when I was returning home from my evening class at seminary when a fellow approached me and asked if I had any money so he could buy some food. I do not hand out money to strangers for fear that they might spend it on drugs, alcohol, or the like. Instead, I offered to buy him a meal, and he said, "Fine." Then God prompted me and said it would be better to bring him home, cook him a meal, and offer him a place to stay. I obeyed what God had quickened to my heart. The man stayed with us two days and the second day, received Christ as his personal Lord and Savior. I praise God for this. What started out as something very small turned out to be glorifying to God in more than just a minute way because of an openness to God's voice via constant awareness.

Responsibility to Constantly Pray

> She who is a real widow, and is left all alone, has set her hope on God and *continues* in supplications and prayers *night and day*.
>
> —I Timothy 5:5

> Praying earnestly *night and day* that we may see you face to face and supply what is lacking in your faith.
>
> —I Thessalonians 3:10

> Moreover as for me, far be it from me that I should sin against the Lord by *ceasing* to pray for you, and I will instruct you in the good and right way.
>
> —I Samuel 12:23

Prayer is absolutely essential if the Body of Christ is to prosper spiritually in the work of God. I know that personally nearly every major spiritual victory that I have had in my life I can attribute to other Christian brothers and sisters being diligent in prayer. This being the case, how important it is that we intercede on behalf of members of the Christian body (Bounds, 2010; Offner et al., 2013). Intercede not just during devotional times or intermittently, but also throughout the day.

Apostle Paul, in many of the letters he wrote to various churches, shared that he was not only praying for them but also praying constantly (Colossians 1:9; 4:12; II Thessalonians 1:11). What a prayer life he must have had to pray for all these fellowships constantly and pray for many other fellowships besides. Yet Paul did not mention his continuous prayers to frustrate the believer but rather to exhort him to the experience of a similar prayer life. For Christians to experience such an intense prayer life, they must not only rely on God but also ask God to help them rely on Him (Psalm 61:2). Humanity's fallen state is so deep-rooted that many of believers' prayers are not prayers of seeking God but pleas to God to help them seek the Lord. In the case of seekers who are just beginning to practice the presence of God, it is foolish to begin to seek God in constant prayer without asking God for help toward this end in the first place.

The challenge is great if we are to have a life of such prayerful intercession. We will find ourselves praying for even a majority of the people we pass on the street and whom we see face to face. If we witness the sin of a brother or sister, we will immediately lift it up before the Father and ask that God initiate a work of completion in him/her and to continue to multiply the areas of fruit in that person's life. And what great joy there is when God has raised a Christian family member up in our heart so that we have an overwhelming desire to pray for that person again and again. The Christian body needs these kinds of intercessors if it is to reach its full potential of growing in grace. There is commendation from above when a believer holds up friends, relatives, and even strangers in long-lasting prayer for months, years, and even decades. Such exemplary cultivated prayer is more essential than we dare suppose. For especially with strangers, it may be that we are the only person praying for that individual and the release of God's hand upon that person's life may be up to us. It is sad to think of the dying souls that walk amongst the church in the entire world. It is even more disheartening to cogitate on the fact that millions of these are not brought consistently before the altar by other Christians. Such great needs, but few long-lasting prayers. God calls us to prayerful living and intercession for our entire lives (Psalm 116:2).

If Jesus were to walk among the likes of us today, He would rebuke us for our prayerlessness (Job 21:14, 15). For outside of prayer, only a worldly concept of life remains, and there is not truth in this (Daniel 9:13). I fear that there are times when we can go a long period of time continually aware of God only to grow weary of giving our all to God (Isaiah 44:23). To become weary in the process of so important a part of prayer as intercession, is to move toward a sudden crippling of the Body of Christ. This is not to say that everything comes to a stop with the cessation of intercessory prayer, but rather *something* usually does, and it is often an event of significance (Bonhoeffer, 1959). Do not wonder that God does not work in the lives of others as we know He can when we do not constantly intercede. God's promises are often contingent on human action. We should not wonder why God's promises are only partially fulfilled when we have not carried our weight of responsibility in the form of continuous, intercessory prayer. As Serampore Carey once said, "Prayer –secret, fervent, believing prayer—lies at the root of all personal godliness."

REFERENCES

Chambers, O. (2008). *My utmost for His highest*. Discovery House Publishers.

Clairvaux, B. (1949). *The steps of humility*. Harvard University Press.

Murray, A. (1979). *Abide in Christ: The joy of being in God's presence*. Whitaker House.

Murray, A. (2004). *A life of obedience.* Bethany House.

Offner, H., Larsen, D., & Larsen, S. (2013). *A deeper look at the fruit of the Spirit: Growing in the likeness of Christ*. InterVarsity Press.

Orr, C. E. (2009). *How to live a holy life*. Floating Press.

Peterson, J. (2003). *The insider: Bringing the Kingdom of God into your everyday world*. Navigator Press.

Piper, J. (2011). *Desiring God: Meditations of a Christian hedonist*. Multnomah.

Tozer, A. W. (2013). *The pursuit of God.* Gospel Light.

Wiersbe, W. W. (2005). *Devotions for renewal and joy: Romans and Philippians.* Honor Publishing.

CHAPTER 8

WISDOM AND CONSTANT-PRAYER AND COMMUNION WITH GOD

WISDOM INCREASES ONE'S SPIRITUAL POTENTIAL

Wisdom and Depth of Christian Walk

Seek the Lord and His strength, seek His presence continually.
—I Chronicles 16:11

Blessed are they who observe justice, who do righteousness at all times.
—Psalm 106:3

There are many Christians who love the Lord. There are fewer Christians, however, who have a love of great depth in their relationship with God (Tozer, 2013). Though there is a respectable crop of Christians who share their faith, have a consistent Quite Time, etc., few have the depth of faith that God desires His children to have (Piper, 2011). Even most of the spiritual leaders today do not appear to have the wisdom and the depth of Christian walk that the old saints had. The

---

The Power of Constant Prayer and Communion With God, pages 95–104.
Copyright © 2024 by Information Age Publishing
www.infoagepub.com
All rights of reproduction in any form reserved.

96 • THE POWER OF CONSTANT PRAYER AND COMMUNION WITH GOD

Martin Luthers, the Brother Lawrences, Thomas a Kempis' despite this age's massive population advantage over ages past, are almost impossible to find in modern society (Augustine, 2010, 2015a, 2015b). The key difference between these old saints and the Christian today is found in one word: wisdom. The wisdom of the saints of old made them a different breed, far deeper in their walks than those of their day and well ahead of those in comparable positions to theirs in today's world (Augustine, 2010, 2015a, 2015b).

It is a sad conclusion that I come to, now that the introduction has been laid. For somehow, somewhere the reborn Christian community has left wisdom behind as one of the most important traits to possess if the disciple is to have a steadfast walk with God. Perhaps it is because of man's prosperity; being spoiled by modern society and desiring be to spoiled more. Perhaps it is because he does not understand and/or remember what it is to be utterly spiritually deprived. Perhaps it is because life has become so complex and there are so many diversions, that the believer does not think he has the time required to seek after the spiritual wisdom that is needed for a deep walk with God.

I have known many foreign (i.e., non-Western) Christians in my life. It does not take much insight for me to see that the average non-Western Christian's faith is noticeably deeper than the Western Christian's. There are believers all over the world praying that Christians in the advanced sections of the world would not be so soft. There can be no question about it, there is a tremendous need in the Christian body to press on towards a greater depth and meaningfulness of walk. This kind of walk can only at attained by diligently crying out to God for His wisdom. For in crying out to God for wisdom, the follower of Christ has guaranteed a future of growth. This is because once a Christian has been a droplet more of wisdom, this wisdom will inevitably lead the believer back to God. In fact, we can determine true wisdom as opposed to counterfeit wisdom by whether it is a train of thought which leads us back to God. Wisdom is a driving force from God that acts through ourselves to bring us unto Himself that we might have God's perspective on life and His character, leading to a life of holiness and godliness.

Wisdom has a highly under-estimated function in the growth process. Wisdom serves to lay the groundwork for future growth (Graham, 2015). Our potential for greater growth is determined by our intensity and extent of wisdom. With wisdom comes maturity and right priorities before God (I Corinthians 13:11; Philippians 3:7, 8, 10). We can best understand the relationship between wisdom and our potential in Christ by considering this illustration. Picture a person trying to dig a well up a mountain (for the growth process is much more difficult than building a well into the top of a mountain, working down). The man has a source of water which rises as he digs to greater heights. The water is the level of maturity that one has attained. The water can only rise as far as one has dug. Shortly after a person has dug, the water rises to the level of the progress of his digging. The maturity we have in Christ can only rise insofar as we are wise in the ways of the Lord. Our maturity cannot rise about our wisdom!

Wisdom and *constant* active habitation under the wings of God are inextricably connected. The cycle that results from their interaction can have tremendous beneficial effects. Again, wisdom drives us to God. Wisdom, then directs us to constant interaction with God. The more we commune with God, the more we come to know God and take on His wisdom. The wisdom, in turn, again leads us into a steadfast interchange with God. It is not difficult to see how conducive wisdom is to a steadfast walk of faith by the believer (Isaiah 33:6).

It is a beautiful trait to seek after wisdom. God is the first one to recognize the purity of the believer's heart in such a venture. In His recognition and appreciation of His servant's desire, God will produce circumstances which serve to increase the believer's wisdom in Christ. There are two kinds of gifts that God is most willing to bestow upon His followers. The first is what God Himself desires to be accomplished. The second is the desires of the believer's heart (Psalm 37:4, 5). In the case of wisdom, if a believer longs for wisdom, the situation is now one in which both God and the believer desire the same thing to be done. In such a case, it is the Bible's promise that such a work will be accomplished (John 15:7).

This is why the prayers that God is most willing to answer are those in which the believer will glorify God, by putting on more of God's character. God always desires that a person would have more of His character, when a believer enters into this same desire, the promise of John 15:7 holds (I Kings 3:1-10). For many are the promises in the Bible that God will give without holding back present opportunities to ask for the comforts of life, deep down wishes, etc. However, for the person who truly and wholeheartedly seeks after the will of God for his life, he will claim such verses that he might have more wisdom. The church and each individual must ask oneself *"Which type of person are each of us?"* The former may lead to an easier life, but what it comes right down to is which is to be preferred, an *easy life or a heavenly life*? May we not be surprised when we find that these two lifestyles are antipodal.

Someone once said that what humans need is a little less knowledge and a little more understanding. It is wisdom that leads to understanding in the spiritual realm (Daniel 12:10). A child of God can know the Bible backwards and frontwards, but have very little understanding of its contents and practical significance; and therefore have little in the way of wisdom. Another person once said, *"It's not important how many times you've been through the Bible, but how many times the Bible has been through you."* Wisdom does. not merely come from studying the Word of God but also interacting with God in the "ins and outs of life."

Gain or Loss of Depth Is Dependent On the Time One Spends With God

And the Lord will guide you continually, and satisfy your desire with good things and make your bones strong; and you shall be like a watered garden, like a spring of water, whose waters fail not.

—Isaiah 58:11

98 • THE POWER OF CONSTANT PRAYER AND COMMUNION WITH GOD

Look carefully then how you walk, not as unwise men but as wise, making the most of the time, because the days are evil. Therefore do not be foolish, but understand what the will of the Lord is.

—Ephesians 5:15-17

The amount of time spent in fellowship with the Lord is like a shovel that digs the well of wisdom (referred to earlier) which determines the extent of our holiness. Ephesians 5:15-17 is a good passage for Christians in search of wisdom in their daily fellowship with God. First, we are exhorted to be cautious in how we go about the Christian walk. In a very literal sense we can only know along what avenues to venture and whether our destination is on the road on which we currently travel, if we ask the Almighty God. The best way to ascertain whether each given avenue we take is the correct one is to ask God this question as a practice come that moment when we meet an intersection in our journey through life. There are numerous intersections in the roads of life; each of varying degrees of importance. While it is customary for a person to seek God's counsel when he rests at a major intersection, it is less customary when he reaches minor intersections. It is a human tendency to seek God during the times of major crises and decisions in his life. However, it is just as important to seek Him in every "trifle" matter as well. A few "trifle" courses of action are as important as one major decision. It is a tragedy when we fail to come before God with a key quandary, for these should be given to Him, too. Nevertheless, it can be equally unfortunate if we fail to consult God concerning three of four relatively unimportant issues in our lives.

We, as human beings, prefer to be able to define events in absolute terms. We enjoy the freedom of being able to call one set of circumstances or decisions significant and another insignificant. But life is not as easy as this. It is not always true that the variation of significance between events is that discernible. For instance, if we think back to the time that we received Christ, we can probably recall the person(s) who was the central instrument of God in bringing us to a saving knowledge of the Lord Jesus Christ. For the sake of example, we can assume that this central figure was a neighbor. Now, quite obviously, the decision to give our life to the Lord is the most important decision we can make. However, we could have hardly foreseen the importance of deciding to move into the home we did (and thereby have this Christian as a neighbor) and the decision to get to know this neighbor on more than a superficial level. We can take this example a step further. Say a person receives Christ as a result of meeting a Christian who is street witnessing in front of a supermarket. If that person has never made that decision to go to the supermarket at that particular point in time, it may have been a long while before he ever received Christ. Hence, the decision to go to the supermarket, though seemingly of no account, actually had some very real salience in the long run. We must therefore be slow to label a particular decision as being of little value and as having little impact on our lives. Finally, one more example which will drive home this point even further. In the same example involving the

Wisdom and Constant-Prayer and Communion With God • **99**

supermarket, say this person had a choice of turning right or left after he went out the exit door, and this is the direction the person decided to go. Minutes later, this man/woman who left the supermarket received Jesus Christ as their Lord and Savior.

On the surface it would seem that, without question, the decision of whether to turn right or left after leaving a supermarket is hardly worth mentioning. Yet in this case, it apparently was significant. With examples such as these occurring in the lives of many every day, the distinction between an important and an unimportant decision is blurred. It is evident that everything under the sun is important to God! There is not one decision in life that is too small to come before God and ask for his divine guidance! This even refers to turning to the right or left while leaving a store. Now it is evident that what is being shared here can be taken to extremes. First, most of the time when we leave a store God will not give us specific directions because it really does not make too much of a difference which direction we go. Second, what is being shared here is not meant to say that we should ask God what we should do in all our paltry decisions. One need not ask God, *"Okay, God, I'm out of the supermarket, which way do I turn?"* Rather what is being encouraged here is a continual state of communion with God such that *if* God did *ever* tell a person to turn left after leaving a supermarket, he would be sensitive to God's voice. *We will only hear God's voice only insofar as we actively listen for it.* If we have left our communication with God back with our devotional reading, we are not going to hear God's voice much during the day unless God chooses to raise His voice considerably. If we are not aware of God, we will only hear God's voice when God raises His audibleness.

The ultimate reality is that Christians most often come before God with a grand problem rather than a piddling decision. This leads to a tendency for church adherents to have God's wisdom in some of the large areas of decision-making, but not the small ones. A child of God will be the recipient of God's wisdom in those aspects of life in which one communicates with God the most (James 1:6, 7). The result is a paradox similar to the one that goes, *"If man can put a man on the moon, why can't he cure the common cold?"* There are many counselors who seem to have an answer for every major counseling problem in existence, but when it comes to their own day to day affairs, they have few. The same is true with people, as a whole. It has always struck me as rather ridiculous how some people could stand their ground in God in the most adverse circumstances, but completely over-react to minor everyday happenstances and irritations. Much of the reason lies in the failure to commune with God, rather than asking for His wisdom only in the worst of times. Even the smallest annoyances are meant for our good that we may attain more wisdom. Therefore, wisdom should be sought (Job 5:27). We must genuinely press-on to seek wisdom in all aspects of our lives, if we are to truly be wise pursuers of God (Hosea 6:3). Wisdom does not come by relaxing and waiting for tragedy to strike our lives that we may gain a greater understanding of it. Rather, wisdom is obtained by longing for it in our innermost

100 • THE POWER OF CONSTANT PRAYER AND COMMUNION WITH GOD

being. Only when we seek wisdom with a major drive in our lives, will wisdom pour forth from our life and lips (Acts 6:10). Now we may claim that a wisdom concerning life's extensive difficulties is all that is required to make it through life. There is a great problem with such a perspective. First, one must rightfully question a person's wisdom (whether it is his own or another person's) if the Jesus follower knows only how to glorify God in life's major encounters and not its minor ones. This is because, in essence, the former is made up of a cluster of the latter. Secondly, an individual might, *"make it through life"* being wise in only those situations of crisis, but he will hardly be experiencing an abundant life in Christ.

It should also be noted that while communion with God increases the Christian's godly wisdom, the lack of communion with God decreases it. There is a misconception apparent in the world today that once a person has wisdom, he cannot lose it. However, this belief is quite false. Wisdom can fade with time much like an atrophy of muscle tissue occurs with the lack of use. If a believer has a true wisdom which is from God, it will manifest itself in a believer's lifestyle. King Solomon at one time was the wisest man in all of Israel. Nevertheless, as he grew in pride, he came to the Lord less and less, but was instead fascinated with his many wives and concubines. Solomon went a step further by falling into idolatry along with his wives. This can hardly be called wisdom. Solomon, who had been wise enough to know that God was the only source, now had lost some of that wisdom. He may have known intellectually that God was the only source, but there was a notable difference between this and wisdom.

If Christians become proud, they too can lose the wisdom of the Lord. Pride is one of the primary causes of a lack of wisdom (Swindoll, 1998). Pride causes believers to become lax in the consistency of their fellowship with God. As this happens, their wisdom fades. Christians may not even realize they have lost a degree of wisdom. That is until they humble themselves before God and return to Him in fullness of heart. As Christians move from this point they soon discover that they have slipped back more than they thought, for they have to learn the same lessons of the past over again. If we are in a position in which we find ourselves having to learn the same lessons many times over, it is probably because we have lost some of our wisdom from God by a deficiency of prayer and communion with Him (Bounds, 2010; Peterson, 2003). Oh, that this would never again happen to us; and it will not if we remember what Thomas a Kempis said, *"When Thou are present all things are delight, but when Thou are absent, all things are loathesome."*

WISDOM AND HUMILITY

Recognizing the Whole Source

> I will establish his Kingdom forever if he continues resolute in keeping my commandments and my ordinances as he is today.
>
> *—I Chronicles 28:7*

Wisdom and Constant-Prayer and Communion With God • 101

So, Aaron shall bear the names of the sons of Israel in the breast piece of judgment upon his heart, when he goes into the holy place, to bring them to continual remembrance before the Lord.

—Exodus 28:29

In keeping God's commandments, believers will discover that in keeping them, the church is wise indeed. The disciple will also discover that if he or she has kept God's commandments, in a large part, between God and oneself he or she will be wiser still. There is humility and meekness in wisdom. In James 3:13 the student of God's Word discovers a verse worth of a considerable amount of meditation. *"In the meekness of wisdom."* Powerful! In Matthew 11:25 Jesus reveals that it is the humble and lowly that are often the recipients of God's wisdom. If a Christian is truly wise, his or her wisdom will ultimately lead one to conscientious humility (Bonhoeffer, 1959; Clairvaux, 1940; Offner et al., 2013). True wisdom is recognizing that a human being in one's own being is totally void of wisdom, keeping a firm desire to put forth nothing that represents self, materialism, and pretentiousness. James 3:17, on the other hand, captures the true nature and intent of God's wisdom. God's wisdom is far greater than humanity's (Job 12:17).

Laying hold of the concept that the only true wisdom is from above version must consequently juxtapose to an all-encompassing knowledge that the first stage of wisdom is to recognize our own lack of wisdom (Proverbs 4:7). It is with this recognition that we receive the wisdom of God (Daley, 2009; Froehlich, 2014; author, 2003b).

It is much like a story of two glasses of dirty water that are filled to the brim. One fellow comes along and upon seeing that both glasses are filled with dirt and bacteria, offers to pour orange juice in each until all the dirt and bacteria are purged out that both may prove drinkable. One glass refuses to accept the offer, asserting that his contents are good enough to satisfy anyone. The second glass accepts the offer, confessing that his contents are polluted and that he needs a new fresh filling from above. How is the first glass ever going to become undefiled unless it first admits to his dirtiness and receives the far better fluid? The second glass, on the other hand, will indeed be purified and receive the better fluid because it confessed its lack and the pourer's ability to fill that lack. So, it is with Christians. Before we can receive the rightness of God's wisdom from above, we must first confess our lack apart from Him.

The only solution to the sobering fact of our lack of wisdom is to seek God with the totality of our being (Proverbs 22:17-21). How likely it is among those such as we, to think that we increase the earth's wisdom by our presence (Job 12:2). When indeed our wisdom existed in God before it did in us. It is far more likely that our human inconsistent behavior introduces some unique confusion, adding evidence for the fallen state of humanity. I praise God that the Lord still specializes in bringing to light that which is dark (Job 12:22). God is unlimited in the ways in which He works to enhance the believer's wisdom. There is no greater example of this than Creation. No Christ follower is so wise that he or she cannot still learn from creation! It is a disciple of wisdom and humility who can still learn spiritual truths to be applied to his life, by observing the life of an infant. *True wisdom cannot exist without humility*! If a child of God continually shares his thoughts of wisdom and boasts about his spiritual knowledge, the Bible calls such a man a fool (Proverbs 10:14, 17:27, 19:20, etc.) *"With the humble is wisdom."* (Proverbs 11:2b)

III. WISDOM IN DAILY PRACTICE

So David left Asaph and his brethren before the ark of the covenant of the Lord to minister continually before the ark as each day required.
—I Chronicles 16:37

The above verse is significant because it calls the believer to *"minister continually."* If the seeker is open to the wisdom from the Lord such that he is receiving input from the Lord as to how to interact with the practical situations of life, he will minister both to the Lord and to those around him. Wisdom in practical terms is following many of the subjects discussed here and putting them into practice. The result will be that, by God's grace, the Lord's wisdom will be manifested.

In counseling numerous people throughout the years, I have had many opportunities to rely on God's wisdom while coming to grips and confessing my lack of wisdom. While I was a phone counselor, I especially encountered numerous situations in which God's wisdom saved the hour. One situation I encountered was with a girl (we'll call her Joan) who called up and said that in a three-month period of time she was going to kill her mother. She intended to kill her by taking a butcher's knife and stabbing her three times in the back. Joan had called literally hundreds of times before and was beyond the *"pleading for help"* stage, yet unable to be helped by anyone. The second time I talked with her I realized that the situation was totally above my head. There was no way in my finite human wisdom that I could even adequately handle her case. I prayed to the Lord for His wisdom that my words would be pushed back and His uttered forth. It was at that point that God's Spirit really began to move. Joan had been extremely unwilling to talk before, but with God's hand released we talked for 2 1/2 hours that night. God moved in a tremendous way. The more I prayed, the more of His wisdom He gave me. After those 2 ½ hours had run their course, God worked such that Joan promised me she would not kill her mother. The subject never came up again. God had won!

Another situation that called for God's wisdom was one in which a woman who had just ingested a bottle of deadly pills called, wanting someone to take care of her pets after she died that night. Again, the situation was totally out of my range of natural wisdom. But I prayed to the Lord for His wisdom and He came through. By God's grace the woman received Christ as her personal savior and to the best of my knowledge is alive and well today.

Wisdom and Constant-Prayer and Communion With God • **103**

Now these situations that I have shared are major ones. In major events such as these, it is often easier to realize that God's wisdom is required than fathoming this fact in everyday situations. Nonetheless, anything less than God's wisdom no matter what the circumstance is not enough wisdom. God's wisdom applies to any condition (Wiersbe, 2005). If a person wants to know how to show love to another, God's wisdom is the answer. I recall one sister in the Lord who held a low self-concept and appeared to have trouble receiving love from people. God had given me a great compassion towards her and love for her (though everyone involved knew our relationship was strictly brother/sister), but she was not open to God's love through me. I came before the Lord and asked Him how I could love her so that she would receive God's love. God's response was that she would respond to a great big hug. I followed God's instructions and hugged her, hoping that she would open up to God's love. God's wisdom prevailed, for after I hugged her, she said to someone beside her, "Now that's love!" God's wisdom can be applied to the solution of any problem. Even if a seeker does not know if we should put our pants or bed sheets in the wash, since there is only room for one or the other, that individual can ask God. If we say to ourselves, "I have a problem," we should straightway realize our need for God's wisdom and God-the giver of wisdom, for the solution. As we grow in constant prayer to God, we will learn to come before God each and every time. Surely *"heavenly wisdom is the fountain of earthly peace."*

REFERENCES

Augustine of Hippo. (2010). *City of God* (Dods, M. Peabody, Trans.). Henrickson Publishers.

Augustine of Hippo. (2015a). *Brainy quotes.* Retrieved on April 2, 2015 from: http://www.brainyquote.com/quotes/quotes/s/saintaugus124552.html

Augustine of Hippo. (2015b). *Brainy quotes.* Retrieved on April 2, 2015 from: http://thinkexist.com/quotation/do_you_wish_to_rise-begin_by_descending-you_plan/263998.html. , p. 1.

Bounds, E. M. (2010). *Purpose in prayer.* Blackstone.

Bonhoeffer, D. (1959). *The cost of discipleship.* Macmillan.

Brady, B. V. (2003). *Christian love.* Georgetown University Press.

Chambers, O. (2008). *My utmost for His highest.* Discovery House Publishers.

Clairvaux, B. (1949). *The steps of humility.* Harvard University Press.

Daley, R. J. (2009). *Sacrifice unveiled: The true meaning of Christian sacrifice.* T & T Clark.

Froehlich, M. A. (2014). *Courageous gentleness: Following Christ's example of restrained strength.* Discovery House Publishers.

Graham, B. (2015). *Quotations book.* Retrieved March 26, 2015 from: http://quotationsbook.com/quote/38480/

Hayford, J. W., & Bauer, R. H. (2011). *Penetrating the darkness: Keys to ignite faith, boldness, and breakthrough.* Chosen Books.

Murray, A. (1979). *Abide in Christ: The joy of being in God's presence.* Whitaker House.

104 • THE POWER OF CONSTANT PRAYER AND COMMUNION WITH GOD

Murray, A. (2004). *A life of obedience.* Bethany House.

Offner, H., Larsen, D., & Larsen, S. (2013). *A deeper look at the fruit of the Spirit: Growing in the likeness of Christ.* InterVarsity Press.

Orr, C. E. (2009). *How to live a holy life.* Floating Press.

Peterson, J. (2003). *The insider: Bringing the Kingdom of God into your everyday world.* Navigator Press.

Piper, J. (2011). *Desiring God: Meditations of a Christian hedonist.* Multnomah.

Swindoll, C. R. (1998). *Joseph: A man of integrity and forgiveness: Profiles in Character.* Nashville: Word Publishers.

Tozer, A. W. (2013). *The pursuit of God.* Gospel Light.

Wiersbe, W. W. (2005). *Devotions for renewal and joy: Romans and Philippians.* Honor Publishing.

CHAPTER 9

GOD'S HOLINESS AND CONSTANT-PRAYER AND COMMUNION WITH GOD

ACTING OUT OF AWE

Silence and Rest in the Presence of God

For when he sees his children, the work of My hands, in his midst; they will sanctify My name; they will sanctify the Holy One of Jacob, and will stand in awe of the God of Israel.

—Isaiah 29:23

But may all who seek thee rejoice and be glad in thee; may those who love thy salvation say continually, 'Great is the Lord.'!

—Psalm 40:16

It is God who in His holiness is enthroned (Psalm 22:3; 47:8). It is up to the individual Christian to act upon this fact (Piper, 2011). To go unaffected by the holiness of God is to miss out on one of the most matchless of Christian experi-

---

The Power of Constant Prayer and Communion With God, pages 105–115.
Copyright © 2024 by Information Age Publishing
www.infoagepub.com
All rights of reproduction in any form reserved.

105

ences. There is an awareness of God such that a follower acts on what God tells him to do. There is also a constant awareness in which the believer only receives an impression of the holiness of God in which no words are spoken, but rather the impression of God's holiness precludes the importance of words. It is one thing to come to a place in which a person has a distinct awareness of God's voice. It is another experience indeed to seek to serve God as a result of a heightened understanding of His silence (Clairvaux, 1940).

It is rare that the Christian is most overwhelmed with God's holiness in the midst of oral communication with Him. Rather, it is during those periods of irrevocable silence that God's holiness peers through even the thickest clouds of stubbornness and doubt to refresh him in the living reality of the perfection of a personal God. If His holiness were not overwhelming enough, His holiness manifested on such an intimate level lifts this fact to even higher plateaus (Jeynes, 2005). The reality is that God loves His children so much that He is not willing to keep His holiness hidden, but instead has chosen rather to descend to those to whom He shows His love the most and disclose Himself again and in an even more miraculous way. To fellowship with God in moments in which His holiness is arrayed before him in total magnificence is one of the greatest miracles of all.

It is customary in these times for the believer to feel uncomfortable in the midst of God's silence. Human beings do not naturally like silence unless it follows an overexposure to the world's stimuli. If people are not with others, they turn on the TV, radio, or stereo to keep them company. How long does modern humanity willingly function awake in silence? It is sad to say that this very fact extends over to the Christian experience as well. Few disciples of Jesus enjoy the silence of God (Bounds, 2010). Thousands enjoy God speaking to them, whether it is through His word, in prayer, or in a message. Some become so accustomed to God speaking on the spot that they become noticeably uncomfortable when God's voice rests in silence. Consequently, there is a lot about the character of God that Christians fail to intimately associate with. There are facts of God's character which can only be revealed in silence. We need to uncover more of God's revelation to us in the audibleness of His silence. We may sit down to pray with Him and if God does not speak first, we will speak, when God wants silence and our undivided attention. Our relationship with God has parallels to relations with other people, in this regard. There are times that with two pretty well-acquainted people in a room, both feel somewhat uncomfortable with silence and most likely one will attempt to initiate a conversation to break the quiet. *Intimacy, on the other hand, allows for silence and even cherish silence.* One beautiful aspect of a marital relationship is the fact that the husband and wife often become close enough so they can still love each other and receive love from one another, in the ambience of silence. *As a Christian draws closer to another human being, he fears silence less and less.* Similarly, as a Christian draws closer to God loving him more each day, he fears silence less and less!

God's Holiness and Constant-Prayer and Communion With God • **107**

It is essential for the Christian to realize that even those most aware of God may have difficulty becoming acclimated to His revelation of His holiness in silence. Even those most aware of God would often prefer to talk with Him rather than remain silent before Him. God is an enthroned King and we need to recognize that sometimes to dominate the course of a conversation with the King is uncalled for, unprofitable, and rude (Psalm 22:3; 44:8). This is not to say that God will not accept our claim to the guidance of a conversation. After all, He loves us and is quite concerned with what we think and is quick to put up with us. Nevertheless, it is one thing for God to accept our desire for controlling the conversation; it is another thing to do what God would really prefer. How profitable can our communion with God be if we always insist that the direction of the conversation go in the way we desire it rather than it in the way God would choose? To illustrate this point, an extreme example will be given.

If John Doe constantly prays to God and shares with God, but it is almost always about sports, of what profit is the communion? God has not really accomplished what He set out to do, i.e., make John Doe a new creation in Christ. God has not accomplished his ultimate goal because John Doe has not permitted Him to. Similarly, though we may not desire to talk about sports with God, when we are continually bringing up unimportant concerns, anxieties we should have given to God, or frivolities off the top of our head, how is God going to reach our heart with His glory? The entire world is of course filled with His glory, but in constant prayer with Him, we must allow His glory to infiltrate our heart that He might claim it as His permanent home (Isaiah 6:3). *"Live in Christ,"* said Samuel Rutherford, *"and you are in the suburbs of heaven. There is but a thin wall between you and the land of praises you are within one hour's sailing of the shore of the New Canaan."*

The challenge with regard to constant prayer and awareness of God is a very steep one. Even in achieving a more continual relationship of activity with God, the seeker must seek to have the flow of communion be guided by God and not oneself. This does not mean that a person cannot guide the flow at times when his or her heart is burdened or a seeker needs to talk with the Lord and smile because that individual senses His listening ear. What it does mean, however, is that we should realize that we can obtain the greatest benefit from constant prayer if we humble ourselves to desire to have the kind and level of communion that the Lord wants rather than what we ourselves want. If the believer wants to concentrate on loving the individual, he needs to let God have His way. Once the individual has permitted God to have His way, that person will discover that what God wants to discuss during the course of praying is of much more value and pertinence to the situation, than what the disciple himself wished to discuss. In this case, loving the individual was more important than understanding him (although God may often prefer his children to understand a person before loving him, or sometimes instead of loving him (Brady, 2003). The key to submitted to God's desire as to the type of communion is a silence before Him in recognition of His holiness (Tozer, 2013).

108 • THE POWER OF CONSTANT PRAYER AND COMMUNION WITH GOD

In the midst of meditation on God's holiness, the believer comes to a realization that every desire he has is belittled before the transcendent holiness of God (I Samuel 6:20; Psalm 8:4). In doing so, believers surrender their rights to do what they want that they might do God's will and surrender the desire to commune only about what they want that the heavenly Father might complete a richer work than the believer had ever dreamed (Wiersbe, 2005).

Desiring to live a life of awe before the Lord does not mean shuddering at every turn. Rather, it means to lay our mind to rest on the holiness of the Lord and that is nothing but a feast. Terror and hatred may fly by the believer amidst a sinking world, but the Christian can be uplifted and cheered by the unfaltering presence of God and have an attitude of celebration hand in hand with His Lord (Proverbs 15:15). In fact, the Scripture states that to honor the Lord is strongly connected to a joyful strength under the protection of the pinions of the Most High (I Chronicles 16:27). That attitude of a disciple of Christ's has towards sin and holiness, as a result of his or her meditation upon the humanly elusive holiness of God, is magnificent and praiseworthy in and of itself (Tozer, 2013). For while being exposed to the holiness of God, it is true that people cannot help but desire to partake in more of that divine character until it consequently becomes more of themselves by an exultant submission before God to His triumphant Holy Spirit.

What is perhaps even more breathtaking than this is the transformation of people's attitude towards sin. For in the joy that a person has as a result bathing in the holy presence of God, one does not carry a heavy load of guilt for not meeting up to the standard of holiness which is God. *If a devotee has a burden of guilt upon his shoulders, he has not interacted with the holiness of God.* One important aspect of God's holiness is His love and forgiveness. *God's holiness cannot be taken apart from his love and forgiveness.* It is humanity's attempt to separate these facets of God's character that often leads to self-condemnation on the part of various guilt-ridden Christians. As has been stated, if a Christian experiences the holiness of God in the practice of Bible-based meditation, joy should result rather than condemnation. In resting in the thoughts of the holiness of God, the Christian comes forth with a desire to be purer before God in the fact of His holiness, not willing that God should see sin in his heart (Habakkuk 1:13). But at the same time, the believer has a tremendous sense of the eternal redemption that is his in Christ because of Christ's perfect holiness.

Our view of a perfect, holy God is quite similar to a dog show conception of the perfect dog. In the mind of the dog show judges, a dog must be debonair, graceful, dignified, and have perfect muscle tone. This makes the dog seem distant and almost not alive. The dog is considered more of a piece of cold art to be observed rather than an animal with whom one interacts. But the real perfect dog, being man's best friend, is a dog who is warm, lively, playful, loyal and loving. Such a dog which may not have dignity, but rather makes us feel like a million dollars when everyone else is grumpy. We have made God's holiness into a dog show-like coldness and perfection rather than the warmth, liveliness, love, and

God's Holiness and Constant-Prayer and Communion With God • **109**

forgiveness, which truly make up the holiness of God. Out of God's holiness, God forgives and *"when God forgives, He removes the sin and restores the soul."*

AFFECTED BY THE HOLINESS OF GOD

What Character Trait of God One is Most Struck by, He Becomes

> And He said, 'My presence will go with you and I will give you rest'.
> *—Exodus 33:14*

> The Lord is just in all His ways, and kind in all His doings.
> *—Psalm 145:17*

To fellowship with God in His holiness is to become holy. God's promise in Exodus 33:14 is not only a promise of guidance, but a promise of the manifestation of holiness. The more seekers are in union with God and recognize His everlasting presence, the more the holiness of God will rub off on them. Psalm 145:17 goes along with the verse in Exodus. Fellowship in God's presence will undoubtedly lead to a spiritual personality and more justice and kindness.

Beyond becoming more like God, as a result of communing with Him, lies the fact that a Christian becomes like Christ in those aspects of Christ's life with which one is most impressed. If a believer is most impressed by God's grace, over time, God's grace will especially be manifested in that disciple's character. If a believer is most impressed by God's power, he will grow a great deal in having God's power work through his life, etc. *What a person loves most about God, in time he will become! It is therefore important to have a balanced concept of God.* To admire God's wrath far and above any of God's traits is to ask for trouble. And to love any other given trait of God's without development in appreciating God's other traits can also be asking for trouble.

Fellowship, with a profound realization of God's holiness becomes in and of itself a call to holiness. A large number of the proclamations of God's holiness that appear in the Bible are also in and of themselves calls to upright living (Genesis 17:1; Leviticus 11:45; 19:2; 20:26; Isaiah 6:1-8; Matthew 5:47; I Peter 1:15, 16). God desires His holiness to humble us, but also to call us to a life of greater holiness. To awake to a life of holiness we must first confront what is holy, i.e., God (Isaiah 52:1). *We will arise first in those areas in which we have been most impressed by the reality of God.* The more we soak in God's holiness, the more aspects of God's character we will *"fear,"* as to lead to growth of character. Inconsistence in the Christian life greatly results from the failure to continuously bathe in the adoration of God's holiness. Too frequently we fellowship with God enough and in sufficient depth to recognize His more apparent traits, e.g., God's

110 • THE POWER OF CONSTANT PRAYER AND COMMUNION WITH GOD

grace and power; but we fail to go beyond this, to search deeper and come to know God more than in this relatively shallow sense.

> O the depth of the riches and wisdom and knowledge of God. How unsearchable are His judgments, and how inscrutable His ways!
>
> —*Romans 11:33*

To even begin to go beyond the surface to the richer dimensions of the Triune God, we must spend a large amount of time having our spiritual senses excited by fellowship with God. We must come before God, petitioning God for a greater appreciation and knowledge of His holiness. Very few lay people are willing to put in the energy to make God's holiness a part of their lives merely by constantly being exposed to it. Sadly, few ministers are also willing to put in this time. The result is an anemic ministry—whether it be anemic sermons, counseling, or manifestation of God's power. *The church today suffers from anemia!*

The main reason why there are not many deep sermons coming from the pulpit, is *because there are not many deep ministers of God!*

Oh, that we might come to know God in a richer way, that more of our anemic conditions would vanish. Let us worship God in all His holiness and *reach up with our hands to God that he would see that we desire him to reach down to us!*

Is not this what the beginning of true holiness is? For

    a.   Milk toast Christianity says, *"God reach down all the way, for I cannot come up"* (see below);

    b.   Self-righteous Christianity says, *"God, I'm coming up"* while

    c.   True holiness Christianity says, *"I cannot come up God, I can only reach up with my hands and tell you that I need you and long for you to reach down."*

The difference between (a) milk toast Christianity and (c) true Christianity is a willing and fervent heart, aching to be used of God for His glory.

The difference between (b) self-righteous Christianity, and (c) true holiness is a humble heart, i.e., a knowledge that we can do no good thing on our own. True holiness is a state of rest, not fleshly striving (Hebrews 4:3, 9). It should be noted, however, that there is a difference between striving by the flesh and striving by the power of the Holy Spirit (Colossians 1:29).

It was stated previously that the aspect of God that a believer stresses the most he will become. This being true, it is very important that a devotee have the proper set of priorities. Many Christians today have incorrect priorities as to which are the traits of God that God most wants us to have. Some are convinced that it is knowledge, other believe it's understanding the prophetic passages of the New Testament; still others think having the gift of healing or evangelism is the most important. To the extent that we have these attributes on the top of our priority list,

God's Holiness and Constant-Prayer and Communion With God • 111

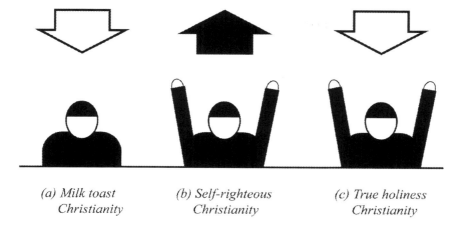

(a) Milk toast (b) Self-righteous (c) True holiness
Christianity Christianity Christianity

FIGURE 9.1 The Difference Between Milk Toast Christianity, Self-Righteous Christianity, and True Christianity.

we are immature Christians. However, to the degree that we have love for God and neighbor at the top of our priority list, we are mature Christians. For the Bible clearly states that love should be the primary trait of God that a person should seek to have in his character (Luke 10:27). Intellectually the reader may nod his head and say, "Well of course, the Bible says that love is more important than anything else. Everyone knows that." But the question is, do we know this in our hearts? Can a man's neighbors and friends tell he has love as his first priority by looking at his life? When people describe us to others in one or two words, how would they describe us? Would love be the first word they would use? What would the first word be that God would use in describing us to others?

Somewhere the Christian body has left love behind with regards to giving it the undivided attention that it deserves. Within the ministry we hear of faith teachers, prophetic teachers, holiness teachers, and praise teachers. *But what ever happened to the love teachers?!* The Lord promises that when one becomes a Christian a person is a *"new creation."* (Galations 5:24; 6:15; Ephesians 4:24; II Corinthians 5:17). But this is only made possible by God's love for man. A Christian can walk in righteousness, not in evil, purely because of the love relationship that he has with God (Isaiah 57:2; Psalm 34:14; 37:27). Apart from a love for God and neighbor and God's love for him, such a command would be impossible to follow. On the bottom line, a man's walk with God can only be satisfying as long as he loves God enough to desire to feed off of Him for his sustenance (John 6:35). One fact that remains—if it is true that the aspect of God that we emphasize the most we become, *should not our emphasis be on agape love?!*

ON WHOSE BEHALF DOES A MAN ACT?

The meek shall obtain fresh joy in the Lord and the poor among men shall
exult in the Holy One of Israel.

—Isaiah 29:19

Meditate in your heart upon your bed,and be still.

—Psalm 4:4b

INTRODUCTION

In the final section of this chapter, I would like God, through this book, to help
expound on two points already stated. First, that the realization of God's holiness and humility go arm in arm (Isaiah 41:14, 15; 57:15). Secondly, that God's
holiness understood more deeply develops into an exhortation towards holiness
(Zephaniah 2:3). The disquisition of these ideas will be directed towards a greater
inhalation of why the phenomenon of fellowship with God in His holiness, not
only leads to a desire to stand among the holy mountains in maturity, but a cogni-
zance of who we act on behalf of, that is to say, God Almighty.

THE HOLINESS OF MAN VERSUS THE HOLINESS OF GOD

Dwelling in the midst of conscious communion with God in His holiness can
result in a very different and more Christ-like type of holiness than if we do not.
The reason is very plain: the human definition of holiness is contorted because
of human's sin. Without continual communion with God, that a person might be
"resurrected" when necessary, the Christian will inevitably become holy greatly
in terms of man's conception of holiness, which is not necessarily holiness as
defined by God.

The most marked demarcation between what Christians conceive to be holiness and God's holiness is that people's idea of holiness tends to lead to self-
centeredness, while God's results in quite the reverse (Offner et al., 2013). Human
holiness is geared towards achieving an advantage in lifestyle over the average individual and to bring joy to oneself. Holiness as viewed by God is for the sole purpose of bringing glory to God; with any individual benefit as a blessing from God
inherent in the growth process itself (James 1:25). The question that should be
addressed, then, is whether we desire to be holy purely for God's glory or whether
selfish motives are involved. Certainly, we must say there is not one individual
alive who can say his or her motives are absolutely pure in this regard. I know
myself too well to think that I even come close to perfect motives. Nevertheless,
*to what extent a person's motives concerning holiness are pure before God will
determine just how holy that person will become* (and conversely, how much he
will be holy only in the sense of man's definition). To the degree that people have

God's Holiness and Constant-Prayer and Communion With God • **113**

impure motives regarding holiness they will (1) exhibit ostensibly good traits that can be best measured by a ruler, (2) their self-righteous attitude will show in that they consider themselves holier than others on the basis of those indicators that can be best measured with a ruler; (3) the individuals will get much more of the glory than they deserve and God will get much less. These three points warrant some elaboration:

1. *Exhibit ostensibly "good" traits that can be best measured by a Ruler*—A friend of mine (henceforth called "Joe") once shared with me about how he used to be this type of Christian. And since his example epitomizes what I mean by this point, I will refer to his example. Joe was looked up to by several believers, especially with regard to his soul-winning efforts. Soul-winning is one of those things that, up to a point, can be measured. Unfortunately, the human view of holiness is such that the more people a person has brought into the Kingdom (the idea that man brings people into the Kingdom is in itself a misconception, for it is truly God that does the work by His Spirit), the more spiritual that individual is. Joe saw holiness in a similar manner and so sought to win more souls into the Kingdom greatly because he thought it would make him more holy and gain points for him both with God and men. As a result, he soon came to regard people as "targets" when he shared the gospel with them. Naturally, if a given person received Christ, Joe scored a bullseye. Now it should be noted that there is nothing wrong with seeing as many souls as possible enter the Kingdom. But if a believer does it to earn points with man and/or God, he has a definition of "holiness" generated by humanity, not by God. The follower of the Lord is considered holy by humans simply because God used that person to lead 10-12 people to Christ in a year. This is not holiness.

2. *Their self-righteous attitude will show in that they consider themselves holier than others on the basis of those indicators that can be best measured with a ruler*—Forgive me saying so, but I am often suspicious of people who consider the essentials of holiness to rest in activities that are easiest to measure, e.g., number of Quite Times per week, degree of church attendance, number of souls saved, etc. In fact, I am suspicious of myself when I find myself placing too great an importance on such things as can be measured. Sooner or later, when I use easily measured criteria, *I am bound to compare myself to others*. Often the comparison occurs in a judgmental way either in the form of self-righteous or self-condemnation, depending on which end of the scale we think we are at. Church attendance is one of the most frequent scales used, simply because it is so easy to measure. People know how often they go to church and have a pretty good idea how often others do. Bible reading is not

quite as obvious, but by simply asking another person about his Quite Time, this figure can also be ascertained.

What is so fascinating is that it is probably those aspects of life which are most difficult to measure that are most important to spirituality. Love and humility, for instance, are very difficult to measure, and is best left up to God. Even if a person had all the data about the secret lives of those he was comparing himself to, measurement would be difficult. Constant awareness of God is very important for holiness, but it is not only difficult to measure with regards to ourselves, but virtually impossible with regards to others.

It is easy to see if at any given moment a person is attending church; harder to see if he is reading the Bible; harder still to tell if he is loving; and virtually impossible (at any given moment) to tell if someone else is aware of God! *When we attempt to compare ourselves to others, which inevitably requires some degree of measuring, we are revealing that we really do not know what holiness is! For as difficult to measure as holiness is, it can only be ascertained by God!* It is therefore confirmed in our hearts: we do not know what holiness is as we should. True holiness/consecration is, as someone once said, *"going out into the world where God Almighty is and using every power for His glory."* Whether or whether not we "look holy" according to such measurements we need to remember the true statement that *"reputation is what men think you are. Character is what God knows you are."*

3. *The individuals will get much more of the glory than they deserve and God will get much less.*—It is unfortunate that man's nature is to assign glory to himself first and foremost and that often he glorifies God only as an afterthought. "Holiness" with selfish motives often results not only in outwardly impressive behavior, but a situation in which the believer takes the credit himself, rather than giving it to God. *One of the simplest ways to determine whether a person's actions were done for the glory of God or for selfish motives is to see whether the person gives the glory to God or takes it himself!* If after a person has been thanked for his thoughtfulness or compassion, he says, "Well, I realize not too many people do it, but I wanted to please God," we can tell that there was a substantial amount of selfishness involved in the action. For God has not received the glory. If another person were to hear that statement, it would not be apparent to him that God was directly responsible for the action taken. If, on the other hand, a person thanked for the same deed said, "Well, if it was helpful, *praise God!*" we could tell there was within this act, a substantial desire to glorify God. It is a true statement *"we think little about God if we think much about ourselves."*

Glorifying God as the Only Source

God desires that His holiness be known (Ezekiel 39:2). It is part of man's responsibility to make that holiness known (Murray, 2004; Orr, 2009; Peterson, 2003). For man to desire to fulfill this responsibility he must realize that in God there is much to boast about, but in himself, there is nothing (Hosea 11:9). In all frankness, the state that we must reach in order to desire above all to glorify God only, is a difficult position to reach. Yet God can work in a magnificent manner through our meditation and fellowship in God's holiness. The Lord wants to do this in order to lead us into an unforgettable recognition of our depravity in comparison to God's holiness. Oh, to dwell under the wing of God and realize what a mighty wing it is! To confront God in His holiness is to confront who we are in all our need and spiritual ineptitude. If it is true that we cannot conceive of God's holiness, neither can we enter into a realization of our absolute lack without the holiness of God in our lives. Though we may move towards an understanding of our failure to be as Christ, we do not understand the whole of it. Nor do we desire to understand the whole of it because we fear that we could not live and bear what we had been shown. Nevertheless, the more we bathe in His holiness, the more we can be made aware of who we are before God. God is indeed the only source. The source can only be that which is Holy as He; and there is only one. God Almighty is the only source. In the midst of God's holiness we, despite of our stubbornness, finally being to gain an understanding that we should glorify that source.

REFERENCES

Bounds, E. M. (2010). *Purpose in prayer*. Blackstone.

Brady, B. V. (2003). *Christian love*. Georgetown University Press.

Clairvaux, B. (1940). *The steps of humility*. Harvard University Press.

Murray, A. (2004). *A life of obedience.* Bethany House.

Offner, H., Larsen, D., & Larsen, S. (2013). *A deeper look at the fruit of the Spirit: Growing in the likeness of Christ*. InterVarsity Press.

Orr, C. E. (2009). *How to live a holy life*. Floating Press.

Peterson, J. (2003). *The insider: Bringing the Kingdom of God into your everyday world*. Navigator Press.

Piper, J. (2011). *Desiring God: Meditations of a Christian hedonist*. Multnomah.

Tozer, A. W. (2013). *The pursuit of God.* Gospel Light.

Wiersbe, W. W. (2005). *Devotions for renewal and joy: Romans and Philippians.* Honor Publishing.

CHAPTER 10

GOD'S FORGIVENESS AND CONSTANT-PRAYER AND COMMUNION WITH GOD

GOD'S WILLINGNESS TO FORGIVE

God's Willingness to Forgive Even the Greatest Sins

> And Jesus said, 'Father, forgive them, for they know not what they do.' And they cast lots to divide His garments.
>
> —*Luke 23:34*

> And I have been with you wherever you went, and have cut off all your enemies from before you; and I will make for you a name like the name of the great cries of the earth.
>
> —*I Chronicles 17:8*

How fast we are to forget that God is extremely willing to forgive us of all of our evil deeds and inclinations (Kruschwitz, 2001). It seems that when we

---

The Power of Constant Prayer and Communion With God, pages 117–128.
Copyright © 2024 by Information Age Publishing
www.infoagepub.com
All rights of reproduction in any form reserved.

118 • THE POWER OF CONSTANT PRAYER AND COMMUNION WITH GOD

sin, there are times when we feel we are tugging God with a rope that He might forgive us and bestow His blessings upon us once more. But such is not the case (Kruschwitz, 2001). God is more willing to forgive than we suppose. God does not forgive begrudgingly. Rather, He forgives as an act of love and any love which God gives is given freely and with enjoyment. We are prone to viewing God's forgiveness as a matter of obligation on His part (Kruschwitz, 2001). God has to forgive us because He died on the cross for us, is our mode of thinking. Given that we sin so often, He must not want to forgive us, but because of the cross, He does anyway. We do not like to admit that we think in such terms. We know this is false intellectually. But in the process of confronting our sinfulness once again, at times these are our thoughts. Oh, that we might know that the willingness to forgive that God demonstrated by dying on the cross for us, still reigns in His heart today. For if it were necessary that God would have to die again for each sin we commit, He would do that. Each time God forgives us, it is with a willingness that He would go to the cross and die for us, even for that very one sin.

God is clear in His Word that He will forgive even a sinner's greatest misdeeds (Matthew 18:24-35). God longs to forgive His children (Mark 11:25; Psalm 143:11). This fact stands true even when the believer has gotten himself into a sinful dilemma, which only that Christian is responsible for. The verse quoted above, I Chronicles 17:8, tells us of God's leading and the fact that He paves the way for those He loves and is with them unceasingly. It is amazing, but the Lord holds faithful to this promise even with one so prone to sin as we (II Timothy2:13).

The Lord instructs His children in His Word to bless those who revile and to pay back good for evil (Romans 12:14, 17, 19; I Corinthians 4:12). The believer finds these verses very difficult to live up to, if not impossible. Yet it is God who is able to bless and love His children, though they are inherently rebellious and self-willed (Minith, 2004). How tremendous a feat it is that while God commands His people to overcome evil with good, that is exactly the principle by which He acts towards His children (Romans 12:21). In each sin we commit, i.e., each evil deed we do against the Lord, it is not God's purpose to give a lesson, but to overcome our evil with His good. In fact, the *only way to permanently overcome evil is with good! God overcomes our evil with his forgiveness that evil may be permanently defeated in our life*!

There are many people who build a fortress against the refreshing savor of the forgiveness of Christ (Kruschwitz, 2001). These people do so because they are convinced that they have committed a sin that is too large to forgive. It would take ages to count the number of believers who suspect that they have committed the "blasphemy of the Holy Spirit." The Lord did not design this verse to be the subject of self-condemnation as multitudes use it to be. A believer in whom the Holy Spirit is active need not worry about such an offense. Nevertheless, it is clear from this discussion that human nature is far more conducive to worry, anxiety, and guilt than it is receiving forgiveness. Indeed, we may well imagine that to receive forgiveness for what is said to be a ghastly sin is among the most difficult

God's Forgiveness and Constant-Prayer and Communion With God • **119**

of human feats. To believe that a past act that haunts, angers, and bites need not haunt, anger and bite God by Christ's blood is a colossal, unimaginable actuality. It is unfortunate, but true, that humans often estimate the extent of God's forgiveness of a particular sin on the basis of the permanency and depth of the sin's effect on their hearts (Minith, 2004). If a believer sees the effects of a particular sin as still living with him, he will find it very difficult to receive forgiveness from God (Montague, 2011). If, however, believers view the effects of a sin as existing only in the past tense, perhaps because they have grown a lot in the Lord since the sin was committed; they will be better equipped to experience the fullness of the forgiveness of God.

Two points may be noted from this fact. First, it is often the case that Christians find it easier to receive forgiveness for a sin that they committed before becoming a Christian than a sin that they committed after becoming a Christian. The reasoning simply follows from what has already been stated. Christians will often view the effects of a sin they committed before their conversion as either not living with them or living with them only to a minor degree, because of the fact that Christ has wrought the work of a new creation. Whereas, Christians will more likely view the effects of a sin they committed since becoming a Christian as still with them because they are, notwithstanding, very much like the person they were when they committed the sin. This is why Joseph's brothers were so greatly haunted by the sin they had committed against Joseph (Genesis 45:1-15; 50:15-21).

I recall knowing a woman who had committed fornication after becoming a believer and was riddled with guilt because of this. She was riddled with guilt especially because she knew that she really had not grown much as a Christian since then. Deep down inside I was concerned as to whether she was still capable of committing the same infraction. As it turned out, her fears were justified because she became vulnerable in the same general area again. The guilt was heavy, because the growth had been small.

Second, the importance of growth and rededicating one's life to the Lord should be noted. If a devotee is growing in the Lord at a brisk pace, and that person has rededicated one's life often, he will rightly sense his "newness" in Christ and acknowledge a separation that exists between himself now and his sinful ways of the past. The growth-oriented Christian is less likely to have a keen guilt-producing awareness of past sins, because the effects of these sins no longer live with him to such a great extent. Each "rededicating" of his life to the Lord also serves to create a sense of renewal that lends itself towards conceptualizing large past sins as something that "other person" (i.e., himself before the rededication was made) committed. It is evident, then, that those who grow quickly in the Lord and are rededicating their lives to the Lord frequently are more likely to open their hearts to Christ's forgiveness (Murray, 1979).

Imagine two people who have a bad experience in Honolulu, Hawaii. The first fellow lives in Honolulu, the second person is a world traveler. The first man has trouble forgetting the incident because every time he goes to work he passes by

120 • THE POWER OF CONSTANT PRAYER AND COMMUNION WITH GOD

where his bad experiences took place. He is reminded of the incident, day after day. The world traveler, however, has moved onto many places in the world. After a time, he almost totally forgets about his bad experiences in Honolulu. When he does remember some of the experiences, he passes off the thoughts as relating to just Honolulu and the past, and not the here and now.

The same concept holds spiritually. It is much easier for the believer who is moving at a brisk pace to put the past behind him and receive God's forgiveness. Like the world traveler, he can say, "That experience/wrong occurred at *that* stage in my life and does not relate to the here and now." So, on the other hand, the Christian who has not moved on in his or her walk with God cannot make such a statement. He has not left *that* particular stage of one's life. Hence, that person is reminded of the experience/wrong, time and time again; and finds oneself unable to receive God's forgiveness.

Though growth is conducive to having Christ's forgiveness implanted in the Christian's deepest expanse of understanding, it is rather foolish to wait until a higher level of maturity has been achieved to accept Christ's forgiveness. Mary Magdalene did not wait to grow to receive Christ's forgiveness (Luke 8:2; Matthew 27:56; 28:1), neither did the woman caught in adultery (John 8:1-12) or the blind man, Bartimaeus (Mark 10:46-52). One of the best ways of receiving God's forgiveness is to meditate on God's holiness and to dwell in the presence of God, allowing God to consume oneself in the Lord's holiness (this is why this chapter is greatly related to Chapter 9) (Jeynes, 2009). In the midst of the holiness of God, the believer will come face to face with his utter wretchedness apart from God (Romans 7:24). Too frequently we are afraid to receive God's forgiveness in this matter. We are willing to meditate on God's holiness, but are unresponsive to God's desire to reveal ourselves for who we are in our lack. It would be the last thing one needed, to be revealed for the lowly person that one is. Yet, *it is the very refusal to be exposed in his spiritual nakedness before the holiness of God that prevents the believer from experiencing the totality of the forgiveness of God*! For when the Christian, bathing in the holiness of God, is revealed for the sinner that he or she is, does one realize firstly, a person's spiritually naked state and the vast void that exists between God and humanity.

Second, the unutterable love and forgiveness of God is demonstrated in the filling of that void by the blood of Christ. At such a time, man realizes that all his strivings are useless and that even his most righteous deeds are impotent and defenseless before the complete perfection of the Almighty God. It is then that he comprehends that in himself he is entirely helpless in his case before God and his only hope is to plead the blood of Christ (Murray, 2004; Piper, 2011; Tozer, 2013). It is Christ's blood that is the only means by which the infinite gulf can be closed. Forgiveness has been received (Swindoll, 1998).

If Christians look at the Bible, they will discover that this principle is proved true again and again. When Bartimaeus, the blind man, needed to receive Christ's forgiveness, he did not run to Christ attempting to make him (i.e., Bartimaeus) feel

God's Forgiveness and Constant-Prayer and Communion With God • **121**

better about himself. Rather, Bartimaeus, upon being exposed to the unutterable holiness of Christ, said, *"Jesus, Son of David, have mercy on me,"* recognizing his wretchedness without Christ (Mark 10:47, 48). It was at that point in which Bartimaeus received the healing and forgiveness of Christ (Mark 10:47-51). Two similar accounts involving blindmen in Matthew reveal the same thought (Matthew 9:27-31; 20:29-34). Mary, the sister of Lazarus who was considered a great sinner, received her forgiveness after she too had understood her nothingness without Christ. She demonstrated this understanding by unceasingly kissing Christ's feet, wiping them with her hair and anointing them with ointment (Luke 7:36-50). Similarly, the Canaanite woman with a demon possessed daughter acknowledged Christ as the only source for everything and herself as nothing. Her cries of *"Have mercy on me, O Lord" and "Lord, help me"* illustrate this point (Matthew 15:21-28).

When these people came before Christ, Jesus *did not rebuke* them in order that they would be made low, but rather His very holy presence ensured this. His words were then ones of forgiveness and because these people were humbled, acknowledging their nothingness, they received Christ's forgiveness. Similarly, today, when believers come before God, though they have not the holiness of Christ before them, they can meditate on God's holiness. God does not rebuke in order that the disciple of Christ be made low, but His very presence in holiness ensures this. The words of God that follow are ones of forgiveness and because the Christians see themselves as they are laid out before God's presence, they receive God's forgiveness. To genuinely acknowledge God's forgiveness of sin is to desire to be humbled. To desire an internalized knowledge of God's forgiveness requires that people be constantly aware of God; and more specifically, constantly kiss the feet of the Lord.

Understanding That God Enjoys Forgiving Results in Less Guilt

Who will sustain you to the end, guiltless in the day of our Lord Jesus Christ.

—I Corinthians 1:8

If the Lord had not been my help, my soul would soon have dwelt in the land of silence. When I thought, 'My foot slips,' thy steadfast love, O Lord, help me up. When the cares of my heart are many, thy consolations cheer my soul.

—Psalm 94:17-19

People tend to feel some sense of guilt if what they do forces another person to make actions that they know that person does not enjoy. Often Christians have such an attitude deposited in the recesses of his heart, when it comes to forgiveness. Because disciples of Jesus know that God hates sin, they necessarily assume that God hates to forgive. How often I have heard words like, "Oh, there I did it again, Now God is going to have to forgive me." But nothing could be further from the truth. God wants to forgive; that is why Jesus was nailed to the cross. God wanted to forgive His people enough that He was willing to sacrifice His only Son to accomplish this end (John 3:16; Romans 5:8). While God may hate sin, He enjoys loving and hence forgiving His people (Kruschwitz, 2001). When God talks about a "cheerful giver," He implies that anyone who is not cheerful in his or her giving really is not giving, anyone who is not cheerful in his loving, is not loving, etc. (II Corinthians 9:7). The same principle applies to forgiving. If God did not forgive His people cheerfully and willingly, He really would not be forgiving at all (Nehemiah 9:17; Matthew 9:2). God's hatred for sin is overshadowed by His abundant grace and mercy towards the sinner (James 2:13). Praise God that God is so willing to forgive that as someone once said, "When God forgives, He not only removes the sin, but restores the soul."

In Psalm 94:17-19, the passage quoted at the start of this section, verse 18 reads, *"When I thought, 'My foot slips,' thy steadfast love, O Lord help me up,"* depicts God's forgiveness. First, the fact of sin weighs believers down, but through the cleansing by Christ's blood, the weight is released and Christians are helped up. The fact of sin in people can potentially cause them to continually slip from the exalted position God has chosen for them (Psalm 94:17). Nevertheless, the blood of Christ makes believers pure in the sight of God, remaining exalted before God because when the Father looks upon those born-again, He sees the perfection of Jesus. God desires to lift up His followers by forgiving them. There is no need for guilt because the believers are, in the first place, guiltless through Christ; and in the second place, God enjoys forgiving His children (Kruschwitz, 2001). No matter how frequently Christians sin, the same precepts remain (Luke 6:36). God would never command His children to forgive if He Himself were not infinitely more forgiving Himself (Matthew 18:21-23; Luke 6:36, 37).

Understanding God's desire to forgive ultimately leads to less of a sense of unhealthy guilt (Kruschwitz, 2001). Unfortunately, one of the reasons that Christians feel guilty, when they are placed in a position in which they need forgiveness from God, is because of the manner human beings have treated them when they required a human's forgiveness (Minith, 2004). It is a rare breed of individual that consistently enjoys forgiving people. There are times when, whether we realize it or not, we make others feel guilty when we are reluctant to forgive. As a result of this phenomenon, most folks discover it difficult to conceive of God not demonstrating a similar reluctance. Rather than feel guilty, Christians have the option of lying back and bathing in the forgiveness of God, realizing more than ever the extent to which God loves them. With a greater comprehension of the pleasure God has in loving and forgiving His people, the devotees no longer separate themselves from fellowshipping with God because of guilt; but capitalize on this opportunity to allow the forgiveness of God to embrace them in order to experience the fuller reality of the love of God.

God's Forgiveness and Constant-Prayer and Communion With God • **123**

It's much like this single young lady named Shirley who loves to listen to classical music. Over the years she courts a number of young men. But when it comes the time when she reveals her great love for classical music, the young men always make a face. When this young lady wants to play her violin, each of the young men have the attitude. "Do you have to?" It took much of the fun out of the relationships for Shirley. She really desired to marry a man who had that interest in common with her.

In the course of her next relationship, Shirley again expressed her love for classical music and offered to play her violin. To which her companion responded, "Fantastic! I love classical violin!" Shirley was shocked by the positive response and felt a freedom to be herself with her dates that she had never before had.

Surely, we too will be amazed at the positive response of God with regard to forgiveness, as Shirley was with her boyfriend's response to her love for classical music. And just as Shirley felt a new freedom as a result, we will sense a new freedom too when we are touched by God's forgiveness.

RECEIVING GOD'S FORGIVENESS AND DRAWING NEAR TO HIS THRONE

Thou does keep him in perfect peace, whose mind is stayed on thee, because he trusts in thee. Trust in the Lord forever, for the Lord God is an everlasting rock.

—Isaiah 26:3, 4

Let us draw dear with a true heart in full assurance of faith, with our hearts sprinkled clean from an evil conscience and our bodies washed with pure water.

—Hebrews 10:22

For we have not a high priest who is unable to sympathize with our weaknesses, but one who in every respect has been tempted as we are, yet without sin. Let us then with confidence draw near to the throne of grace, that we may receive mercy and find grace to help in a time of need.

—Hebrews 4:15, 16

A born-again disciple of Christ can be bold and not fearful with his Lord, only when he has God's peace settled deep within his soul. *Peace is one of the least discussed aspects of Christian maturity and yet it is one of the most needed. No man can claim to be separated from the world unless he has a peace in which he consistently places himself under the wing of God!* A lack of peace is one of the last aspects of worldliness to go. Certainly, any Christian who has undergone any degree of commitment at all, senses a new peace. However, while peace often the first sign of God's indwelling and therefore one of the earliest areas of growth that

124 • THE POWER OF CONSTANT PRAYER AND COMMUNION WITH GOD

the disciple experiences, it is one of the most difficult areas in which to have any sense of completion. It should therefore come as no surprise to the Christian that one of the first areas Satan will try to upset in the life of the mature Christian is his peace. "The child of God" a beloved believer once said, "has two great marks about him. He may be known by his outward warfare as well as his inward peace."

With peace comes an awareness of the reality of God's promises. This is why inner peace is often one of the first changes that takes place in the new believer's life. God desires to comfort the new Christian with the reality of His promises. In the mature Christian, peace remains a reminder of the reality of God's promises. If Satan can chip away at this base in the believer's life, through anxiety, worrying, etc., he has set the stage for what could possibly be a major offensive against even the most steadfast lover of Jesus. If the Christian loses his peace, watch out! In such a case, not only is the disciple made vulnerable in a general sense, but also discovers within oneself an inability to come before God's throne with boldness and receive forgiveness.

Given the importance of peace in receiving the full extent of God's forgiveness, it is evident that it is to the Christian's advantage (and obviously to God's advantage) to seek to maintain a peaceful surrender to the will of God. In seeking God's peace, a seeker pursues mercy and hence life (Proverbs 21:21). God's promise in the verse initially quoted from Isaiah 26 is that God will grant peace to the person whose mind is solidly entrenched in the thoughts of God. Therefore, practicing the presence of God is essential to peace. Upon obtaining God's peace it is then that the Christian can come before God's throne with boldness and an assurance of the "ever-existence" of God's love towards him. It is before the throne of the that the Christian can be upheld by the arm of God (Proverbs 20:28). The believer can be weak and beaten by the winds of the world, but if he or she has God's peace, it is no matter for this person to come before God and receive forgiveness (Romans 5:2, 6). It is hard to receive a gift in which a person is not at peace in receiving it (Romans 5:15). Before the throne of God, the Lord can remind the individual that despite one's weakness this person is a chosen vessel of God's by His grace and for His glory (Deuteronomy 7:6).

Did you ever feel tense and have opportunity to listen to the waves come in at the seashore? There is a tranquility that results when we listen in such a way. When we listen to the sea as it whirls in a restful sound upon the seashore, it is like there is a message of peace in the sound of the waves. It is hard not to have some sensation of peace when we hear the waves in this way. The waves spell out to us some constancy in life and serenity that gives peace to our souls. It is a similar experience when we tune ourselves in to hear the voice of God. In God's voice we hear the constancy and consistency amidst this world of turmoil. We hear a constancy of God's purposes and God's love. It is hard not to have a great peace in our hearts when we hear God's voice of constancy. Surely, it is constant prayer to God that gives us peace.

THE INFLUENCE OF HEART KNOWLEDGE
OF GOD'S FORGIVENESS

Principles By Which God Works

> For if you forgive men their trespasses, your heavenly Father also will forgive you, but if you do not forgive men their trespasses, neither will your Father forgive your trespasses.
>
> *—Matthew 6:14*

The above verse is a prominent principle by which God works in forgiveness. This verse and others like it (Mark 11:25, 26; Ephesians 4:32; Colossians 3:13) are often taken merely to refer to consequences which extend to the afterlife. And while this is true, as far as it goes, the consequences of not being forgiving exist in the present life as well. When an individual does not have a spirit of forgiveness, there is a tension that exists between that person and God. When such a person comes into contact with God, he is confronted by Him to live up to a standard of Christlikeness. Subsequently, he comes face to face with the fact he is not at peace with God.

An unforgiving heart is a sin that can easily creep into our heart without even being aware of its existence (Kruschwitz, 2001; Offner et al., 2013). It is only when the Christian kneels before the Savior that the state of his heart revealed to himself. It is sad that we should allow our unforgiving heart to eat away at our walk with God before God finally points it out to us. What is worse is that the born-again disciple frequently fails even to allow God to point out his sin when alone with Him. But instead is closed to the possibility that his attitude must be made pure by the Living God.

It is unquestionable that the unforgiving heart causes a marked deterioration in relationships. If another person commits a sin against us and afterward our interaction continues with that person for some time, the bitterness will emerge and somewhat defile the reminder of the conversation. If it is the case that unforgiving individual has several occasions to interact with the individual that offended him, these interactions will also be affected. Even attempts to love that person are at least somewhat thwarted by the unforgiving spirit, because the overflowing love of Christ is partially capped. Even the same acts of love towards this individual are dampened in their meaning both for the giver and the receiver. Sometimes it takes weeks, months, and even years to unlock a bitterness that springs forth from an unforgiving heart. And it is at such a time that the individual is finally cognizant of the many interactions in which he did not allow the fullness of the love of Christ to grasp the other person (Hebrews 12:15).

Given the potential evil that an unforgiving heart has and the knowledge of the principles by which God works concerning forgiveness (Psalm 18:25), this sin is definitely a transgression that a Christian should seek to prevent straight-away. Practicing God's presence is again the answer. If believers bathe in the presence of

God, they become quickly aware that God's response towards the offender's sin is quite different from theirs. *The most essential difference is that upon seeing a sin, God's immediate concern is for the person who sinned, while man's essential concern is with himself!* In coming toward this realization, believers can, if they so desire, deal with their lack of forgiveness, asking God to remove their stubbornness of heart wholly to the people who offended them once again. *To the degree that a Christian overlooks the fact of one's bitterness, the bitterness will extend its territory such that an entire relationship can be spotted with hurt.* This explains why small disagreements and hurts can often lead to major upsets in relationships. Even if unforgiveness results from matters like who should use the restroom first, or whether an individual should mow the lawn or take out the trash, etc., a heap of bitterness can result if the unforgiving heart is not treated. A good way to treat the unforgiving attitude is to meditate on the forgiveness of Christ, using the Bible or otherwise. By practicing God's presence, a believer can meditate on the forgiveness of Christ even in the process of the event taking place. What a cleaner heart the believer can place before the eyes of God if he is more aware of him.

The Forgiving Heart

But I will hope continually, and will praise thee yet more and more.
—Psalm 71:14

Blessed are the merciful, for they shall obtain mercy.
—Matthew 5:7

There are multitudinous implications of truly knowing God's forgiveness that have not been touched on so far. Principally among these is that the freedom a person has in being forgiven can now be exercised to forgive others. *The believer can forgive others in so much as that individual has personally experienced the forgiveness of Christ.* It was after Abraham was forgiven for lying to Pharaoh about Sarah, his wife (Genesis 12:10-20), that he was able to forgive Lot for his self-centeredness and rescue him from his kidnappers (Genesis 14). It was following God's forgiveness of Moses' murder of the Egyptian that Moses was able to demonstrate a magnanimous spirit of forgiveness towards the Israelites (Exodus 32:33; Numbers 12:13).

Though we may be forgiven by God through the shedding of Christ's blood, we must receive and bathe in what Christ has already accomplished at the cross. If we do not receive the fact of Christ's forgiveness, Christ's blood will very little impact on our ability to forgive (Matthew 18:23-35). As it is to God's glory to forgive, it is also to man's glory to forgive (Proverbs 19:11). If we want to glorify God by the Christlikeness we demonstrate in forgiving others, we must first have a strong sensation of God's forgiveness (Colossians 3:13). It is far more than coincidence that the Bible's commands to forgive often follow a reminder of the splendor of the forgiveness of Christ (Ephesians 4:32; Colossians 3:1).

The reasoning behind why humans are able to forgive most when they themselves have encountered the forgiveness of Christ is as follows:

The person who has truly yielded to the fact of Christ's forgiveness:

1.   Has come to grips with the truth of one's (and therefore, man's) depravity apart from God; he has (following from 1) a realization of how many great wrongs Christ has forgiven of him;
2.   (also following from 1) one has a sense of his equality with all humankind, i.e., that all humans are 1) depraved and 2) have been forgiven of many sins.

In contrast, the person who has not yielded to Christ's forgiveness:

1.   has not come to grips with the truth of one's depravity apart from God. That individual either is too stubborn and proud to admit one's depravity or admit it, but this fact upsets him so much that he does not know how to deal with it;
2.   he does not have an understanding of how many wrongs Christ has forgiven of him. Either he does not understand how sinful his behavior is in the first place, or if he does understand, he soon forgets many of his past behaviors (James 1:22-27);
3.   he does not have a sense of his equality with all mankind. He either thinks he tries hard to be good or is good enough to be forgiven or on the other hand, does not think he deserves to be forgiven because he is so bad (and though it be true that no one deserves God's forgiveness, if this realization tends to lead to rejection of Christ's forgiveness, it is foolishness) and worse than most people.

The man who has yielded to Christ's forgiveness can forgive because he has come to grips with his own depravity *and so can more readily accept and forgive the depravity of others* (Matthew 6:12). This type of person can also forgive others because he or she knows how much Christ has forgiven that person. Any way that another person may offend him is nothing when compared to the plethora of sins that have mounted on one's account against God. In recognition of how great a volume of sin Christ has pardoned that individual of, how could that person not forgive others? Finally, the one who has yielded to the cleansing work of Christ can forgive others because he has a sense of his equality with mankind. He does not think himself better than others, and believes that he has substantially less to be forgiven of than other people (I Samuel 24:10-12; 26:9). He knows in all his being that all men fall *far short of God's glory*! One knows that every sin another person commits, he in himself could easily commit (Chambers, 2008). That person is well aware that it is only the grace of God that saves him from sinning even to a greater extent than he already does.

And so, we enter again into the vast realm of God's forgiveness. For not only does God enable us not to sin against Him, but when we do, He forgives us, as we are faithful to confess our sins unto Jesus (Augustine, 2010, 2015a, 2015b; Brady, 2003).

REFERENCES

Augustine of Hippo. (2010). *City of God* (Dods, M. Peabody, Trans.). Henrickson Publishers.

Augustine of Hippo. (2015a). *Brainy quotes*. Retrieved on April 2, 2015 from: http://www.brainyquote.com/quotes/quotes/s/saintaugus124552.html

Augustine of Hippo. (2015b). *Brainy quotes*. Retrieved on April 2, 2015 from: http://thinkexist.com/quotation/do_you_wish_to_rise-begin_by_descending-you_plan/263998.html. , p. 1.

Brady, B. V. (2003). *Christian love*. Georgetown University Press.

Chambers, O. (2008). *My utmost for His highest*. Discovery House Publishers.

Jeynes, W. (2009). *A call to character education and prayer in the schools.* Praeger.

Kruschwitz, R. B. (2001). *Forgiveness*. Baylor University.

Minith, F. B. (2004). *In pursuit of happiness: Choices that can change your life*. Fleming H. Revell

Montague, G. T. (2011). *First Corinthians*. Baker Academic.

Murray, A. (1979). *Abide in Christ: The joy of being in God's presence*. Whitaker House.

Offner, H., Larsen, D., & Larsen, S. (2013). *A deeper look at the fruit of the Spirit: Growing in the likeness of Christ*. InterVarsity Press.

Piper, J. (2011). *Desiring God: Meditations of a Christian hedonist*. Multnomah.

Swindoll, C. R. (1998). *Joseph: A man of integrity and forgiveness: Profiles in Character*. Word Publishers.

Tozer, A. W. (2013). *The pursuit of God.* Gospel Light.

CHAPTER 11

DISCIPLINE AND CONSTANT-PRAYER AND COMMUNION WITH GOD

DISCIPLINE IN OBEDIENCE

Only take heed, and keep your soul diligently, lest you forget the things which your eyes have seen, and lest they depart from your heart all the days of your life; make them known to your children and your children's children.

—Deuteronomy 4:9

Command the people of Israel to bring you pure oil from beaten olives for the lamp, that a light may be kept burning continually. Outside the veil of the testimony, in the tent of the meeting. Aaron shall keep it in order from evening to morning before the Lord continually; it shall be a statute forever throughout your generation. He shall keep the lamps in order upon the lampstand of pure gold before the Lord continually.

—Leviticus 24:2-4

The Power of Constant Prayer and Communion With God, pages 129–140.
Copyright © 2024 by Information Age Publishing
www.infoagepub.com
All rights of reproduction in any form reserved.

130 • THE POWER OF CONSTANT PRAYER AND COMMUNION WITH GOD

The life of discipline is one of the most foundational aspects of Christian growth (Minith, 2004; Swindoll, 1998; Wiersbe, 2005). Discipline is, of course, in and of itself a virtue (Wiersbe, 2005). But more than that, it sets the foundational work for a rapid process of maturing in Christ (Jeynes, 2010, 2014; Orr, 2009). So often when we fall victim to the wiles of the devil it is because we have failed to press on in assuring the development of consistent habits of discipline (Augustine, 2010; 2015a,b; Bounds, 2010). Satan attempts to eat away at those areas of discipline in which God is moving in our lives, that he might undermine the assurance of continued victory in Christ. This fact leads us to the discovery of an interesting phenomenon. When Satan chips away at certain areas of discipline, the negative results are rarely immediate, but rather long term. Various disciplines such as prayers, a Quiet Time, meditation on the Word, memorizing verses, etc., once undermined may not have their impact felt immediately. This can lead many who become slack in their disciplines to become complacent. This person can have the attitude of, "I have not dug into the Word for several days, and I don't feel any different." Nevertheless, spiritual deterioration may be right around the corner. Discipline is foundational for fruits of the Spirit such as love, patience, and joy. Take a Christian's discipline away and he will not feel an immediate effect necessarily. But it will erode the fruits of the Spirit slowly until the effect is even more devastating than the first.

There is a definite discipline required in obedience (I Corinthians 9:25-27). The believer must yield his whole being to God, serve, and love God with all his heart (Romans 6:12; Joshua 22:5; 23:11). The emphasis that God places on obedience as the most important aspect of discipline occurs constantly (I Kings 2:3; 8:25; I Thessalonians 5:6). Four key words which cut into the idea of discipline as a means to a strong Christian walk are found in Deuteronomy 4:9, the verse quoted at the head of the chapter: *"Keep your soul diligently."* There is a very strong sense in which the believer must keep an eye on his tendencies towards action not only as dictated by the Spirit of God, but also by the flesh. *A man slips back into old sin when he has failed to watch the actions of the flesh and the temptations of Satan often enough and soon enough to engage in a Holy Spirit-led counter attack*! If a believer takes his eyes off the activities of his adversaries long enough, the next time he looks, he may discover that he is in their grasp (Chambers, 2008; Daley, 2009; Froehlich, 2014). It is when the follower of Christ is caught off guard in this manner that he tends to lose his fire for God and even fall into various and sundry forms of idolatry (Deuteronomy 4:23; 11:16; 12:13, 27a). It is typical for the average Christian to scoff at such a thought as it pertains to his own walk with God. However, the first traces of a loss of fire and the rise of idolatry are almost always subtle. Satan will only try to attempt what he can get away with. *It is frequently the case that Satan sabotages just enough fire and love for God and produces enough idolatry in a person's life so that he does not notice it*. In other cases, Satan works slowly yet efficiently enough so that a believer finally comes to grips with his loss of zeal and increased idolatry, unaware that it did not result from any sudden change, but weeks, months and perhaps years of cautious work by the Prince of Liars himself (Hayford & Bauer, 2011; Montague, 2011).

Discipline and Constant-Prayer and Communion With God • **131**

It is then apparent that discipline in the Christian's life is essential to preventing the type of spiritual deterioration that has just been elucidated. Not only is discipline required in the usual sense, but also a type of discipline which observes the soul diligently on a continual basis. The Bible calls Christ's disciples to always be wary of where they go along the path of life; making sure that they remain on the straight path of the ways and purposes of the Lord (Proverbs 4:26; 16:17; Ephesians 5:15). In the Leviticus scripture, also quoted at the beginning of this chapter, we see that the Lord desires that the light of the lamp stand burn *continually* and that the procedure within the house of the Lord be kept in order *continually*. Because the Body of Christ is now filled with the Holy Spirit, the Body of Christ is now itself God's house and temple (I Corinthians 6:19, 20). And just as God desired that His house (tent) have a lamp continually burning and be in order continually, so He desires that for his present dwelling house, the Body of Christ. God desires that lamp stands (the church) have lights burning in the hearts of the Body of believers, symbolizing the power of the Holy Spirit within the church (Revelation 1:12, 19: Zechariah 2:4).

Secondly, God desires an orderly maintenance of the functions of the Body of believers, including an assurance of the continuation of light (the Holy Spirit) emanating from the lampstand (the church). This maintenance requires discipline. And one should note that God requires that His body be enflamed with the Spirit and disciplined *continually*.

Christians may assume that they are maintaining a walk which radiates with the light of Christ. But the Word of God warns against self-deception in this regard (Luke 11:35). There is a darkness that can be more extensive than a darkness of which one is aware. Constant awareness of God tunes believers into God's calculation of to what extent the light of Christ shines in them. What better source of evaluation to go to than God Himself.

DISCIPLINE AND PRAYER

Continue steadfastly in prayer, being watchful in it with thanksgiving.
—Colossians 4:2

I will take my stand to watch, and station myself on the tower, and look forth to see what He will say to me.
—Habakkuk 2:19

Discipline in prayer requires watchfulness. There is almost by necessity an element of watchfulness in any prayer (Bounds, 2010; Murray, 1979, 2004; Peterson, 2003). Prayer is the main instrument of God given to man through which the spiritual walls of the Evil One are destroyed and his attacks stifled. To enter into prayer is to launch ourselves in the midst of a spiritual battle. If, in his prayer, the believer touches the realm of God, he or she will undoubtedly become aware of the spiritual encounters taking place that one had not been aware of before (Psalm

132 • THE POWER OF CONSTANT PRAYER AND COMMUNION WITH GOD

102:7, 8). There is therefore a distinct element of watchfulness in prayer (I Peter 4:7). *Prayer is required for the most effective watchfulness.* And if a disciple is watchful, he or she is therefore disciplined.

The facts that have just been stated have incredible ramifications for practical Christian living. When followers of Christ want to stand up against the powers of darkness at work in their own or another person's life, prayer is a salient first step towards the effectuation of that goal (Graham, 2015). If believers sense that they are being restricted by sin in their lives, they must pray and watch, that God might help them define what the sources of those restrictions are. If they anticipate an arrayment of the forces of evil against them, they must pray and watch in order to determine whether their anticipation is warranted, and if it is, of what nature the attacks are most likely to be. If children of God are confused about their present spiritual condition, they must watch and pray, that God might reveal to them a cross-section of what is actually taking place in his life.

It is self-evident that for the disciple who practices watching and praying actively, confusion and unanticipated defeat will sharply decrease. How much more will this be true for those who practice constant prayer and watchfulness! *Praise God*! As the practice of constant prayer and watchfulness becomes more perfected in his life, the Christian will discover that its maturation ultimately produces a type of spiritual radar system. The result is that the devotee becomes very sensitive to the activities of God Himself and the flesh as they work upon him and those around him or her. God calls the believer to have this type of "radar system," especially with regard to Christ's Second Coming (Mark 13:33-37). This "radar system" has such an overwhelming impact that the follower of Christ quickly takes note of the fact that Satan becomes so frustrated that he opts to attack full steam when the believer's radar is down; in order that he might gain ground before the believer resumes his state of constant prayer and watchfulness. Watchfulness being essential to discipline, the effect of constant prayer and watchfulness upon our overall discipline are nothing less than amazing.

We are encouraged to watch more diligently when there is something to watch for. Certainly, the Second Coming of Christ and the vicious activity of Satan are something to watch for. I recall working as a security guard while at college. I was always a lot more aggressive in my watchfulness once I learned there was a rapist loose on the premises. Because the existence of the rapist meant there was something very serious to be on the watch for. As a result, my discipline as a security guard increased and I was more completely constantly aware of the goings on around me. The same principle applies to us as Christians. When we are careful to watch for the Second Coming of Christ and the activities of Satan, we become more disciplined and exhibit more constant awareness as a result.

DISCIPLINE AND THE HEART

Keep your heart with all vigilance; for from it flow the springs of life.
—Proverbs 4:23

Discipline and Constant-Prayer and Communion With God • **133**

Need it be said that our heart requires discipline (Jeynes, 2010, 2011; Piper, 2011; Tozer, 2013). Surely, if obedience requires discipline, the heart must also. If the heart is the source of the springs of life, the springs of obedience must flow out of it also (Orr, 2009). Though the discipline and watchfulness of the heart require the most persistence, it can also be one of the most rewarding aspects of discipline. In the heart lies the many roots of undisciplined behavior which if allowed to run their course, subsequently turn into sin. The desire to have a disciplined heart culminates as we seek to glorify God and God only, totally oblivious to the demands of the world system; for it is God who tests the heart (I Thessalonians 2:4). Few men see into our heart, but God knows its contents totally. He who tries to please men will seek actions that are right; he who tries to please God will seek to have a heart that is right. For this man knows that if our heart is right before God, the actions will follow.

When God judges the Body of believers, He will first look at the hearts (II Corinthians 5:10; Matthew 7:21-23). This is why God will judge our words so strictly; for from the tongue flows the abundance of the heart (Matthew 12:36, 37; Luke 6:45). One of the key notes of the Sermon on the Mount is the idea of glorifying God through a heart attitude rather than actions that can be readily discerned as good and evil by men (Matthew 5:22-27; 6:1). This mode of pleasing or displeasing God refers not only to the areas mentioned by Christ, but also to virtually every aspect of Christian living.

If we are unloving and selfish in our heart, though we do not seem to show it in our actions, it is nevertheless selfishness (Brady, 2003; Kruschwitz, 2001). If we are stubborn in our heart, though our actions (as seen by men) may not indicate it, we are nevertheless stubborn. To call sinful thoughts in the heart anything less than sin is like calling a plant which is developing a complex root system, but has not yet appeared on the ground surface, anything less than a plant. Yet herein lies a great error in how nearly every Christian, not excluding myself at times, handles sin. We act to thwart sin when it has appeared on the "surface," like the plant, having evidence itself in our actions. Mistake #1: We should have sought to root out the sin—when it was still taking root in our heart. We then proceed to attempt to remove that sin from our "repertoire" of sinful behavior.

Mistake #2: We should have sought to extirpate the sin at its source, the heart, rather than just remove it partially by attacking its outward manifestations.

It is the man of God who is concerned with seeing the roots extirpated. He knows that God sees the entire plant. As far as this man in concerned, whatever sin *God* sees must go. As for the man, who in his own estimation seeks God, whatever sin *man* sees must go. This hypocrite shall eventually fall, for the roots still implanted will bud forth sin quite rapidly.

It is the devil that convinces man that ill-feeling in the heart cannot curse and cannot destroy. The Lord warns that "roots" can cause man befoulment (Hebrews 12:15). If man underestimates the potential destructive power that is in the roots of sin, God does not. If Satan knows that a person will fight only sin that is noticeable, he will keep the grass low that he might maximize the amount of sin in a Christian's life without risking an incurrence of loss should the Christian call upon the Lord to back him in spiritual warfare. There is a level at which a Christian gets angry at sin, angry enough to fight it until defeated (Offner et al., 2013). *The level of sin at which a disciple of Christ gets angry enough to fight greatly determines how much sin in his life* (see chart). If we do not become very disturbed with our sin until it is evident to others, Satan will allow the sin to be evident just enough so that we do not venture to fight it. The reason Satan does not want us to fight is because Satan is bound to lose. God says that the lover of Christ is dead to sin and that Christ gives victory, which victory ensures victory once war is declared (Romans 6:10, 11:1 Corinthians 15:57).

The Christian forgets that Satan is not after an out and out battle with God, for the Prince of Darkness would surely lose. Satan's playground is only what man gives him. Any major overt spiritual strikes by the devil are only as a result of desperation, out of fear that he will lose his ground (Matthew 4:1-9; 16:18-20; Revelation 19:11-21). During such strikes, we can be certain that if we stand steadfast in the mighty forces of God, that victory will be right around the corner (Matthew 4:11; John 19:30; Revelation 19:11-21; 20:1-3, 10).

If lovers of God become angered by sin at the root level, they will discover that *relatively* little sin will be noticeable because they will be allowing God to attack their sin at the roots and encouraging Satan to keep those sins down to a lower level.

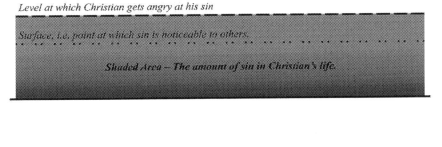

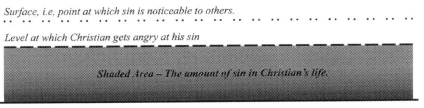

FIGURE 11.1- When Sin is Noticeable to the Believer and to Those Around the Believer-Satan Does Not Want the Christian to Notice Sin

Discipline and Constant-Prayer and Communion With God • **135**

The Christians who experience continual communion with God that their heart might be subject to God's disciplining hand will suffer less from sin, but not only that, they will also be more able to function within a lifestyle that emphasizes grace. The believers who live in a realm in which they seek to do godly acts firstly will have an estimation of themselves that fluctuates with their behavior. Because of circumstances, behavior fluctuates much. Hence, their estimation of themselves will fluctuate much. Some days they will think highly of themselves, other days low. The emphasis will be on how well they performed this day, and not God's grace. *Behavior fluctuates much, but the heart fluctuates less.* The heart gradually grows in subjection to God. As a result, our estimation of ourselves fluctuates little when we emphasize the heart. We are aware of growing closer to God, but at the same time know our need for God's grace. *Behavior fluctuates around the state of the heart* (Figure 11.2).

To focus on behavior is to focus on ourselves. To focus on the heart, is to focus on God! Though it is true that the extent we act like Christ we are like Christ (i.e., his heart is Christ-like); circumstances often interfere in the direct relationship between these two. The result may be that we are actually growing, but circumstances prevent the behavioral realization of that growth until after those circumstances have passed. For instance, a woman may be growing in the Lord, but because of family problems she is upset and irritable and this growth has not yet manifested itself in her behavior. She must not esteem herself lower as a result, but rather acknowledge her heart growth and receive God's grace. There are some of the spiritual benefits that can be derived from a heart disciplined life.

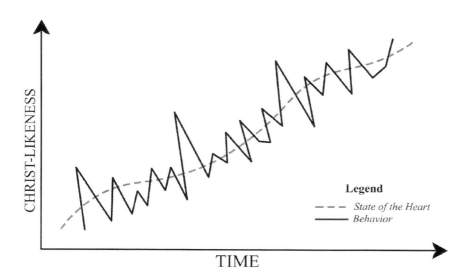

FIGURE 11.2- The Relationship between the State of the Heart and Behavior

DISCIPLINED AND THE SENSES

I said, 'I will guard my ways, that I may not sin with my tongue; I will bridle my mouth, so long as the wicked are in my presence.'

—Psalm 39:1

Happy is the man who listens to me, watching daily at my gates, waiting beside my doors.

—Proverbs 8:34

Of all the section titles, this is undoubtedly the vaguest. Yet, there is a necessity of maintaining discipline, with regard to man's five senses: sight, hearing, smell, taste, and touch. Many Christians fall because they have many other areas of their lives disciplined, but not the areas which relate to the senses. Discipline, with regard to the senses, is of particular importance because the activity of the five senses has a strong connection to several key human drives. Sight, for instance, can be related to the hunger drive, sex drive, materialistic drive, etc. If Christians are not careful to set their eyes on those things which are pleasing to God, they will be prone to getting caught up in Satan's net (Psalm 25:15). Hearing can be an active instrument in the drive for control over circumstances (being nosey and listening in on other peoples' conversations is an expression of this desire for control) as well as self-preservation (fearing sounds in the darkness). Smell and taste can relate to the hunger drive and touch to the self-preservation and sexual drives. The prominence of believers' watchfulness over the activity of their senses becomes quite pertinent to experiencing a consistency in their walk with God. Thousands of Christians would walk fairly consistently with Jesus, were it not for undisciplined drives which upset the progression of their spiritual growth.

Proverbs 8:34 quoted at the head of this section refers to two of the senses: hearing and sight. This verse encourages disciples to listen to the Lord as opposed to the voice of the word of Satan; and to set their eyes on the things of the Lord, to watch for God and His leading, rather than wandering where the caprice of the flesh may venture. In our daily lives, we have quite a variety of voices we can listen to. We can be nosey and listen to the conversation of others or we can listen to the subtle whispers of the devil. What people hear will inevitably lead them to action. And if Christians do not exercise continued discipline over what they allow to enter their minds through this sense, they will find themselves acting in a way that is both at times incomprehensible as well as rebellious against the Living God. In the case of the sense of sight, the program for combat is much the same. Many a person's lack of discipline over the wanderings of the eye has led many to get caught into a tight trap of lusting after the opposite sex or the material attractions of this world. The modern world is filled with constant allurements in both these areas and many more; and if Christians' eyes are not directly on the Lord instead, they will surely fall (Proverbs 4:25).

Discipline and Constant-Prayer and Communion With God • **137**

The senses of taste and smell need to be guarded especially with regards to food. Many people become overweight because they allow their sense of taste to grow out of such control that it becomes as important to satisfy their taste and their hunger. In which case, such these people can consequently eat well after the hunger is gone as their desire for God. If believers have discipline over their taste buds, sweets will pose no temptation. Christians who have a disciplined taste drive fill find their taste totally satisfied in the goodness of the Lord (Psalm 34:1).

Though the tongue be important in reference to taste, it is even more so in connection with speech (though it itself it is not a sense). Psalm 39:1, quoted at the head of the chapter, underlines the discipline of speech. A human's tongue is by nature undisciplined and unruly (James 3). Only by the Lord's help can it be tamed (Psalm 141:3).

Martin Luther knew the power of the tongue well when he said, "When people slander others they remark: I do not say this because I wish to slander him nor do I want it told behind his back." Another person once said, "Gossip is like mud thrown again a clean wall; it may not stick but it leaves a mark." And "though words break no bones, they can break hearts." Joham von Goethe also had strong words concerning the tongue. "Insinuations are the rhetoric of the devil." Finally, an anonymous Christian Saint once spoke these words: "In the multitude of words you may recognize boastfulness."

DISCIPLINE AND SUBMISSION

And going a little further, He fell on His face and prayed, 'My Father, if it be possible, let this cup pass from me; nevertheless, not as I will, but as thou wilt.'

—Matthew 26:39

If the disciple is to be consistently submissive, whether it be to God or his fellow man, his submission must be based on a disciplined life. In the verse just quoted, Jesus displays a solid discipline. Without the disciplined lifestyle Christ could not have submitted to the Father. For in His manhood, Jesus did not desire to go to the cross (Hebrews 12:2). Likewise, there are many avenues on which God calls His children to travel on which they are not prone to go and at times may even be detestable to them. At such times, the Christian's response is greatly reliant on the amount of discipline that has been built into his life. Discipline to entrust himself to His faithful Creator, believing that God will fulfill His promises.

Submission requires discipline because eventually the servant of God will be required to do something he does not want to do. In fact, *the extent we are submitted to God really is not tested until God asks us to do something we do not want to do.* Nevertheless, when we submit to God in such an instance, a good deal of growth results (Hebrews 5:8). Oh, that we may grasp more of the submission of our Lord. He exhibited a submission beyond comprehension (Mark 14:36; Luke 22:42; Matthew 26:39, 42).

Yes, submission requires discipline and who was more disciplined than the Lord? Think of a maid and her employer for a moment. The maid comes to clean house for her employer once a week. The maid lives a life of constant submission to her employer; as much as any employer-employee relationship could name. Because of this constant submission on the part of the maid, she becomes quite a disciplined individual. In fact, if you ever cared to notice a fact about human nature, most of the time maids are substantially more disciplined than their employers. This is because submission breeds discipline. Similarly, as we submit to the wishes of God, we will find that discipline increases in our life as well.

DISCIPLINE AND SPIRITUAL BATTLES

The shatterer has come up against you. Man the ramparts; watch the road; gird your loins; collect all your strength.
—Nahum 2:1

Be watchful, stand firm in your faith, be courageous, be strong.
—I Corinthians 16:13

Rejoice in the Lord always; again, I will say, Rejoice, let all men know your forbearance. The Lord is at hand.
—Philippians 4:4, 5

Lest Satan deceive us, it requires discipline to stand any chance in the multifarious spiritual battles that we encounter. In fact, it is the disciplines of the Christian's life that the Evil One often challenges most intensely, believing that if he can undermine these aspects of the disciple's life, the Christian is nearly defeated. Temptation, by its very nature, challenges the Christian to either stand fast in his disciplined way of life or abandon it. To become angry is to abandon the discipline of self-control; greed is to abandon the discipline of simplicity; lust is to abandon the discipline of a pure thought life. A disciplined life in Christ is a key thrust toward defeating Satan's attempts at drawing us away from the presence of God and walking in His statutes. If the believer is undisciplined to begin with, it is very easy for him to be lured into more undiscipline. The person, who does not have control over his emotional and spiritual faculties, will soon discover that the devil can gain partial control over him or her easily enough. If such a person is a non-Christian, one can be led into doing evil quite constantly (Genesis 6:5).

Nevertheless, even the most steadfast Christians are tempted often. The strategy of the devil differs with such an individual. Rather than direct attack, the devil must first convince the believer that his discipline in the area of his life being challenged is not worth pursuing. Often the Evil One will venture to persuade the

Discipline and Constant-Prayer and Communion With God • **139**

devotee that the type of discipline he is seeking to undertake is drudgery and is not at all enjoyable. He will attempt to convince the believer that the latter's effort is as a result wasteful and that true enjoyment rests in "letting go" rather than in discipline. It takes less than we would like to admit to stun us with such a ploy. Especially during these times when we are either sick or tired, it can be easy to agree with the devil's arguments. This being true, it is no wonder that God calls His children to awake, be cleansed and start to fight, rather than surrender to perverse reasoning (Psalm 119:9; Romans 13:11).

Apostle Paul warns that if followers of Christ are not disciplined in their walks with God, they can easily be hypocritical (I Corinthians (9:27). To stand fast against the wiles of the devil, they must be watchful (I Corinthians 16:13; Nahum 2:1). These believers must be cautious concerning the activities of Satan, but more than this, they must be careful to keep their eyes and minds on God. Church attendees should lay their thoughts upon the products of God's grace and rejoice in all the activities of God, doing each continually (Philippians 4:4, 5). Minds that are filled with the thoughts of the greatness of God and hearts overrunning with joy, whatever the circumstances, are two of the greatest defenses against spiritual attack. To do each takes discipline. Notice that Philippians 4:5 states, regarding rejoicing, *"Let all men know your forbearance."* It takes forbearance and hence discipline to continually rejoice. II Corinthians 10:4, 5 exhorts the believer to *"take every thought captive to obey Christ."* To fulfill such a demanding commandment also requires discipline. Spiritual battles are a constant phenomenon in the Christian life and a ready spiritual artillery must be had if victory is to be realized. A human does not, in and of oneself, have spiritual artillery, but must look to the Lord to fight the battles. To have God fight our battles, we must first allow Him to do just that. Yet too frequently when we are in the midst of struggle, we forget that He *is* available to fight our battles. Ah, that we might bask in His presence all the day long, as a continual reminder that He is always ready to fight for us, because we are His children. Amen.

REFERENCES

Augustine of Hippo. (2010). *City of God* (Dods, M. Peabody, Trans.). Henrickson Publishers.

Augustine of Hippo. (2015a). *Brainy quotes.* Retrieved on April 2, 2015 from: http://www.brainyquote.com/quotes/quotes/s/saintaugus124552.html

Augustine of Hippo. (2015b). *Brainy quotes.* Retrieved on April 2, 2015 from: http://thinkexist.com/quotation/do_you_wish_to_rise-begin_by_descending-you_plan/263998.html. , p. 1.

Bounds, E. M. (2010). *Purpose in prayer.* Blackstone.

Brady, B. V. (2003). *Christian love.* Georgetown University Press.

Chambers, O. (2008). *My utmost for His highest.* Discovery House Publishers.

Daley, R. J. (2009). *Sacrifice unveiled: The true meaning of Christian sacrifice.* T & T Clark.

140 • THE POWER OF CONSTANT PRAYER AND COMMUNION WITH GOD

Froehlich, M. A. (2014). *Courageous gentleness: Following Christ's example of restrained strength*. Discovery House Publishers.

Graham, B. (2015). *Quotations book*. Retrieved March 26, 2015 from: http://quotations-book.com/quote/38480/

Jeynes, w. (2010). Religiosity, religious schools, and their relationship with the achievement gap. *Journal of Negro Education, 79*(3), 263–279.

Jeynes, W. (2014). School choice and the achievement gap. *Education and Urban Society, 46*(2), 163–180.

Hayford, J. W., & Bauer, R. H. (2011). *Penetrating the darkness: Keys to ignite faith, boldness, and breakthrough*. Chosen Books.

Kruschwitz, R. B. (2001). *Forgiveness*. Baylor University.

Minith, F. B. (2004). *In pursuit of happiness: Choices that can change your life*. Fleming H. Revell

Montague, G. T. (2011). *First Corinthians*. Baker Academic.

Murray, A. (1979). *Abide in Christ: The joy of being in God's presence*. Whitaker House.

Murray, A. (2004). *A life of obedience.* Bethany House.

Offner, H., Larsen, D., & Larsen, S. (2013). *A deeper look at the fruit of the Spirit: Growing in the likeness of Christ*. InterVarsity Press.

Orr, C. E. (2009). *How to live a holy life*. Floating Press.

Peterson, J. (2003). *The insider: Bringing the Kingdom of God into your everyday world*. Navigator Press.

Piper, J. (2011). *Desiring God: Meditations of a Christian hedonist*. Multnomah.

Swindoll, C. R. (1998). *Joseph: A man of integrity and forgiveness: Profiles in Character*. Word Publishers.

Tozer, A. W. (2013). *The pursuit of God.* Gospel Light.

Wiersbe, W. W. (2005). *Devotions for renewal and joy: Romans and Philippians.* Honor Publishing.

CHAPTER 12

VISION AND CONSTANT-PRAYER AND COMMUNION WITH GOD

GOD'S VISION, NOT OUR OWN

Let not your heart envy sinners, but continue in the fear of the Lord all the day.

—*Proverbs 23:17*

Jesus said to him, If you can? All things are possible to him who believes.'

—*Mark 9:23*

Many believers strive zealously to acquire and sustain a vision from God. Few are successful in fulfilling a vision from God. The major reason for this failure is that Christians fail to maintain constant communication between themselves and the source of that vision, the Lord God. Most people, once they have received a vision or "burden" from God, attempt all kinds of devices to attempt to employ the vision and make it a reality. This is a grand mistake. For the source of that vision also has a course outlined that He desires to take to fulfill that vision step

---

The Power of Constant Prayer and Communion With God, pages 141–147.
Copyright © 2024 by Information Age Publishing
www.infoagepub.com
All rights of reproduction in any form reserved.

141

142 • THE POWER OF CONSTANT PRAYER AND COMMUNION WITH GOD

by step. A human frailty, however, is to focus on the glorious end-product and pass over the steps that God has ordained are necessary to complete His purpose (Chambers, 2008; Daley, 2009; Murray, 2009; Orr, 2009). Second, those that do experience a respectable degree of fulfillment frequently become tainted with compromise (worldly or otherwise) that stifle the tremendous witness that God had originally intended. Both of these failures result from a lack of continual fellowship with God and an attitude of true humility in which believers firmly recognize that it is God's vision and not theirs; thereby receiving their directions from God. In the first case numerous visions turn into mere dross because the disciple in his flesh tries to launch a vision which only God can do Himself (Job 5:8, 9). Secondly, a large percentage of prodigious ministries, which were enacted based on a vision, become tainted with worldliness. At times this fact becomes so distinct that an individual cannot discern that God has been so kind to share with us the desires and goals that He Himself has for humankind and the love He feels for those who are missing out on a richer experience of His grace (Hayford & Bauer, 2011; Kruesheitz, 2001; Minith, 2004). Though this fear of God be essential, it is rendered impotent unless we have faith to believe that God can complete the work and reach the goal that He has graciously shared with his servants. The servant must take God at His word and believe that God destines no true vision for failure, but rather intends to fulfill what He has set out to do (Joel 2:21; Genesis 6:22).

If Christians have both a fear of God and a belief that God will fulfill His promise concerning the vision, this will lead Christians into a constant reliance on God concerning what paths to take towards the completion of that vision. In fearing God, we acknowledge that God, being the source, must naturally do the directing (Bounds, 2010; Tozer, 2013). And in believing God for His promise in connection with the vision, in humility we must realize that we cannot pump up any such faith on our own merit or energization. We instead must rely on the grace of God to sustain our faith to see the vision through until its time of completion (Augustine, 2010, 2015a, 2015b).

PATIENCE IN REGARD TO VISIONS

For still the vision awaits its time, it hastens to the end—it will not lie. If it seems slow, wait for it, it will surely come, it will not delay. Behold, he whose soul is not upright in him shall fail, but the righteous shall live by his faith.

—Habakkuk 2:3, 4

For you have need of endurance, so that you may do the will of God and receive what is promised.

—Hebrews 10:36

Vision and Constant-Prayer and Communion With God • 143

A vision, once promised, will progress step by step as God promised. But God did not promise that the fulfillment of the vision would necessarily take place at the time desired by God's servant. God cautioned Habakkuk in Habakkuk 2 to be patient concerning the vision He was about to give him. And while the Christian's vision may not be prophetic in nature as was Habakkuk's, the same caution concerning patience applies. There are few particulars which are as frustrating to the Lord's adherents as seeing a vision which they long to see fulfilled, sit by the wayside immobile. If one thing is clear, though, it is that human impatience results from a lack of a heavenly perspective upon the mobilization and fulfillment of the vision. If God's servants are growing anxious over the dormancy of a vision, it is because they are not allowing the direction of the vision to rest in God's hands, but merely in their own (Swindoll, 1998).

It is a typical tendency among humans that after one phase of a vision has been activated, they immediately return to God and say, "Okay, that's done. Now what? Huh? Huh?" and when they receive no response or are told by God to wait, they will commonly anticipate what God would do and act to implement it themselves. In essence, there is too great a human tendency to place the implementation of God's visions into human hands (Montague, 2014; Offner et al., 2013; Peterson, 2003). But such anticipation is unfruitful. For if the Lord is with us, the "burden" we have will come to pass (Joshua 14:12). Believers need not fret over the fulfillment of a vision for its future will be determined by the most skillful hands that there are (Psalm 39:7). Only God can work to accomplish a spiritual cause; humans apart from God's guidance cannot (Job 5:8, 9).

The born-again believer has reason to be joyful, as that individual patiently awaits the Lord to move towards the fulfillment of a vision. God has proved Himself to be faithful again and again in the Bible. The hope a Christian has in any vision from God begins with the Word of God (Psalm 119:74; Joshua 1:8). Herein lies a remarkable relationship between the promises/fulfillments in God's Word and constant communion with God and practicing God's presence allows the Lord to bring to mind the existence of His promises and His remarkable record in regards to fulfillment, i.e., 100% fulfillment (Joshua 21:45). Constant communion with God is a vital part of waiting on God to act to consummate a vision. Because when we are in such close contact with the Lord, He is able to furnish His servant with some of His own patience (Piper, 2011). Surely, no one would deny that when we are around patient people, it is easier to be patient ourselves. This same fact is true with God, yet even to a larger extent. For surely, if the good qualities of those around a person rub off on him, how much more will the good qualities of an indwelling and enveloping God rub off when actually communicating with Him!

Picture a dog owner who wants his two dogs to be patient. One dog shows remarkable patience while the other one does not. The owner will only serve the individual dog's food if they are patient. But one of the dogs is very impatient when it comes to being served his meal. He runs and jumps around in impatience whenever he knows that it is getting close to meal time. As a result, the owner

144 • THE POWER OF CONSTANT PRAYER AND COMMUNION WITH GOD

does not give the impatient dog its food. Meanwhile, the other dog demonstrates tremendous patience. Therefore, without hesitancy, the owner gives the patient dog its food. Time and time again, this happens. The impatient dog sees that it does not receive any food when it is impatient, while the patient dog does. But after a while, by virtue of spending time with the patient dog, the impatient dog learns patience and receives its due reward. Spending time with God teaches us the value of patience and the just reward we will receive if we have patience.

How interesting it is that some of the world's most precious offspring such as oil, wine, and diamonds require years upon years of waiting that complete development may take place. To interrupt the aging process of each before due time would be to greatly depreciate the value of each. The same is also true with the vision/burden which God gives His servant. The greatest vision often requires a long period of waiting until the time has come for deployment. To interrupt the aging process before due time would be to greatly depreciate its value. I fear that, in this "rush, rush" modern age, such is the Christian's tendency. We are all guilty of being depreciators.

THE DEDICATED LIFE

If you are willing and obedient, you shall eat the good of the land.
—*Isaiah 1:19*

The hand of our God is for good upon all that seek Him all the power of His wrath is against all that forsake Him.
—*Ezra 8:22b*

It is doubtless that there is a relationship between seeking the Lord with our full being and receiving that vision which the Lord has so promised. It is a wholly dedicated life that the Lord will entrust with His visions. The Lord dares not entrust a vision so valuable with someone who will squander it for worldly gain or fleshly lusts. There are always those who upon receiving a vision will seek nothing more than to have the vision come to pass. However, God wants a person whom, upon receiving a vision, will seek nothing more than to glorify God. Let it be realized that such an individual entrusts the course of a vision to God. He or she does not seek the work of God's hand, but instead seeks God's face. Such a Christ-follower knows that as one commits to the path that the Lord lays out, ever longing to satisfy the Lord with a dedicated life held fast to the cross, that the rest will follow in due course (Deuteronomy 15:4, 5). If the disciple wants a vision which does not vacillate, that person must not vacillate (Psalm 125:1). The believer who is steadfast in all aspects of his life, will have the steadfast faith that will be an essential ingredient to make the vision a reality (II Timothy 4:7).

The follower's vision, like his life, should be in the Lord's hands. Just as a believer falls if he strives to put his own life in order without petitioning the Lord's energizing power, so he will fall if he strives to make the vision a reality without asking for the Lord's unction. Let no man deceive himself, if he strives in the flesh with respect to his daily walk with God, he will strive when entrusted with a vision! If he does not continually pray with God during his daily life and decisions, he will not pray with God for direction concerning the vision! The outcome of any vision will be a product of the interaction between God's character and that of the believer. When Christ walked the earth, the vision of Christ's sacrifice on the cross was completed in absolute perfection. because the product of the interaction between Christ and God the Father was perfection (Matthew 26:28; Luke 22:24). Naturally, man himself is so imperfect. Nevertheless, the fulfillment of a vision can be a brilliant testimony of the glory of God, if a Christian's interaction with Him has a high quality and is quite continuous.

It is an awesome thought to think that a product of a vision can reflect the quality of our walk with God. It should be stated that the success of a vison must not be considered in terms of what the world defines as success, but what God does. For a vision demands purity and godliness first as an indication of success. If a man acts on a vision such that he does not compromise the Word of God and stands on his convictions, the result shall be considered greater than if more people are reached and won in a ministry which does compromise and whose convictions waver. The ministry which results from a vision will reflect the walk of a person who received it. If a worldly Christian receives a vision form the Lord, he will most likely have a worldly ministry. A godly man who receives a vision from God will most likely have a godly ministry.

A dedicated believer will stay in fellowship with God. He will stand in faith and therefore lose his hope in nothing of what God has promised to him (Colossians 1:23). A man who constantly prays with God does not have his hope swallowed up because his Lord is ever before him. Any time his hope fades in brilliance, he is in such touch with God that he looks ahead of him and his hope begins to return. The Christian who practices the presence of God commits all his ways to the Lord (Psalm 37:4, 5). It therefore takes little out of the ordinary for him to commit his vision to the Lord. He knows that it is God who will win the battle and that if the Lord is with him, the vision shall be fulfilled (Joshua 5:13-15; 14:12).

ALLOWING GOD TO REIGN OVER THE VISION AND THEREFORE HAVING FAITH

Trust in Him at all times, O people, pour out your heart before Him; God is a refuge for us.

—Psalm 62:8

Truly, I say to you, whoever says to this mountain, 'Be taken up and cast into the sea', and does not doubt in his heart, but believes that what he says

146 • THE POWER OF CONSTANT PRAYER AND COMMUNION WITH GOD

will come to pass, it will be done for him. Therefore, I tell you, whatever you ask in prayer, believe that you have received it, and it will be yours.
—Mark 11:23, 24

When a Christian trusts in the Lord concerning the fulfillment of a vision, he is allowing God to reign over the ultimate direction and manifestation that vision will take. When steadfast faith is present, the believer is acknowledging that the development of that vision is in safest keeping when in the hands of God; and any attempt by one to snatch control over its development away from God can only lead to failure. Psalm 62:8, just quoted, asserts the importance of trusting in the Lord concerning a vision, this is when God's full power can be released to make the vision a miraculous reality (Wiersbe, 2005). It should be noted in Mark 11:23, 24 Jesus says that *the Christian's responsibility is to believe the mountain will be moved, allowing God to do the actual working of this miracle. God does not say that a Christian should believe that the mountain should be moved while in the pushing upon the mountain himself.* The same principle naturally holds in regards to a vision from God: The disciple of Christ should have faith that the Lord will accomplish His purpose in regards to the vision, not himself. Rather the disciple should provide a suitable atmosphere for God to work miraculously. As has been noted, one important ingredient for providing this atmosphere is a life of purity and holiness before God (Psalm 96:9).

The Lord calls His servant to commit the vision to Him, and He will see that it comes to pass (Proverbs 16:3). One need take stock in the fact that whatever goal God has in mind, He will accomplish (Acts 27:25). *Humans makes a terrible mistake when, as a result of knowing some of God's goals, they try to accomplish them themselves. People cannot accomplish God's goals any more than an amoeba can accomplish people's goals. Individuals design goals that humans can accomplish, so God designs goals that God can accomplish!*

One needs to commit the vision to the Lord, so that there is a minimum amount of interference on his part throughout the day. The believer needs a faith which will make this possible and this is accomplished through constant prayer with God. In constantly praying with God, God can continually remind us that He is in control and that only He can work effectively towards to fulfillment of that vision. Only God could produce the many fruits in the promise He made to Abraham and the same is true with the Christian (Genesis 12:1-4). If Abraham had experienced a more consistent communion with God, he probably would not have forced the fulfillment of the promise given to him like he did (Genesis 16:1-4). It is during those times of weakness and vulnerability that the Christian will be tempted to take a vision into his or her own hands. In such a vulnerable state, all past commitments not to interfere rest as old relics. The Christ follower views the product of the vision as dying, one's faith is wavering, and he is tempted to intervene to save the seemingly sagging mission.

It is at such times that more than ever we need God's assurance that He is still the captain of the ship and if the vision is truly from Him, the ship will not sink

Vision and Constant-Prayer and Communion With God • **147**

(Brady, 2003; Froelich, 2014; Graham, 2015; Murray, 1979). Oh, that we might believe constantly that the one who dares to share with us His great vision for His Creation is faithful to bring His vision to completion for His Name's sake. Amen.

REFERENCES

Augustine of Hippo. (2010). *City of God* (Dods, M. Peabody, Trans.). Henrickson Publishers.

Augustine of Hippo. (2015a). *Brainy quotes*. Retrieved on April 2, 2015 from: http://www.brainyquote.com/quotes/quotes/s/saintaugus124552.html

Augustine of Hippo. (2015b). *Brainy quotes*. Retrieved on April 2, 2015 from: http://thinkexist.com/quotation/do_you_wish_to_rise-begin_by_descending-you_plan/263998.html. , p. 1.

Bounds, E. M. (2010). *Purpose in prayer*. Blackstone.

Brady, B. V. (2003). *Christian love*. Georgetown University Press.

Chambers, O. (2008). *My utmost for His highest*. Discovery House Publishers.

Daley, R. J. (2009). *Sacrifice unveiled: The true meaning of Christian sacrifice*. T & T Clark.

Froehlich, M. A. (2014). *Courageous gentleness: Following Christ's example of restrained strength*. Discovery House Publishers.

Graham, B. (2015). *Quotations book*. Retrieved March 26, 2015 from: http://quotationsbook.com/quote/38480/

Hayford, J. W., & Bauer, R. H. (2011). *Penetrating the darkness: Keys to ignite faith, boldness, and breakthrough*. Chosen Books.

Kruschwitz, R. B. (2001). *Forgiveness*. Baylor University.

Minith, F. B. (2004). *In pursuit of happiness: Choices that can change your life*. Fleming H. Revell

Montague, G. T. (2011). *First Corinthians*. Baker Academic.

Murray, A. (1979). *Abide in Christ: The joy of being in God's presence*. Whitaker House.

Murray, A. (2004). *A life of obedience.* Bethany House.

Offner, H., Larsen, D., & Larsen, S. (2013). *A deeper look at the fruit of the Spirit: Growing in the likeness of Christ*. InterVarsity Press.

Orr, C. E. (2009). *How to live a holy life*. Floating Press.

Peterson, J. (2003). *The insider: Bringing the Kingdom of God into your everyday world*. Navigator Press.

Piper, J. (2011). *Desiring God: Meditations of a Christian hedonist*. Multnomah.

Swindoll, C. R. (1998). *Joseph: A man of integrity and forgiveness: Profiles in Character*. Word Publishers.

Tozer, A. W. (2013). *The pursuit of God.* Gospel Light.

Wiersbe, W. W. (2005). *Devotions for renewal and joy: Romans and Philippians.* Honor Publishing.

CHAPTER 13

SENSITIVITY AND CONSTANT-PRAYER AND COMMUNION WITH GOD

THE CHALLENGE TO SENSITIVITY

For by their own sword they did not possess the land; and their own arm did not save them; by thy right hand, and thine arm, and the light of thy presence for thou didst favor them.

—Psalm 44:3

For Jerusalem has stumbled and Judah has fallen; because their speech and their deeds are against the Lord, defying His glorious presence.

—Isaiah 3:8

The fact that the light of the presence of God opens the way for victory, leads those who hunger after God to move ahead ever-sensitive of His Spirit's leading (Offner et al., 2013). Constant communion with God is, by definition, being sensitive to God's leading. But sensitivity, as far as this chapter is concerned, means much more than this. *A believer to be sensitive to God requires not only a sensi-*

The Power of Constant Prayer and Communion With God, pages 149–156.
Copyright © 2024 by Information Age Publishing
www.infoagepub.com
All rights of reproduction in any form reserved.

150 • THE POWER OF CONSTANT PRAYER AND COMMUNION WITH GOD

tivity to his leading, but also to his feelings and attitudes. This kind of sensitivity draws the believer into a more mature knowledge of God, never before possible. What people call the knowledge of God is very superficial (Clairvaux, 1940; Daley, 2009; Murray, 1979; Tozer, 2013). Individuals often define the knowledge of God as being something quite intellectual to cover the fact that their knowledge of God is quite perfunctory. *The believer comes to know God through responding to what God tells him to do only to the extent that an army soldier comes to know his drill sergeant through responding to what he tells him to do! The Christian commonly makes a mistake in asking God merely what He wants him to do and not why.* By this I do not mean we should question the wisdom behind what God asked us to do. Rather, this is an important question to ask if we are to understand the true heart of God. For instance, God may ask the disciple to go up to someone and pray with him about a problem. Certainly, God will honor our simple obedience to such a request (Brady, 2003; Murray, 2004). However, we have fallen short of the sensitivity to God that the Lord would like (Chambers, 2008; Swindoll, 1998). If the disciple, in addition to obeying asked why the Lord wanted him to pray, the Lord might reveal to him some of the deep compassion and concern He has for that individual. As a result of being exposed to the thoughts of God, the disciple would have more of the heart of God.

What a joy it is just to set ourselves down on a chair and chat with the Lord. That is, not merely mumbling on about our attitudes and feelings, but rather asking God about *His* attitudes and feelings. He longs to respond to His servants that desire to know the heart of God (Wiersbe, 2005). This is especially true since few are the number of believers who do long to know the heart of God (Minith, 2004). Knowing the heart of God is how the Christian develops the same burdens of compassions and love that God has for His Creation. Many believers fail to have a burden from God because they do not bother to ask God what his burdens are!

Let it be known, that as in Psalm 44:3 (previously quoted), the disciple cannot take the Promised Land God would ideally want for him without the light of God's presence. There are many Christians who upon experiencing victory take pieces of land for the glory of God, but is it the Promised Land? *To know the heart of God at any particular moment and act on this fact is to rest in the perfect will of God. To fail either to know the heart of God or to fail to act on this fact is to settle for a state of permissive obedience.*

Does not both our study of the Word of God and our experience tell us that in fellowshipping with those who have grown closest to God, we are cognizant of gaining a glimpse into part of the heart of God? When we see a Christian with true love, are we not cognizant of now having some understanding of what the heart of Christ must be like (Augustine, 2010; Peterson, 2003; Piper, 2011)?

It is no strange fact of insignificance that the born-again believer is frequently more apt to seek God's hand than God's heart. God's call to the Christian is that he seek God, the source and not God the means toward the result! If a person be attracted to God because of the results He produces, it might as well be another,

Sensitivity and Constant-Prayer and Communion With God • 151

because it is not actually the results that make God unique (John 4:48). While the results that God produces are not necessarily unique, the heart of God is totally unique and totally impossible to completely replicate. Today, God calls His church to arise and seek after and celebrate the uniqueness of God by longing to know His heart (Orr, 2009).

The Practice of Sensitivity to God

My foot has held fast to His steps; I have kept His way and have not turned aside.

—Job 23:11

In God we have boasted *continually*, and we will give thanks to thy name forever.

—Psalm 44:8

To boast of God continually is to be humble continually. Such a Christian is boasting of God and not himself. Such a person realizes that he can do nothing from his own ability, but rather one must rely solely on God. This person realizes he can afford only to be sensitive to God and to the beat of His heart. The result of such intense reliance on God is stated in Job 23:11, i.e., he walks in the ways of God without wavering. Praise God because Job states this with confidence. How else can a disciple of Christ make such a statement, except that he knows the heart of God. But who is so close to God to say that he can always say that he knows the heart of God, and never wavers from the steps that God has ordained for him? I know that I cannot. *It is the humble that consider God's heart, it is the proud that consider their own heart.* And herein begins the proud's fall, for in the heart of men rests deceit and all wickedness (Mark 7:15, 21-23). All that which proceeds from man is meaningless. All that finds meaning comes from God and relies on God (Psalm 94:11). God knows when a believer sets his own heart before God's and knows when he cares to seek God's hand and not His heart (Matthew 19:16-30; Luke 11:29-32). The believer should take heed, for although it is so that God knows when a person does not seek God's heart first, the very fact of God's knowledge of man gives the Christian reason to be sensitive to the heart of God (I Samuel 16:7; Job 31:4; Psalm 44:21; Proverbs 5:21; 16:2; 21:2).

It reminds me of a friend of mine who had several adult children. This friend of mine was not particularly wealthy. It was a shame but neither did her children keep in very close contact with her. But one day she came into a handsome sum of money. Her children found out about this fact. Suddenly, she was receiving phone calls from them constantly. They were so anxious to get together with her. However, my friend was able to perceive that her children were not anxious to get to know her heart, who she was, but instead were interested in her hand of blessing. How sad it is that our behavior with God is not far different.

152 • THE POWER OF CONSTANT PRAYER AND COMMUNION WITH GOD

There are times when believers are confronted with the facts that much of the world is starving; that there are many homeless within a short distance from their door; that there are people all around them who especially that day need to be recipients of the love of Christ. The only way we can grow to act so that these needs may be consistently met is if we are in tune with the heart of God. There is little way for the disciple of Christ to feel the compassion that God feels towards such as these unless he moves his own opinions aside and allows the heart of God to consume him and overtake him with the love of Christ. The Lord reveals His heart to those who would humble themselves before Him and confess that it is far better to have God's heart dominate our thoughts than our own.

Sensitivity to God in the manner mentioned will produce myriad beautiful results. We will be sensitive to the Lord as to where the harvest for catching spiritual fish is ripe and the resultant harvest will therefore be great (John 21:1-6). The believer will also know what he should speak and how he should say it when the time comes (Acts 23:6-8; Matthew 10:18; Luke 21:14). The believer will also be sensitive to the timing of God, i.e., how and when to act such that God will be glorified (Matthew 16:1-4). He will know how to defend the gospel such that the Holy Spirit will touch the heart of the people we are talking to (I Peter 3:15). The Lord is looking for men who will respond to His call (Matthew 4:19). The Lord is looking for people who will readily respond in obedience to what He commands them (Matthew 13:23; Luke 6:47, 48; 8:15). The Lord is looking for people who will be quick to listen for the heart of God and not be so intent on spouting every feeling that they have in their own heart (James 1:19). God is looking for people who will listen to His heart beat close enough to understand its significance (Matthew 13:14). God wants disciples who upon listening for God's heart and understanding its meaning will act upon it that God's will might be done and that God would be glorified (Matthew 7:24-27).

SENSITIVITY TO MAN

Greater love has no man than this, that a man lay down his life for his friends.

—John 15:13

But thou art near, O Lord, and all thy commandments are true.

—Psalm 119:151

There are two important aspects to being sensitive to other people. The first is the willingness to lay down our life for the sake of other people, i.e., to love them no matter what the cost. Second, is an understanding that God is near to enable us to be sensitive to other people. No person can be very sensitive to others in his flesh, he must have the Spirit of God to open his eyes to the needs of others (Augustine, 2015a, 2015b; Graham, 2015).

Sensitivity and Constant-Prayer and Communion With God • **153**

Though we be a seeker of the welfare of other people and desire to be sensitive to them, we must realize that we cannot be sensitive to other humans until we are first sensitive to God. There are so many unapparent needs within each man that the insight of a mere cerebral thought cannot pierce. It is only the Holy Spirit Himself who can uncover the dark corners of such needs (I Corinthians 2:11). Therefore, in order to be sensitive to the needs and desires of individuals, we must be in submissive continual communion with the Holy Spirit.

Being sensitive to the Holy Spirit has parallels in a child's dependence on his parent. Think of a child who is taken by his parent to a place of relative sophistication, at least to a child. Perhaps the child is taken to church or a museum by his parent. At the church, certain statements are heard by the child, but not understood. At the museum certain exhibits are seen by the child, but not understood. As a result, the child tugs the arm of the parents and says, "Mommy, what does this mean?" or "Daddy, what is he doing?" The parent then informs the child and the child understands. The child must have this type of dependent relationship with his parent if he is to grow and act appropriately, in a given situation.

Similarly, there are many situations that require sensitivity that we do not understand. In such situations we must be humble enough to become like children and ask the Holy Spirit, "What does this mean?" or "Why is he doing that?" For surely the Holy Spirit, like the parents of the child, understands far more than we.

As we are sensitive to the Spirit of Christ concerning interacting with people, we will learn more about them than we ever imagined in so short a time. For Jesus Christ knows and is sensitive to all men (John 2:23-25). The Lord Jesus encountered many people with a wide range of various needs. Only because He was (and is) deity did He know that the adulterous woman needed to know that God was supportive of her actions; and needed to be made keenly aware of the love God had for her (John 8:1-8). The Lord Jesus also knew that the beloved apostle Peter needed to be rebuked when he cried out that Christ's soon-coming death should be prevented at all costs (Matthew 16:21-23). In our natural man it might seem that rebuke might have been more appropriate in the first case and only a remark of soft loving disapproval in the second. But Jesus shows us that such logical thinking is often quite inaccurate. What if Jesus had instead rebuked the woman caught in adultery and dealt mildly with Peter's remark? The Christian is faced with similar situations in his dealing with other people. The Christian cannot afford to make such crucial mistakes in his dealings with others. Yet it is often these kind of mistakes that Christians frequently make. Such errors can only be reduced if we are sensitive to the leading and insights of the Holy Spirit (Bergman, 2004; Briscoe, 2013).

There are many situations in life which require sensitivity to God and yet being human, believers have a distinct tendency to live their Christian lives quite haphazardly when it comes to being sensitive to the needs of others. It is indeed an indication that a believer cares when he expresses his willingness to help another person who has expressed a need. Hopefully, all Christians should be responsive

154 • THE POWER OF CONSTANT PRAYER AND COMMUNION WITH GOD

when some needs go unexpressed. The true disciple of Christ cannot walk through life with the attitude that if there is a need it will be expressed, for this is simply not the case. By a strong sensitivity to the leading of God, it becomes the Christian to attempt to have God work to meet even unexpressed needs.

The Christian should not be satisfied if he is used by God to meet those needs which are expressed. For even those in the world are responsive to many of these needs. What separates the believer, as a light to the world, is if he allows God to use him to attempt to divulge what the unexpressed needs are and allow God to work to meet those needs (Philippians 4:19). Sensitivity to God on a constant basis leads the disciple to, among other things, ask what another person's needs are. Sensitivity to God also allows him to pick up on the significance of a particular sentence or circumstance that points out a need, of which he would not have otherwise been aware. Sensitivity to God can give him knowledge of a need in a person's life without a word even being spoken. There have been many times I have walked into a room in which a person is sitting alone and the Lord impressed upon me that that person is lonely. I have then proceeded to talk with that person that God might meet their needs. There have been other times that I have entered a room with a person sitting alone and God has impressed upon me that the person is not lonely. Without relying on the Lord to guide me, I would have no way of knowing who was lonely and who was not. The Lord is gracious to guide me as long as I am willing to be guided. Yet, there are those times when I have walked into a room with a person who was alone and left the room, realizing that I had been too caught up in myself to be sensitive to the Lord concerning the possibility of that person being lonely. I then realize that perhaps there was a need that was unmet. My natural tendency has again manifested itself, that I have a great inclination to look to my concerns first before I look to the needs of others. Subtle as it may seem, this is sin! Nevertheless, I rejoice gladly that my Lord suffered on the cross that I might be forgiven for sins such as these. PRAISE BE TO GOD!

Apostle Paul, though a great man of God, showed insensitivity to the need of the moment when he showed unwise hardness toward John Mark (Acts 15:36-40). In later epistles, Paul showed that he had acknowledged his lack of precious sensitivity to God and appreciated the virtues of John Mark (II Timothy 4:11). The Lord Jesus is, of course, a tremendous example of being sensitive to the needs of other people. When John the Baptist was overwhelmed with doubt upon being imprisoned, Jesus comforted him with assurances that Jesus was indeed the Messiah (Matthew 11:4-6). Jesus was sensitive to the physical and spiritual needs of others, as a whole (Matthew 9:36; Mark 9:26-29). Spiritual needs are usually more likely to go unmet than physical needs because they are less apparent. In fact, *spiritual needs are met so seldom that the recipient is frequently surprised when another person is used of God to meet a need that was unexpressed! This very fact shows that even the dedicated believer is more sensitive to the realm covered by the five senses than the realm of the Spirit!* We know how deprived a person is considered when he is physically blind or deaf, but the believer often does not re-

Sensitivity and Constant-Prayer and Communion With God • 155

alize that unless he sensitizes himself to the voice of God, he himself is to a great extent spiritually blind and deaf. It is a mistake to construct a false dichotomy and assume that since unbelievers are spiritually blind and deaf, believers must be extremely spiritually discerning. To assume the latter is not only logically incorrect but biblically incorrect as well. The phrase, *"Let him who has an ear to hear, listen..." is not only used to refer to unbelievers and their spiritual deafness, but also believers as well* (Revelation 2:7, 11, 17, 29; 3:6; 13:22).

The question emerges: If so many Christians are more spiritually deaf and blind than they are spiritually discerning, why is not the fact obvious to them? The question is simply answered using this illustration. If virtually everyone on earth were physically deaf and blind, the deaf and the blind would not be aware of the unfortunate status of their condition. The same truth holds spiritually as well. Most believers are not aware that they are to a great degree spiritually blind and deaf because most every other is also. It is not unusual for a Christian to initially react unfavorably to another believer who shines like a light and who by his very walk with God shows that he constantly communes with God. The unfavorable response is sometimes natural because witnessing such a shining light is a *reminder of one's own spiritual deafness and blindness.* The ignorance concerning the believer's own spiritual deafness is also sustained by the fact that most believers associate the most with other believers who are at about the same level spiritually. Excluding the Christian who is humble and really committed to growing in the Lord, few followers of Christ desire close fellowship with someone who is a living conviction and a constant reminder that he should be living with far more dedication to Christ than he already is. Whether we will avoid this "shining light" or label him as "weird," etc., the end result is all the same.

How God longs to speak to His people throughout the day, yet, oh, how few listen. And those who do listen, listen far too little. The miracles that can be wrought by listening to God's voice concerning the needs of others are remarkable. How often I am surprised when I survey a room of people (small group or large) and ask the Lord which individuals have needs, that the Lord impresses upon my heart at least one or two. At times God will direct my steps to attempt to meet that person's need. How incredible it is the needs God meets in such a fashion, by His glorious grace. God, by His grace, has chosen to reveal to His people the needs of others and He will share those needs, if we demonstrate that we care enough to ask God what these needs are. It is incomprehensible to think of the number of souls that have been saved and the number of tears that have been caught and the number of hearts mended all because there were born-again believers who chose to constantly listen to the voice of God concerning the needs of others. There have been a phenomenal amount of needs met by being sensitive to God in this way. There is no way I can be convinced that God does not want to meet so many more needs in a similar fashion.

156 • THE POWER OF CONSTANT PRAYER AND COMMUNION WITH GOD

CONCLUSION

Sensitivity to God affects our priorities (Acts 16:25-27); our timing (Luke 10:38-42; John 12:1-8); discerning God's will (Genesis 24:15-27; Matthew 4:18-22), and wisdom in dealing with blatant sinners (I Corinthians 5). If the Christian life is to be our way of life, we must have this sensitivity. The only way to have this sensitivity is to have the sensitivity which God Himself supplies. The Christian is most amply supplied with this sensitivity, when he is constantly communing with God.

REFERENCES

Augustine of Hippo. (2010). *City of God* (Dods, M. Peabody, Trans.). Henrickson Publishers.

Augustine of Hippo. (2015a). *Brainy quotes*. Retrieved on April 2, 2015 from: http://www.brainyquote.com/quotes/quotes/s/saintaugus124552.html

Augustine of Hippo. (2015b). *Brainy quotes*. Retrieved on April 2, 2015 from: http://thinkexist.com/quotation/do_you_wish_to_rise-begin_by_descending-you_plan/263998.html. , p. 1.

Brady, B. V. (2003). *Christian love*. Georgetown University Press.

Briscoe, S. (2013). *Time bandits: Putting first things first*. Multnomah Press.

Chambers, O. (2008). *My utmost for His highest*. Discovery House Publishers.

Clairvaux, B. (1940). *The steps of* humility. Harvard University Press.

Daley, R. J. (2009). *Sacrifice unveiled: The true meaning of Christian sacrifice*. T & T Clark.

Graham, B. (2015). *Quotations book*. Retrieved March 26, 2015 from: http://quotationsbook.com/quote/38480/

Minith, F. B. (2004). *In pursuit of happiness: Choices that can change your life*. Fleming H. Revell

Murray, A. (1979). *Abide in Christ: The joy of being in God's presence*. Whitaker House.

Murray, A. (2004). *A life of obedience.* Bethany House.

Offner, H., Larsen, D., & Larsen, S. (2013). *A deeper look at the fruit of the Spirit: Growing in the likeness of Christ*. InterVarsity Press.

Orr, C. E. (2009). *How to live a holy life*. Floating Press.

Peterson, J. (2003). *The insider: Bringing the Kingdom of God into your everyday world*. Navigator Press.

Piper, J. (2011). *Desiring God: Meditations of a Christian hedonist*. Multnomah.

Swindoll, C. R. (1998). *Joseph: A man of integrity and forgiveness: Profiles in Character*. Word Publishers.

Tozer, A. W. (2013). *The pursuit of God.* Gospel Light.

Wiersbe, W. W. (2005). *Devotions for renewal and joy: Romans and Philippians.* Honor Publishing.

CHAPTER 14

CONSTANT-PRAYER AND COMMUNION WITH GOD AND CONSISTENCY

THE CHALLENGE FOR CONSISTENCY

Introduction

> With open mouth I pant, because I long for thy commandments.
> —*Psalm 119:131*

> Trust in the Lord with all your heart, and do not rely on your own insight.
> In all your ways acknowledge Him, and He will make straight your paths.
> —*Proverbs 3:5, 6*

It may seem at first redundant to assert that consistency is needed in constant prayer to God. After all, does not constant mean consistent? What is meant when it is said that a believer needs consistency in constant communion with God is that he is constantly aware of God one day after the next. Consistency in constant communion means that day in and day out the Christian enjoys continual com-

---

The Power of Constant Prayer and Communion With God, pages 157–165.
Copyright © 2024 by Information Age Publishing
www.infoagepub.com
All rights of reproduction in any form reserved.

158 • THE POWER OF CONSTANT PRAYER AND COMMUNION WITH GOD

munion with his Heavenly Father. It means that neither trials, depression, work, fun, nor extreme blessing can deter from our constancy of active relationship with God. It is very easy to taste of constant communion some days when all is going well and then have God seem far away the following day, because of a sudden change in circumstances. How can a believer enjoy constant communion with God each and every day and hour, without the vacillation that most Christians are accustomed to?

When a disciple of Christ knows what joy there is in sharing and walking so closely with God, it is difficult for him to experience those periods of spiritual dryness that occur when he is only aware of God on and "on and off" level or perhaps even hardly at all. In this regard our walk with God is much like a marriage. One of the hardest marriages to experience is one that starts off well and then goes awry (Brady, 2003; Froehlich, 2014; Graham, 2015; Kruschwitz, 2001). Having experienced a good marriage at one time, it is hard to settle for anything less.

As a disciple abides in the Lord more, sin must decline (I John 3:6). The individual, who is consistent in his communion with God, finds that he parts quickly with the world. He is not constantly communing with God one day and having fatigue and sin overcome him the next day. He has chosen to follow the Lamb of God (Revelation 14:4). He will follow the Lord and fellowship with Him in a spirit of diligence; not just a few days in a week, but all week long. How can a man be double-minded when he persists in gluing his thoughts to the one who saved his soul? *Consistency in constant communion with God is, by its very nature, the solution to and totally inconsistent with double-mindless!*

Consistency in constant communion with God not only means there is heightened quantity of fellowship with God, but there is also a sharp qualitative difference as well. Psalm 119, perhaps more than any other chapter of the Bible, is filled with references to the necessity and excitement of constant communion with God. In Psalm 119:97 the psalmist David talks of meditating all the day long. Meditation denotes quality of communion. It is *impossible to reach perfection in the quantity of one's communion with God, but this being true, it is even more impossible to reach perfection in the quality of one's communion with God!* The reason for this is simple. The quality of communion we experience is dependent on the extent a person can fellowship with the whole of God. Since man cannot even begin to conceive of the whole of God, let alone commune with Him, nothing near perfection can be attained in one's quality of communion.

The challenge now becomes one of maintaining a consistency both in the quantity and quality of a devotee's prayer with God. It may appear at times that quality is being developed at the expense of quantity and vice versa. But if Christians pursue each with consistency, they will see fruit in each. There are days when I am aware of God practically every minute of the day, yet I know I have failed to respond to many of the promptings of my Lord during that same time. Thus, while I have experienced constant prayer with God on a large scale quantitatively, I have not reached the heights of the enjoyment of constant prayer that God would

Constant-Prayer and Communion With God and Consistency • **159**

like overflowing in my life. There are other days when I am not aware of Him as much as I should and yet I am sensitive to His promptings when I am aware of Him. Thus, when I am aware of Him, the communion I experience is of a high quality. It is the all-too-human tendency to desire quality when we have quantity and to desire quantity when we have quality. Nevertheless, the truth remains-if the believer earnestly seeks for both, God will grant him both.

Improving the Quality of Constant Prayer and Communion

Blessed are those who keep His testimonies, who seek Him with their whole heart, who also do no wrong, but walk in His ways.

—Psalm 119:2, 3

The importance of quality to the consistent experience of constant fellowship with God is two-fold. First, once a believer experiences a heightened quality of constant prayer with God, it plants a seed to hunger for more and more prayer with God because the experience is so tremendous. Second once he has reached a certain level of experience, it becomes more difficult to slip out of constant communion. The first reason why the quality of our communion is important simply follows from the fact that the more we taste of that which is good, the more we long for it. It is interesting to note that in Psalm 34, after the psalmist says that he will bless the Lord at all times, in the same breath he invites the reader to *"taste and see that the Lord is good"* (Psalm 34:8). The Christian who is continually interacting with the Lord knows very well just how good this steadfast fellowship tastes. The greater the quality of this communion, the more he is driven to resume this constant fellowship. And the more he is driven to resume this fellowship, the greater its consistency.

The second reason why quality prayer is important, i.e., it becomes more difficult to slip out of communion, can be best understood using an analogy. If the temperature reaches a high of 72 degrees F for the day, it is much more difficult for that temperature to fall to freezing than if the high for the day was only 40 degrees F. So it is with constant communion with God if we are accustomed to maintaining a high level of quality communion with God than if we are accustomed to a low level. The freezing point of interaction with God, i.e., the point at which we are no longer actively interacting with God, is more likely to be reached in the second instance.

The importance of quality in our minute-to-minute interaction(s) with God agreed upon, it now becomes valuable to discuss practical actions we might take to improve the quality of our communion with God. The actions that are going to be specifically mentioned are not designed to cover all the steps a believer might take, but instead are designed to give him insight into what types of options are both available and practical.

First, the quality of our communion with the Lord is enhanced the more we ask the Lord what we should do before any action we may take. This can include various major decisions a person is faced with, but also can include decisions as to when we should have a dinner engagement or even what we should buy at the store. It is good to be continually communicating with while shopping; but how much better it is to shop *with* Jesus, asking Him what we should purchase.

Second, the quality of our communion with God is enhanced as we go out of our way to ask the Lord about the needs of others. It is good to be aware of the presence of God while in the midst of other people. Nevertheless, how much better is a person's interaction with God if he interacts with God asking Him about the needs of others. If, while in a room with a group of people, we asked the Lord outright, "Are there any needs which need to be met among the people in this room?", what compassionate results are possible. As God reveals the needs, the believer then acts to meet the needs, by the grace of God, accordingly.

Third, the quality of our communion with God is enhanced if as we pass by people on the street, etc., we ask God if these people need to be ministered to in any way. It is good to move along in life with thoughts of praise to God. It is even better to be looking for opportunities to love in the midst of some quite ordinary circumstances of life. If God does not direct us to minister directly, He will almost inevitably direct us to pray for that person.

Fourth, the quality of our communion with God is enhanced if we are open to leadings from God in the course of our daily life. Perhaps while in a person's presence, the Christian might ask God if there is a special verse from the Bible or other word of wisdom which might uplift this person in the faith. Or while at home, the Christian might ask God if there is anyone the Lord wants him to call or visit and give such a verse or word of wisom to. Such precise obedience often has tremendous fruit.

Fifth, the quality of our communion with God is enhanced to the extent that we are keenly aware that God is within us (Holy Spirit), beside us (Jesus Christ) and directly around Him (the Father). To be consciously aware that the Spirit of love and power, that Spirit of Pentecost, is within us adds power and depth to our communion with God. To know that we walk hand in hand with Jesus can change the course and enlarge the meaning of each and every step we take. And to know that the Father envelopes him in his love can give the disciple an overwhelming sense of peace, security, and God's love.

Sixth, the quality of our communion with God is enhanced as we seek to have this communion go uninterrupted, even during the course of our sleep. Somehow as we grow in the grace and knowledge of our Lord Jesus, sixteen hours of potential interaction with Him just is not enough. Hence, the believer might take specific actions to see to it that he can enjoy the presence of God in his sleep as well. The believer can ask for God to give him dreams about his Lord, minister in areas of his life that need growth and meditate on the Word of God before going to sleep that his night's thoughts will be pure and centered on the Word of God. What great blessings are manifested when the Lord dominates our thoughts in our sleep (Psalm 119:55). The Lord has ministered to me greatly in my sleep. He has given me, by the riches of His grace, tremendous dreams of my Lord and of heaven. He has given me powerful dreams, woken me up and led me to pray fervently to rededicate my life to Him. He has given me preaching messages and insightful words of counsel in my sleep. Truly God wants to speak to His people while they sleep—one need only ask!

PEACE AND CONSISTENCY IN CONSTANT COMMUNION

The Basic Relationship Between the Two

> Thou dost keep him in perfect peace, whose mind is stayed on thee, because he trusts in thee.
>
> *—Isaiah 26:3*

> And the peace of God which passes all understanding will keep your hearts and your minds in Christ Jesus.
>
> *—Philippians 4:7*

Peace is an essential key to enjoying consistency in our constant communion with God. The verses just quoted assert the strong relationship between peace and constant awareness. Constant awareness produces peace (Isaiah 26:3, 4) and peace produces constant awareness (Philippians 4:7). The typical Christian is too quickly caught up in the things and pursuits of the world (Hosea 12:1). As a result, peace is not as familiar to the born-again believer as it should be and so his mind is not focused on God (Augustine, 2010, 2015a, 2015b; Wiersbe, 2005). The Christian who is not at peace will easily have his mind wander to the problems he faces, the day's agenda, deadlines he has to meet and decisions that require his action (Chambers, 2008; Daley, 2009; Swindoll, 1998). Such a lack of peace leads to double-mindedness which is inherent to the idea of constant communion with God (Piper, 2011; Swindoll, 2008; Tozer, 2013). Double-mindedness means that a person is serving another god (Matthew 6:24; James 1:6, 7). There is a way of the Lord and a way of the world; constant awareness is a resolute decision to walk in the way of the Lord (Nehemiah 5:9; I Corinthians 10:21).

Peace is a seldom discussed topic. One reason it is rarely discussed is because it is not very highly understood. It seems that peace is a sense of harmony with the will and ways of God. Peace is a feeling of one mind and one heart with God. When the Christian is at peace he wants nothing more than for this peace to continue. In a Christian's quest for the continuation of this peace, he will tend to communicate with God. It is difficult to have a pure sense of communication with God when a person is upset or consumed with thoughts of earthly matters. But when the believer is at peace he realizes that he has a peace because his thoughts are tuned into God, the source of peace. To the extent the believer has all of his

162 • THE POWER OF CONSTANT PRAYER AND COMMUNION WITH GOD

thoughts on God he will experience more peace. Because all that does not lead to peace is outside of God. It is when all sources of distraction, worry, and problem-logic are left outside of the believer's mind that peace settles in. He instead puts his thoughts upon God. As a disciple experiences a greater depth of this peace, he seeks more communion with God that his peace might continue. *These thoughts being present, peace may be redefined in Christian terms. Peace is a harmony with God's will and workings and is in its highest essence a state of single-minded communion with God. Constant communion with God is the continuation of non-cessation of this single-minded communion with God. Peace is therefore essential for the enjoyment of the highest quality and quantity of communion with God.*

Christ left His people peace when He ascended into Heaven (John 14:27). He, therefore, left His children with the potential of experiencing an ongoing communion with Him, since peace leads to this constancy of active relationship. Peace is a term which often goes unnoticed but is frequently highlighted in the Scripture. In Ephesians 2:14-17, the word "peace" is mentioned four times. Throughout this passage Christ is emphasized as being the source. In other sections of Scripture, God is stated as being the source of this peace again (John 16:33; II Corinthians 1:2). If God is the source of peace, what makes a believer think that he can arrive at any continuing state of peace outside of abiding in God? It is a common occurrence that the Christian, upon receiving peace in his heart, will neglect to abide in God and in no time at all lose that peace which placed him in that state of communion to begin with. This fact leads to the next section.

Seeking Peace and Keeping Constant Communion With God

Depart from evil, and do good; seek peace, and pursue it.
—*Psalm 34:14*

It has been mentioned that there is a great inter-relationship between constant awareness of God and peace. It has been stated that constant awareness produces peace and peace in turn leads to constant awareness. In this section, the relationship between peace and constant awareness will be more thoroughly discussed. In the verse just quoted, the Lord encourages His followers to seek peace and pursue it. Peace is a quality to be sought. Firstly, peace is a fruit of the Spirit and therefore ought to be sought in its own right. Secondly, peace is to be sought because it is conducive to constant communion with God.

Peace sets an atmosphere which is conducive to constant communion with God and therefore should be sought. Constant awareness is itself a means to peace and therefore helps in achieving the pursuit of peace. Psalm 34:14 states that the Christian should long and seek for peace, not that he should keep in a peaceful state. The reason for this is simply that peace is a quality that is very volatile and very easily escapes us. A person may manufacture a joy or faith, but it is very difficult to manufacture a genuine peace. Either a person has the peace of God or he does not (Murray, 1979, 2004; Orr, 2009; Peterson, 2003). Neither is there any specific regimen a Christian can go through to attain peace (through prayer, etc. can help). He might start praising God if he wants the Lord to fill him with joy, but there is really no corresponding action a person can take to be the recipient of God's peace so quickly. As a result, the Lord calls the believer to pursue peace that in time he might lay hold of its beauty once again. Constant communion with God is the means to this end. With time, the Christian's unceasing communion with God will ultimately lead to his quest being satisfied. Constant communion with God is our longing for peace put into practice. If the disciple lacks peace in his heart, continuous interaction with God is a good first step for realizing the fullness of God's peace.

While a person really cannot keep peace because it is too volatile a quality but can only seek it, the opposite is true about constant awareness. A person cannot seek constant awareness, but only keep it. We cannot seek constant awareness simply because if we are seriously seeking to be aware of God, we will be aware of God. There is no such thing as honestly seeking constant awareness at any moment in time and not experiencing it and furthermore, because our constant communion with God results from an act of the will, unlike peace, we can work to keep it. Therefore, if we want to seek after peace, we can best do that by steadfastly keeping constant awareness. If we want a disposition conducive to a greater quantity and quality of constant communion with God, then a state in which we are experiencing the peace of God is best for that.

God's Desire

Great peace have they who love thy law; nothing can make them stumble.
—Psalm 119:165

And the effect of righteousness will be peace, and the result of righteousness, quietness and trust forever.
—Isaiah 32:17

If born-again believers truly seek after righteousness, they will in time experience the rich and continuous active relationship with God which is constant communion with Him. The result of such righteousness will be peace. In communion with God, we understand more of the mind of God, the fountain of all wisdom and herein lies peace (Proverbs 3:17). In their most steadfast interaction with God, Christians hold onto the wise teachings they have received from God. The assurance of the truth of these teachings, which constitute a major part of the gospel, make for peace (Proverbs 4:13; Acts 10:36). As disciples cry out for God to fill them with the peace from above, through the very expression of crying out to God and listening to His reply they will come to a greater knowledge of God's faithfulness and receive the peace they so desire (Proverbs 1:33; 2:3-5).

164 • THE POWER OF CONSTANT PRAYER AND COMMUNION WITH GOD

God desires that the overflowing of His Holy Spirit be evident in His children's lives (John 7:38). Peace like a river is part of this fullness of overflowing today (Isaiah 48:18). When God speaks of peace like a river, it should be noted that a river is consistently constantly flowing. It is through unceasingly interacting with God that peace can most effectively and consistently flow. Without this unceasing interaction a believer's peace will soon dry up because of its volatile nature. If we rely on yesterday's peace to get us by today, we will not have peace today. Just as if a river relies on yesterday's water to flow today, it will dry up.

That the Christian's experience of peace be complete is important to the Lord. This is evident in His post-resurrection appearances. Upon seeing His disciples for the first time since He had risen from the dead, His first spoken desire for them was that they would have peace (John 20:19, 21). Continuous ever-flowing peace with God takes work and commitment. Most of all, it takes a willingness to receive what Christ wants to give His children. In constantly communing with God, we are expressing such a willingness. With Constant communion marking the Christian's lifestyle, a new empowering takes place in the Christian's life. The believer has a new desire to ever turn to the ways of the Lord herein lies peace (Psalm 119:59). In the decrees of God there lies understanding and in acknowledging the fact that in God rest all heights of understanding and that no such understanding or wisdom exists with ourselves (Psalm 119:99, 100; Proverbs 3:7, 21-23). May the Lord teach His people to seek the very place He desires for them.

May the thoughts written in this book be used of the Lord to minister to those who hunger and thirst ever more after God. May the Lord use this book to satisfy those who hunger and thirst this way. This book is totally for the glory of the only glorious God: to Him every word of this book is dedicated. Amen.

REFERENCES

Augustine of Hippo. (2010). *City of God* (Dods, M. Peabody, Trans.). Henrickson Publishers.

Augustine of Hippo. (2015a). *Brainy quotes*. Retrieved on April 2, 2015 from: http://www.brainyquote.com/quotes/quotes/s/saintaugus124552.html

Augustine of Hippo. (2015b). *Brainy quotes*. Retrieved on April 2, 2015 from: http://thinkexist.com/quotation/do_you_wish_to_rise-begin_by_descending-you_plan/263998.html. , p. 1.

Brady, B. V. (2003). *Christian love*. Georgetown University Press.

Chambers, O. (2008). *My utmost for His highest*. Discovery House Publishers.

Daley, R. J. (2009). *Sacrifice unveiled: The true meaning of Christian sacrifice*. T & T Clark.

Froehlich, M. A. (2014). *Courageous gentleness: Following Christ's example of restrained strength*. Discovery House Publishers.

Graham, B. (2015). *Quotations book*. Retrieved March 26, 2015 from: http://quotationsbook.com/quote/38480/

Hayford, J. W., & Bauer, R. H. (2011). *Penetrating the darkness: Keys to ignite faith, boldness, and breakthrough*. Chosen Books.

Constant-Prayer and Communion With God and Consistency • **165**

Kruschwitz, R. B. (2001). *Forgiveness*. Baylor University.

Minith, F. B. (2004). *In pursuit of happiness: Choices that can change your life*. Fleming H. Revell

Murray, A. (1979). *Abide in Christ: The joy of being in God's presence*. Whitaker House.

Murray, A. (2004). *A life of obedience*. Bethany House.

Orr, C. E. (2009). *How to live a holy life*. Floating Press.

Peterson, J. (2003). *The insider: Bringing the Kingdom of God into your everyday world*. Navigator Press.

Piper, J. (2011). *Desiring God: Meditations of a Christian hedonist*. Multnomah.

Swindoll, C. R. (1998). *Joseph: A man of integrity and forgiveness: Profiles in Character*. Word Publishers.

Tozer, A. W. (2013). *The pursuit of God*. Gospel Light.

Wiersbe, W. W. (2005). *Devotions for renewal and joy: Romans and Philippians*. Honor Publishing.

BIOGRAPHY

William Jeynes has served in ministry for over 45 years and in academics for 31 years. He has served as a missionary/evangelist and he and his wife have counseled thousands of families over the years. As a missionary/evangelist over the years he has been a tool to see over 300,000 people come to Christ. He is a Professor at California State University, Long Beach and a Senior Fellow on the Family at the Witherspoon Institute in Princeton, New Jersey. He graduated first in his class at Harvard University and also graduated from the University of Chicago, where he received the Rosenberger Award for the most outstanding student in his cohort. Bill has ministered in churches in every inhabited continent and in nearly every state in the country. He has spoken a number of times at Yoido Full Gospel Church in Korea, the largest church in the world. He has spoken on family and faith issues for the White House, the U.S. Department of Justice, the U.S. Department of Education, and the U.S. Department of Health & Human Services. He has spoken for both the G. W. Bush and Obama administrations and interacted with each of these Presidents. He has also spoken for former members of the Clinton administration. He has spoken for foreign and UN leaders, Harvard University, Cambridge University, Oxford University, Columbia University, Duke University, Notre Dame University, and the Harvard Family Research Project. His 4-point family and economic proposal given to the Acting President of Korea was passed

The Power of Constant Prayer and Communion With God, pages 167–168.
Copyright © 2024 by Information Age Publishing
www.infoagepub.com
All rights of reproduction in any form reserved.

168 • THE POWER OF CONSTANT PRAYER AND COMMUNION WITH GOD

and became the foundation for their economic and family policy to arise from the Asian Economic Crisis of 1997–1998.

He has about 185 academic publications, including 17 books. He has written for many prominent journals including those at Columbia University, Harvard University (two journals), Cambridge University, the University of Chicago, the London School of Economics, Notre Dame University, and many other universities. He has also written for the White House.

Dr. Jeynes has been interviewed or quoted by the *Washington Post*, the *Los Angeles Times*, The *Wall Street Journal*, the *New York Times*, the *London Times*, the Associated Press (AP), CNN, CBS, NBC, ABC, FOX, Spectrum/Time Warner Cable, public radio, Al Jazeera, the *Teheran Times*, *US News & World* Report, the *Atlantic, Politico, Education Week*, and many other news sources. His work has been cited and quoted numerous times by the U.S. Congress, the U.S. Supreme Court, the British Parliament, the EU, and many State Supreme Courts across the United States. Dr. Jeynes has been listed in *Who's Who in the World* for each of the last ten years and received a Distinguished Scholar Award the California State Senate, the California State Assembly, and his university. Dr. Jeynes wrote the #1 and #2 all-time most cited articles in the half-century history of the journal *Urban Education*. He also wrote the #1 all-time most cited article in the 47-year history of the journal *Education & Urban Society*. He periodically writes columns in the *Orange County Register*, the nation's 14th largest newspaper. He formerly taught at USC and the University of Chicago. Bill has been married for 38 years and has three wonderful children.

Printed in the United States
by Baker & Taylor Publisher Services